THE DARK SIDE

THE
DARK
SIDE

MARK SCHREIBER

INFAMOUS
JAPANESE CRIMES
AND CRIMINALS

KODANSHA INTERNATIONAL
Tokyo • New York • London

DEDICATION

To my mother, Gail
Who made me think of work as play,
And to my father, David,
Who sang me marching songs at bedtime.

Note on Japanese Names from the Publisher:
The names of Japanese who were active before 1868 are given in Japanese
order, surname preceding given name. Thereafter, Japanese names are
given in Western order, surname following given name.

Distributed in the United States by Kodansha America, Inc., 575 Lexing-
ton Avenue, New York N.Y. 10022, and in the United Kingdom and con-
tinental Europe by Kodansha Europe Ltd., 95 Aldwych, London WC2B
4JF. Published by Kodansha International Ltd., 17-14 Otowa 1-chome,
Bunkyo-ku, Tokyo 112-8652, and Kodansha America, Inc.

CONTENTS

FOREWORD

Crime has a stubborn way of cutting through a society and laying bare how things really work. It displays our fears, our prejudices, our taboos and traditions for all to see. It shows, as well, how power is exercised and enforced in a given culture. Foreigners, for example, can learn much about we Americans from studying our outlaws: Jesse James, Bonnie and Clyde, Al Capone, John Gotti, to name a few. But who can cite a single famous bandit of Japan, a nation that has exported so many of its products—along with its crime syndicates—around the globe? Like other sensitive topics, the Japanese are content to let such matters drop quietly from conversation.

Fortunately for us, along comes Mark Schreiber, doing here what he consistently does so well elsewhere—pushing aside the screen that bars the outside world from peering in on Japan. Combining the tools of the translator with those of the journalist and historian, he delves into several centuries of murder and mayhem, taking readers on a unique tour of criminal Nippon. Little is spared, from the details of Japan's nineteenth century gallows to the attractions of Japanese women to murder by poison.

Schreiber's eye for the bizarre and offbeat makes it, to be sure, an entertaining ride. We are introduced to Japan's most notorious criminals, its Robin Hood, Guy Fawkes and Ted Bundy. There are cannibals and peeping Toms, anarchists and crazed cops, femmes fatales and snake oil salesmen. We read of Hei the Demon, the legendary chief of a samurai SWAT team in eighteenth century Tokyo. We learn, too, that Japan's much vaunted koban system of local police boxes actually comes from a Prussian police trainer.

To bring us these tales, Schreiber plumbs obscure Japanese texts, scholarly works and faded newspaper accounts. Drawn from his long running series in the *Mainichi Daily News*, these stories comprise a kind of underground history of Japan, and they are a worthy addition to his first book, *Shocking Crimes of Postwar Japan*. We get not only the color but the sensibility of the day. They remind us of how deep-seated was Japan's historic fear of foreigners, from the burning of missionary Christians to the grisly murders of early Western traders. Other passages touch on gun control and capital punishment, as well as organized crime, corruption and other issues that still resonate today. In the process, Schreiber shows the Japanese for what they are, as fallible and as strange, in their own unique ways, as are the rest of us.

So, thank you, Mark Schreiber, for shining your inquisitive light on these dark corners of old Japan. Those who believe there must be more to the Japanese than trade deals and technology will find a welcome, if ocassionally murderous, kind of enlightenment here.

David E. Kaplan

PREFACE

This book is based on my series "Crime and Punishment in Old Japan,"
which appeared from July 1998 to March 2001 on the Japan Focus page
of the *Mainichi Daily News*. Page editor Mario Di Simine got me started,
and he was succeeded by my colleague Ryann Connell, who supported
me with terse editing and alliterative headlines every step of the way.
Haruo Nishimura, the MDN's former managing editor, passed away
before this work could be completed, but his many kindnesses will not
be forgotten.

Even after more than three decades of living in Asia, I could never
have imagined that some day I would write about medieval and nineteenth century Japan. While researching my first book on crime in
postwar Japan, however, I realized this country has preserved a vast
body of historic accounts of crime and punishment, and I felt moved to
introduce these stories to readers outside Japan. The contents herein
largely reflect my own preferences and discoveries. In the interest of
brevity and readability, I chose to keep details of the legal system, government administration and social structure to a minimum. Perhaps I
shall expound upon these further in a work of expanded scope.

My initial desire to write about the law in Asia was inspired by a
truly great writer and scholar whom I never had the pleasure of meeting: the late Sinologist Robert van Gulik, whose wonderful series of

Judge Dee mystery novels present China's rich and colorful past through historical fiction. I feel Dr. van Gulik's greatest achievement was to nurture an appreciation among Western readers for the "righteous officials" in China's literary tradition.

In the course of writing this work, I was extremely fortunate to receive guidance and encouragement from a number of Japan scholars and writers. Two in particular, Aaron Cohen and William Wetherall, were my teachers in every sense of the word. I would also like to thank my partners in crime writing for their support and encouragement, particularly David E. Kaplan, Gavin Frew, Stanley Guy, Peter Martin, Richard S. Meyers, Laura Joh Rowland and Robert Whiting.

I must also acknowledge the travails of my long-suffering wife, Yvonne, who had to share our small Tokyo home with a veritable mountain of books and paper. Morito Matsuda's enthusiasm for Zeni-gata Heiji piqued my interest in TV period dramas and led me to explore their historic roots. I was helped and sustained in my quest by Robert A. Allen, Ryoko Tamaki, Saeko and Nagatoshi Maki, Takako Kobayakawa, Yoshio Nakamura, Moriichi Uchino, Yoshio Miyamoto, Yumio Nawa-*sensei*, Naohiro Hohashi, Dave Spector, Corky Alexander, Yayoi Uchiyama, Ron Rhodes, Charles Wordell, Burrit Sabin, Antonio Pagnotta, Edwin Karmiol, Stephan Hauser, Erika and Jules Young, Michael Birt, Paul Henriques, Bryan Harrell, James Bailey and Bob Cutts. The staff of Kodansha International went out of their way to support this project. Finally, several individuals in Japan's National Police Agency and the Tokyo Metropolitan Police Department kindly provided me with useful information, but modestly requested their names not be cited. To them let me just say, *Taihen gokuro sama deshita*.

Mark Schreiber
Tokyo
April 2001

E DO
PERIOD

1603–1868

ROOTS OF THE LAW

JAPAN'S TOKUGAWA rulers generally eschewed direct involvement in the enforcement of ordinary criminal cases, but they did put a well-organized system in place. From 1635, the government was organized into the *Roju*, a group of five senior councilors from large fiefdoms, who served the Tokugawa shoguns. Beneath them was the *Hyojosho*, a judicial council that met near the Wadakura gate, close to what is now Tokyo's Palace Hotel. It included three main departments: the *Jisha bugyo*, the overseers of Buddhist temples and Shinto shrines; the *Kanjo bugyo*, the treasury; and the *Machi bugyo*, an office resembling that of mayor or governor. The latter heard ordinary civil and criminal cases (see note on page 237).

At its height, Japan had sixteen machi bugyo around the country, from Hakodate in Hokkaido to Nagasaki in Kyushu, who reported directly to the Hyojosho.

A machi bugyo worked hard to earn his annual stipend of 3,000 *koku* (about 15,000 bushels) of rice. In addition to processing civil and criminal claims, he was also responsible for day-to-day decisions affecting the local townspeople, tax collection, and organizing the fire brigades.

The city of Edo, in its heyday, had two machi bugyo offices, referred to as *Kita* and *Minami*, Northern and Southern. The locations changed

On trial: The accused are brought before the Machi bugyo.

with the times, but for most of the era, the former was at Gofukubashi, near the Yaesu north exit of Tokyo Station, on the site of the present Kokusai Kanko Hotel. The Southern office, or court, eventually wound up adjacent to the Sukiyabashi Gate, just in front of Yurakucho Station. A third bugyo office existed for a short period near Kanda. It operated between 1702 and 1719, after which the system reverted back to two.

The courts alternated, each conducting trials for one month while its counterpart caught up on the backlog of paperwork. The choice of venue and which magistrate an accused criminal appeared before was thus determined merely by timing, depending on which court was in session that particular month.

Outside of the areas under direct Tokugawa rule, provincial lords were usually permitted to exercise autonomous rule, including enforcement of traditional family laws. Some did not hesitate to mete out cruel and unusual punishments, but others were more enlightened and lenient than Edo and other major cities in their sympathy for the downtrodden and their efforts to rehabilitate offenders.

With the Tang Penal Code and other Chinese laws forming the model for law in Tokugawa Japan, Japanese jurists were able to study historic Chinese accounts of court cases. The most widely disseminated was a thirteenth century work credited to an official named Gui Wan-rong and entitled *Tang Yin Bi Shi* (*Parallel Cases under the Pear Tree*). The pear tree, its English translator points out, is an old literary allusion meaning "a just and benevolent official."

The work contains brief accounts of 144 notable civil cases that were recorded between the pre-Han (300 B.C.) and Northern Sung (960–1127) Dynasties. To facilitate comparison, similar cases appear in sets of two. This work entered Japan via Korea in 1619, when it was transcribed and annotated by Hayashi Doshun, a noted sinologue, and remained in use for over two centuries.

In the introduction to his translation of the *Tang Yin Bi Shi* (published in 1956), the famous Dutch diplomat and sinologist Dr. Robert Hans van Gulik explained the popularity of such works among administrators by noting that ". . . nearly all scholar-officials started their career as district magistrates, and the administration of justice formed an important part of their daily duties. The recruitment examinations . . . ill prepared them for this work . . . [and] the case books provided a welcome short-cut to a general acquaintance with the Penal Code and the methods of its enforcement, including also some elementary facts about jurisprudence and the detection of crime. . . .

"The case-books provided the inexperienced scholar-official with reading-matter at once useful and agreeable, and in accordance with approved literary taste."

Here is one example, a case called "Kao Fang compares cloth," which he cites.

In the time of Shi-tsung (954–59 A.D.) of the later Chou Dynasty (914–60 A.D.), when Kao Fang was Prefect of Ts'ai-chou, a man of that place called Wang Yi was robbed with violence. Five men were arrested, put in prison and thoroughly interrogated. When the stolen goods were indeed found with them, all five confessed and were going to be subjected to the supreme penalty. Kao Fang, however, had the stolen goods brought and examined them. Summoning Wang Yi he asked him whether the garments he had lost were made out of one piece. Then Kao Fang had the size and texture of the garments checked and found that they were different. The prisoners then declared that they had been falsely accused. When Kao Fang asked them why they had confessed, they stated that they had been unable to stand the flogging, and had only desired to die quickly. After a few days, the real robber was apprehended and the five men were acquitted. Kao Fang later served under the Sung Dynasty, and ended his career as executive assistant to a minister.

The story provides a magistrate with at least four useful pieces of advice:

1. Ascertain that testimony does not contradict the evidence. (E.g., do not base rulings solely on confessions.)

2. Avoid hasty decisions.

3. Recognize the obligation not only to administer justice, but to redress wrongs.

4. Competence reaps career rewards.

Although the microscope, fingerprinting and blood typing were still a long way in the future, medieval Japan had pathologists, who were known as *kenshikan*, with a grasp of basic forensic science.

Their text was a book entitled *Xi Yuan Lu*, or "Instructions to Coroners," written in 1247 by a Chinese official named Song Ci. Literally it means "record of the washing away of wrongs," but the title has also been rendered as "A Manual for the Prevention of Injustice." This work, one of the earliest treatises on forensic science, was studied and used for hundreds of years in China

The manual was updated with new commentary in 1308 and transmitted to Japan, probably via Korea, as the *Sen'en Shuroku*. It was translated into Japanese in 1736 by a physician named Kawai Naohisa and published in two volumes in 1768 under the title *Sen'en Rokujutsu*.

Song Ci was a remarkable man for his times, and it shows in his manual, which ran the gamut of everything from deaths resulting from drunken brawls to accidental drownings, poisonings, suicides and even criminal malpractice by physicians. Song Ci advised magistrates to be especially suspicious of cases of sudden death with no discernible wounds. One passage reads:

> Look to see if the face is bruised or swollen on one side. These are usually cases of smothering the nose and mouth. Strangulation by a scarf or cloth leaves no marks, but the neck becomes hard. Be sure to look for signs of hands and feet being tied. The tongue will probably have been bitten. And the pubic area and buttocks may be swollen from having been stood upon. If none of these signs is present, examine the throat for mucous and swelling. These might indicate death from diphtheria.

As science progressed, notations were added by other medical examiners that corrected or elaborated on Song Ci's work.

Unfortunately some magistrates were too busy (or lazy) to concern themselves with unexplained deaths, and delegated investigations to ignorant and inexperienced subordinates. Cases were often mishandled because of a lack of effort at the initial stage of the investigation. To make matters worse, fortune tellers, priests or undertakers were often the first ones outside of family members to view a body. These people were not only unreliable as witnesses, but could be bribed to ignore suspicious circumstances.

Song Ci was not merely a scientist, but also an official who fully understood the social environment in which the law functioned. He was very much aware of how easily corruption could thwart the administration of justice, and he warned grimly, "Although the investigating official may conduct the proceedings honestly, if his subordinates accept bribes, they can completely distort the findings. Later, they may have to pay for their misdeeds, but in the meantime they will have cost an innocent person his or her life."

Thanks to this manual, an official dispatched to view a corpse, although not trained in the modern sense, had a rudimentary knowledge of how to spot death under suspicious circumstances. If he suspected poisoning, he might insert a *gin saji*, an elongated device made of silver, into the back of the deceased's throat. If it immediately showed spots of tarnish, for instance, this might indicate a murder by poisoning.

The one exception to this was *suishi*, deaths by drowning. Edo's many rivers, ponds, canals and wells made it a paradise for suicides, and they occurred so frequently it came to the point that the authorities simply disregarded them.

A Shrewd Kyoto Jurist

In his chronicle *Honcho Oin Hiji* ("Parallel Cases under the Cherry Tree"), first published in 1689, popular author Ihara Saikaku (1642–93) related cases heard by the *shoshidai*, the shogun's regional deputy for Kyoto. Ihara's book does not refer to judges by name, but simply uses the general term *gozen*, "His Lordship."

Most of the cases of which Ihara wrote involved Itakura Shigemune (1586–1656), himself the son of a judge named Itakura Katsushige (1545–1624). Itakura the elder had been a Zen priest for thirty years before taking the position of *shoshidai*.

From the way he held court, it is easy to see why people of the times regarded Shigemune as a rather inscrutable character.

"Before conducting a trial," the book's introduction notes, "Shigemune would make obeisance to the west, then hide himself behind a *shoji* door and grind tea while the court proceedings went on. No one questioned him about his peculiar behavior, and he did not bother to explain his actions until many years had passed. Then he explained that he first prayed to the deity of Atago for spiritual guidance, after which he retired behind the door to avoid being swayed by physical features into censuring or favoring someone. By the evenness of the ground tea, he knew his heart was calm enough to make a decision on a case."

One of Itakura's legendary cases involved a silk weaver named Ono who found himself saddled with heavy debts and saw no recourse but to sell off his property and leave Kyoto. To help him, ten members of the weavers' guild contributed a total of 100 *ryo*. But when Ono awoke on New Year's morn and looked for the money to repay his creditors, he and his wife were aghast to find the entire fund missing.

The disheartened weaver and his wife saw no recourse but the suicides of themselves and their children.

Suspecting foul play, the guild appealed on the man's behalf to Judge Itakura, who ordered all ten guild members to appear in court with their wives. "If you have no wife," he said, "bring a sister or niece." The judge ordered each member of the guild and his wife (or other female relative) to carry a large Chinese drum, suspended between the ends of a long pole, all the way from the court to the judge's residence and back.

For the ten days that followed, each couple appeared at court in turn. By then, the judge knew who the thief was. When a wife had whined, "You gave your share. How can they do this to us?" her husband whispered, "Shhh! Just hold on a little longer. It's not easy to steal 100 *ryo*." Unbeknownst to the couple, their remarks had been overheard by a Buddhist priest whom the judge had enlisted to ride inside the drum. Courts in those days had no compunctions about this early form of wiretapping.

In another celebrated case, on a late autumn night in the 1660s, the body of a man in his early forties was found on the road outside the Byodo-ji temple, an arrow protruding from his rib cage. The man still grasped a string of prayer beads in his left hand.

The deceased was identified as a merchant who sold pipes and smoking accessories in front of the Daibutsu, the Great Buddha statue.

The previous night he had attended a *nembutsu* mass and was apparently on his way home when the killer struck.

When the man's grieving widow appeared before the judge, he asked, "What was his behavior like recently? Do any of his close associates come to mind?"

The wife named two men in particular. "Four or five years ago, they met frequently. But suddenly for some reason their association ended."

The two were summoned to the court and questioned, but neither appeared to have a motive for the crime. The first told the judge, "The victim and I used to compete in *kemari* [kickball, a popular pastime in those days]. But my skills surpassed his and we eventually drifted apart."

The second said, "Several years back, the victim and I competed for the favor of a courtesan named Kagetsu, who works at Misuji-machi. But it was a friendly rivalry, and we never once quarreled over her. Kagetsu is still in the business; if you doubt my words, please ask her yourself."

No matter how the judge looked at the matter, both men appeared innocent of any wrongdoing. Finally, he said, "You are both men of means. So please give his widow a solatium of one *kamme* to help with funeral expenses."

This was a considerable amount, equivalent to over 1 million yen today, and certainly more than was customary, especially for a lapsed friendship. The judge watched the men's expressions carefully. One man winced upon hearing the excessive sum; the other seemed to take it in stride.

The judge finally told the widow, "You are childless. Therefore after one hundred days of mourning, you are free to remarry." He then issued a strange command: "Take the arrow and bury it beside the ashes of your husband."

Months passed. One night the following spring, residents of the neighborhood where the killing occurred were aroused from their beds by a woman's screams: "Help! It's a thief! Please come quickly!"

Men rushed into the street waving clubs and other makeshift weapons. One of them carried a short bow and arrow. Constables, who had been lying in wait, hustled him off to the court.

The arrow buried in the slain man's grave was dug up and compared with the one in the man's possession. They proved identical.

"The woman who cried out was the widow of the man you killed last year," said the judge. "What I don't understand is why you did it. What was your grudge against him?"

Confronted with the evidence, the man confessed. "After I became accomplished at archery, I began shooting at cats and foxes. I felt the urge to shoot a human being. Late one night when no one was around, I shot him."

The man's archery skills were to cost him his own life.

This story contains a mystery within a mystery. It has been suggested that Ihara's tale of the murderous archer is an allegory referring to the execution of Christians in Kyoto nearly a half century earlier.

These Christians had resided in an area called Daiusu-machi, the "Daiusu" believed to be a corruption of the Latin word *deus* ("god"). During a festival in 1619, in protest against what they perceived as Shinto idolatry, the Christians shot arrows into a *mikoshi* ("portable shrine"), causing considerable consternation. For their sacrilege, more than seventy believers were burnt at the stake.

In support of this hypothesis, the scholar Isoo Munemasa points out the similarities in pronunciation of "Daibutsu-mae" and "Daiusu-machi." In any event, the weapon of choice in both cases was the short bow.

Edo's Legendary Magistrate

Among the legendary exploits of the machi bugyo of Edo, the greatest of them all perhaps was Ooka Echizen (1677–1751). His full title was Ooka Tadasuke, Echizen no Kami. He began his career at age thirty-five as an obscure magistrate. His abilities caught the eye of Tokugawa

Yoshimune, the reform-minded shogun, and in 1717, he was promoted to machi bugyo of Edo's southern court, where he presided until 1736, making him the third longest-serving governor-magistrate of the Edo period.

Judge Ooka gained a legendary reputation for his integrity and ability to serve the interests of justice. As part of his duties, he also made an effort to influence the language. In 1723, he banned the usage of *shinju* ("heart center"), the popular term for a suicide pact, which in his view romanticized what was an illegal act. *Shinju* itself was an artificial term, created by puppet theater and kabuki dramatist Chikamatsu Monzaemon (1653–1724) for the title of his 1703 play *Sonezaki Shinju*, which was based on a actual incident occurring only two weeks before.

To replace it, Ooka coined a new bit of legalese, *aitai-jini*, or "mutual death." Unfortunately this term never really caught on, and he would no doubt be displeased to learn that Chikamatsu's term remains in popular use to this day.

As Ooka's fame spread, apocryphal stories about his exploits were complied into a book known as *Ooka Seidan*. Many were extrapolated from earlier tales, originating both in Japan and China, that are regarded as embellishments but with at least some basis in fact.

"The Case of the Bound Jizo," is one such tale. One day, the story goes, a kimono merchant came to Ooka's tribunal to report that an entire cartload of bolts of cloth had been stolen while he took an afternoon siesta by a temple, in the shadow of a statue of Jizo, a guardian god.

Constables were sent to investigate. As no witnesses could be found, the judge decided that exceptional measures would be needed to solve the case. After pondering the matter, he decided that the statue of Jizo, a god whose job was to protect travelers, had been derelict in its duty.

Ooka instructed his constables to return to the scene of the crime and arrest the statue. No doubt shaking their heads in bewilderment over this strange order, the men grunted as they lifted the heavy stone Jizo from its pedestal, bound it with ropes, and began to pull it back to

Ooka's court in an open-wheeled cart used in those days to transport criminals.

Naturally, these strange goings-on attracted the attention of the people in the neighborhood where the theft had occurred. They fell in behind the cart and followed it into the compound at Sukiyabashi and up to the *shirasu* (literally "sand bar") where litigants knelt before the judge.

The spectators were astonished to see Ooka angrily scold the Jizo for negligence—after which he ordered the rope bindings to remain in place until the Jizo arranged for the stolen goods to be returned to their owner!

Hearing this, the spectators erupted in nervous laughter. Ooka, infuriated by such a lack of decorum in his court, berated the spectators and then slapped a heavy fine on them for contempt. The crowd started to wail piteously that they could not afford to pay such a stiff fine. Pausing for dramatic effect, Ooka reconsidered briefly and then told them, "I am willing to settle for a token fine. Each of you must give to the court a small swatch of cloth [measuring about six centimeters square]. But if even one person among you fails to pay this token fine, the full amount will apply."

The people rushed to comply. When they returned with the token fines, Ooka told the old man who had been robbed to examine the swatches of cloth. Halfway through the lot he spotted a sample of goods that matched one of the bolts of stolen material. Ooka ordered the suspect's residence searched, and a portion of the stolen goods was recovered. Under further questioning, the man revealed the identities of his confederates, and an entire gang of thieves was apprehended.

Ooka then walked up to the statue of Jizo and personally removed the ropes still binding it, all the while acknowledging its part in recovering the stolen merchandise. The constables then returned the statue to the grounds of the Nanzo-in temple.

While it is generally acknowledged that these events never took place, the existence of the Jizo itself is beyond dispute. Edo's townspeople even adopted the custom of reporting thefts to the statue, at which time they would replicate the actions of the famous judge by tying a piece of rope around it. The statue became known as *Shibarare Jizo*, the "Bound Jizo."

Originally in Azumabashi, in Sumida Ward, the Nanzo-in temple was relocated to Katsushika Ward on the city's eastern outskirts after the Great Kanto Earthquake of 1923. Here, the one-meter high Jizo stands beneath a protective roof, covered from head to foot in meter-long sections of straw ropes attached by visiting worshipers.

Although the custom of tying a rope around the Jizo has come to take on a less ominous meaning in recent years, a few of the temple's visitors, it is said, stand before it as robbery victims asking for the Jizo's help in recovering lost property. Straw ropes are available from the temple for 100 yen each.

The *Shibarare Jizo* statue. Legend has it Judge Ooka Echizen ordered its arrest in order to apprehend a gang of thieves.

LAWMEN AND THEIR ASSISTANTS

YORIKI ("SERGEANTS") and *doshin* ("constables"), the men who carried out law enforcement in Tokugawa times, were members of the samurai class and often inherited their jobs. *Yoriki* literally means to "give power"; *doshin* means "same heart." In Edo, these officials lived in a communal neighborhood along a canal (Hatchobori) that connected to the Sumida River, and the expression *Hatchobori no danna* (a master of Hatchobori) eventually became a euphemism for the cops.

The communal neighborhood helped provide better security for officials' families, and its location gave them a relatively short commute to the places they went most often—the city's northern and southern courts and the main jail.

Throughout most of the Edo period, yoriki numbered 50, divided into two brigades (for the northern and southern courts) of 25 each. The number of doshin fluctuated, ranging from a low of 150 to a high of 240. The latter were divided into two brigades assigned to the respective courts. This means that the city of Edo relied, at the most, on 290 officials to carry out its law enforcement. In contrast, the modern Tokyo Metropolitan Police Department employs over 10,000.

The yoriki and doshin performed many other duties in addition to police work, such as fire watch, ceremonial and administrative jobs. Perhaps at any given time, about twenty-eight doshin were involved purely in police work, and of these, only a dozen were actually on patrol—this in a city with a population of between 500,000 and 1 million souls. Even if people back in the old days had been exceptionally law-abiding—which they certainly were not—the number of cops was clearly insufficient.

Sergeants did not wear what qualified as uniforms, but dressed quite smartly and styled their hair in a distinctive manner. They shaved their foreheads and sideburns and wore a comparatively short topknot, a style that allowed them to affect disguises that would permit them to move unrecognized among either townspeople or the samurai. They carried two swords and a *jitte*, a short truncheon. This was brandished about as a symbol of authority, but seldom used to wallop offenders. When serving on fire duty, sergeants wore fire-resistant headwear and cloaks designed to ward off sparks and flying debris. A common sight as they moved around Edo would be one or two men leading horses by the bridle, and flanked and followed by a retinue that included a pair of constables, one or two lance carriers and a porter.

Constables, who spent much of their time patrolling Edo's neighborhoods on foot, wore more practical garments than the sergeants, which they changed according to the season. In addition to swords, they carried a jitte inside the breast of their kimono. Their sash belts were worn low on the stomach, and they affected a distinctive swagger as they walked about.

Sergeants generally made their appearance at court at 10 A.M., and worked until about 4 P.M. The constables started working two hours earlier but also knocked off around 4.

The yoriki, considered as equal in rank to *hatamoto* (retainers to the provincial lords), received an annual stipend of two hundred *koku* of rice. Their residences covered from two hundred to three hundred *tsubo* of land, a fairly generous amount, but this had to include a stable for their horses. The homes were recognizable by a distinctive *kabuki-mon* gate with a heavy crossbeam and pillars. Doshin had to be content with one hundred tsubo. (A middle-class home today might be less than thirty tsubo, but can stand two or three stories high.)

One source estimated the average yoriki's annual wage as equivalent to a little less than 4 million yen today. On this, he had to support the members of his extended family, one young understudy, two servants, and two housemaids. The wages of the doshin were paltry by any criteria, only a fraction of that of the yoriki; perhaps what would be equivalent to about 40,000 yen per month. Thus, both yoriki and doshin depended on income from other sources, including favors, gifts and, of course, outright bribes. Today's notorious system of rewarding "underpaid" public officials with gifts and even cozy jobs after their retirement, in exchange for deferential treatment, clearly has its roots in the practices of Tokugawa times.

Police Spies

Punishment during the Edo period was swift and stern, but not every offender was punished. True, those who committed the worst excesses could be flogged, tattooed, banished from Edo, sent into exile on some remote island or deprived of their heads. But police also found it practical to offer more lenient treatment to some in exchange for their cooperation as spies and informers. Such a system predates Edo times and is said to have roots as far back as the Heian period (794–858).

Circumstances made this dependence on snitches unavoidable. As noted earlier, the city, with a population estimated at between 500,000 and 1 million, employed some 290 police officials at the most. Since they performed many other tasks, only about 28 doshin were engaged in law enforcement work, such as patrols and investigations. This meant that perhaps only a dozen were actually on the job at any given time.

Much of the slack had to be taken up by the private sector—gatekeepers and watchmen—and through collective measures by citizens such as neighborhood watch groups. The spies and informers may have proved the most effective of all.

Such men went by a variety of names. In Edo, they were called *okappiki* (or more politely, *goyokiki*). In the provinces around the Kanto region, they were referred to as *meakashi*; and in the Kansai region they were called *tesaki* or *kuchitoi*. They developed their own hierarchy, and the more accomplished even organized networks of "subcontractors," with as many as seven or eight subordinates, known as *shitappiki*, who were in many cases dependent on the *oyabun* ("boss") for their income. Each day, the head spies' assistants would cross the city to converge near Hatchobori, the area where police officials lived, and pass on the information, rumors and gossip they heard in their neighborhoods.

The okappiki and their minions moved about unrecognized by the ordinary citizenry, serving as eyes and ears for the officials. By the 1850s, such men may have numbered between five hundred and one thousand in Edo alone. Thanks to their numbers, their network was quite effective. Indeed, it was said that if a fugitive from the provinces managed to sneak into Edo, he would invariably be spotted, identified and apprehended within three days.

Okappiki received an annual stipend of 1 to 3 *bu*, paid out of the policeman's own pocket. (The cops, underpaid as they were, made up for such outlays by accepting favors or bribes.) Most okappiki earned their living through commerce, such as small family-operated cateries or hair dressing establishments, which had the advantage of putting them in daily contact with a large number of people.

Historians' views differ as to whether or not the spies were permitted to carry a police truncheon. Having no official standing, they were not authorized to make arrests. Instead, they would lead a criminal into a trap, which perhaps explains the use of *okappiki*, literally meaning to "give a little pull."

The spies had no official status, and were generally regarded as a necessary evil. Nevertheless some of them came to be trusted by the constables (who had to be addressed respectfully as *danna*, or "master"), and when the situation warranted, spies were even provided with a document that certified to their trustworthiness. There were others who played both sides of the law. If a criminal had money, some police spies could be bribed to look the other way, or even supply police with false or misleading information. Moreover, their subordinates tailored the details of the information they provided according to the amount of the income they received. Miserly cops received a commensurate amount of data.

In a system where abuses were rife, judges and administrators were understandably ill at ease over this dependance on spies to carry out law enforcement. Yoshimune, the eighth Tokugawa shogun, officially proclaimed that the spies "blemished the dignity of the law," and demanded the system be abolished. Bans were placed on the okappiki system at least twice, once in 1712 and again in 1789. These acts, however, failed to halt the practice.

While detailed historical records about the exploits of individuals are few, the okappiki gained literary recognition by carving out a solid niche in popular fiction during the first half of the twentieth century. Three of the best known were the subjects of hundreds of stories. Mikawacho no Hanshichi was a creation of Kido Okamoto, who set his 68 stories between 1841 and 1867. Teishi Yokomizo wrote approximately 200 works about Ningyo Sashichi, an okappiki active from 1815 to 1840. Kodo Nomura penned 386 stories about Zenigata Heiji, a man who apparently enjoyed remarkable longevity as the stories in which he appears span a period from 1641 to 1830. While entirely a fictitious character, Zenigata Heiji boasts the particular distinction of having a stone monument to his memory. Erected by fans in 1970, it can be seen on the grounds of the Kanda Myojin shrine, close to his old neighborhood not far from Akihabara Station.

Apprehension and Arrest

When word was received from a paid snitch or other source that an outlaw had been spotted, Edo's arrest squad would swing into action, armed with a variety of exotic contraptions. At night, a team of policemen and their porters would carry several *chochin* (portable corrugated

Jitte truncheons

paper lanterns) marked with the characters *goyo* ("official business") and other forms of illumination. If needed, they could don the medieval equivalent of body armor and other protective gear.

Old woodblock prints show examples of *hashigo-tori*, which involved using four portable ladders to form a square around the criminal, leaving him boxed in like a violent baby in a play pen.

Edo authorities took exceptionally strict measures to keep firearms out of the city and shootouts seldom occurred. But many criminals carried dirks, and the average desperado was somewhat less docile than those of modern times since he had nothing to lose—judges were seldom reluctant to impose the death penalty.

To subdue criminals, the cops assembled a collection of specialized paraphernalia. These were generally grouped into items for thumping; restraints; warning devices; and weapons that could be grasped, thrown and pulled in, like cowboy lassos.

The basic instrument of law enforcement, the jitte, was a short truncheon made of iron (less often of wood), usually with a string and tassel attached to the handle. The forged iron jitte varied widely in length and their shafts could be circular, hexagonal or octagonal. (The ones sold in novelty shops today are usually circular and chrome plated.)

Many, but not all, jitte were distinguished by a short, protruding *kagi* ("hook"), running about one-fifth the shaft's overall length. In close combat, an adept user could first deflect and clench a sword blade, and then, with a twisting and pulling motion, use his jitte as a club, striking the throat or solar plexus and subduing the attacker. Nevertheless, one did not confront a swordsman when armed only with a jitte without a great deal of practice and, hopefully, some backup. Schools of jitte techniques were finally standardized in Edo during the reign of Shogun Yoshimune, but numerous variations persisted in other parts of the country.

The police arsenal also included long poles to keep samurai at bay, so they could not deliver a slash or stab with their swords. The predecessors of these weapons originated in China and were brought to Japan by fighting priests between 1532 and 1569, and at least one European import is known to exist. Called a *Namban-bo*, it had iron pincers on the end that would snap shut and grasp the target like a mechanical hand.

Police even had access to a primitive form of Mace known as a *me-tsubushi-gu*, which used a gunpowder charge to propel hot sand or a chemical irritant into a violently resisting fugitive's eyes.

If the criminal refused to surrender without a struggle, he would be roughed up, but every effort was made to capture him alive. Through the sheer force of numbers offenders were pursued, cornered, and if they continued to resist, pummeled, stunned or pierced with small puncture wounds until they were overcome. Once caught, they were trussed up with short lengths of rope, whose colors varied according to the season, e.g., blue for spring, white for autumn, red for summer and black for winter. (Iron handcuffs were also available for this purpose.) They would then be tossed into a *banya* (holding pen) until they could be interrogated and brought to trial.

Despite TV period dramas showing a machi bugyo on horseback leading a contingent of cops to make a bust, it was almost unheard of to find a magistrate at the scene of an arrest. The exception of course would be the Hitsuke Tozoku Aratame, head of Edo's serious crimes squad, but his work did not require him to judge cases.

History does record a few cases when judges mounted up for a raid.

Roping them in: Constables used ladders and a variety of other exotic instruments to apprehend criminal suspects.

One occurred in 1644, when five *ronin* ("masterless samurai") and a sumo wrestler objected to the poor quality of services at an establishment in the Yoshiwara and went on the rampage, taking some of the women as hostages and holing up in one of the brothels. The incident occurred just at dusk, when business was at its most brisk, and the commotion threatened to spread among the other patrons.

The word was sent out, and eight sergeants, forty constables and a bevy of attendants converged on the quarter to quell the disturbance—in other words, nearly all the policemen on duty at the time. It was also probably the first and only time in history that magistrates from both northern and southern courts converged on a crime scene simultaneously.

The Yoshiwara was located quite a distance from Edo's two courts, and who knows, it's quite possible their honors merely used this as a pretext to take a look-see, having no other legitimate cause to make an appearance in Edo's most famous pleasure quarter. Nine years earlier, the shogunate had issued an edict prohibiting high-ranking samurai from entering brothels or theaters.

The Bottom Rung

One of the more severe forms of punishment in Tokugawa times was *hinin teka*, or demotion to "non-human" status, which was usually coupled with confiscation of one's assets. This immediately plunged an individual to the bottom of the social order, below the samurai, farmers, craftsmen and merchants. The *Osadamegaki Hyakkajo* ("The Edict in 100 Sections") prescribed this sentence for survivors of love-suicide pacts, as well as for having sex with a female relative; injuring one's former wife after divorce; for acts of petty thievery; or for collecting verses in *mikasa-tsuki*, a type of gambling pool in which people composed verses and the winner was picked by an umpire.

Old records from the Nagasaki court show it was common for parents or other close relatives to petition the court to confer hinin status on an incorrigible son or relative, perhaps in the hope of straightening him out, or as a means of disinheriting him, or to prevent his misbehavior from resulting in a punishment imposed against the entire family.

A clear distinction existed between the hinin, who had come by their non-status via the legal system, and the so-called *eta*, who were born into it. For the former, there was always the possibility that after several years of roughing it they could obtain amnesty and recover their former status. This was not an option for the latter group, a permanent underclass of butchers, curers of animal hides, and many other occupations, including wandering mendicants, blind musicians and masseurs, fortune tellers, street performers, makers of wind chimes and certain types of pottery, and, in rural areas, people who worked at a job known as *yamamori*, keeping a watch for illegal loggers and forest fires. Another source of revenues, and a fairly lucrative one according to some accounts, came from ties with *bakuto* (professional gamblers and forerunners of the yakuza).

Hinin were, in addition to being tightly controlled within their own group, subject to special laws that did not apply to other social classes. These included concealing their status as a hinin and a prohibition from dealings or relationships (including marriages) with ordinary citizens.

Although the system was officially abolished in 1871, discrimination against their descendants remains a serious social issue even today. The distinctions between the two groups were important, but possibly for reasons of expediency, many reference materials dealing with crime and punishment apply the term *hinin* to both groups. At the risk of oversimplification, this writer has done the same, subject to the precautionary points noted above.

Edo's outcast population was not especially large; one estimate put them at slightly over five thousand. Many lived communally in about twenty hamlets scattered on the fringes of the city. The one in the north, in Asakusa adjacent to the Yoshiwara pleasure quarter, was headed by a man with the hereditary name of Danzaemon. The southern community, near Omori, had its own boss, Kuruma Zenchichi, who was subordinate to Danzaemon. The top men had a modicum of status and were permitted to carry a sword. They also had the power of life and death over the people they oversaw and were, when ordered by the government authorities, required to execute those of their own community who had been found guilty of crimes.

Some hinin were obliged to beg for their livelihood; others were consigned to the lowest and dirtiest forms of work, such as transporting corpses and preparing them for burial. Hinin were also indispensable at the city jail in Kodenma-cho, where they worked under a boss named Chobei. Another of their tasks was to tattoo criminals with distinctive markings, usually on the forearms and, for the more incorrigible cases, on the forehead as well. Hinin worked as assistants in the torture chamber; before executions, they tied the mask over the eyes of the condemned and restrained them to make the swordsman's task go smoothly. This bit of work finished, they stripped clothing from the corpse and washed the blood from the severed head. Afterwards, they wrapped the heads and torsos in straw matting and transported the remains, slung from a pole, to the burial site.

Although outcasts were typically not identified by name in historical records, they were labelled in many old woodblock illustrations showing scenes of torture, executions and the processions around the city that proceeded execution for more serious crimes.

Hinin were actually entrusted to perform two types of public executions: *haritsuke* ("crucifixion") and *hi-aburi* ("burning at the stake"), the obligatory punishment for arsonists. The term *crucifixion* is really a misnomer; a more fitting rendering would be "death by perforation." After hoisting the condemned onto the crossbeam, two hinin crossed the ends of their *yari* (long spears) in front of his face. On the command of the presiding authority, they alternatively thrust their spears into the left and right sides of the torso. The trauma resulted in death within a minute or two, but the spear thrusts continued to a count of twenty or thirty by which time the condemned had long since lapsed into unconsciousness or death. The coup de grace, called *todome-yari*, was delivered by a cut, starting from the right, that transversed the throat.

Meticulous records were kept of the related costs for these activities, and bills were presented to the authorities for services rendered.

Despite their lowly status, other outcasts, including women, performed humane tasks at two facilities, shelters that dispensed rudimentary social services. Japan's first *hinin-goya* was established in 1671 in Kaga province (Ishikawa Prefecture). It was to continue operating for two hundred years.

From 1687, Edo authorities entrusted hinin with the operation of similar shelters, called *hinin-tame* or simply *tame*, that provided care for the indigent, the homeless, or those who had collapsed on the city's thoroughfares. Additional land was allocated to expand the facilities in Asakusa in 1689 and in Shinagawa in 1700.

The tame also ministered to people who suffered from the rigors of torture during police interrogation, and they became prototypes for a prison hospital, nursing prisoners who had become severely ill in jail. While under the care of the hinin, the prisoners were fed nourishing meals, kept warm in winter and occasionally visited by physicians, who dispensed medication. They remained at the facility until they died or recovered enough to return to jail. Other shelter residents were minors who had been sentenced to exile. Too young to be jailed with the criminal population, they were kept in confinement until they reached fifteen, the age at which their punishment could commence.

The shelters also took in people found innocent by the court but who had been rendered homeless in the interim, usually due to the stigma of having been arrested and jailed. The facilities were initially run as private enterprises but were soon operated with public funds. Old records show that during the year 1858 the Asakusa facility hosted 374 people, of whom 26 were women or children.

When the outcast system was abolished by law in 1871, the hinin involved in penal activities, like the samurai, were totally disenfranchised. They lost not only their special status, but also their exclusive jobs.

BEHIND BARS

UNDER EXTRAORDINARY circumstances, authorities temporarily freed criminals from Edo's jail on the condition that they return of their own accord. It took a major fire to make this happen, but in olden times prisoners kept to this kind of honor system. When a conflagration broke out in the city just after the Lunar New Year in 1841, the prisoners were released with orders to "return within three days." They did, with no exceptions. From the 1650s to the 1860s, similar events are said to have occurred over a dozen times.

This is not to say that prisoners never escaped. Few succeeded, however, and the ones who tried received heavier punishment. The jailer on duty at the time of the escape would lose his job and be banished from the city.

One famous escape was made by a thief known as Daijiro. While in jail awaiting sentencing, he refused meals for about six days, until he convinced the jailers that he was ill enough to warrant transfer to the *tame*, a holding area in Shinagawa maintained for sick prisoners and minors. After relaxing for a few days he "recovered." En route back to the regular jail, he bribed his guard to let him rest at a teahouse in Takanawa and while in the toilet removed the ropes binding him and disappeared through a back door. He showed up at the home of a lady friend in nearby Shirogane and the two of them attempted flight from the city.

The couple was captured and thrown back in jail. Before he could be brought to trial, he bribed a guard to supply him with a saw and spent the night furtively cutting through one of the cell's wooden bars. This did not give him quite enough room to squeeze through, but by this time it was already morning. The following night he started to cut through a second bar, but an honest *nezuban* (night guard) caught him in the act. He was moved to a high-security cell where he was restrained with manacles and wooden stocks on his feet. Daijiro, his paramour and the jailer who supplied the saw all received the death sentence.

The facility where this excitement occurred was known as the Denma Rogoku. An earlier facility had apparently existed in Tokiwabashi but in the late sixteenth century or early seventeenth century it was moved to Tokyo's present-day Chuo Ward. Denma had the advantage of being near Hatchobori, where the police officials lived. It was to remain in use until 1875, when a western-style prison was finished in Ichigaya. The site of the old jail, just beside Kodenma-cho Station on the Eidan Hibiya subway line, is presently home to a small park and two Buddhist temples. Its *Kubi-kiri Jizo*, a small stone deity erected in its southeast corner—a location determined by *fengshui*—marks the place where executions were held. *Kubi-kiri* means "decapitation."

Japan's largest jail, Denma Rogoku covered an area of about 8,640 square meters—a small city block. It had a wall topped with sharpened bamboo staves pointing inwards to discourage escape. From the outside, it was not especially imposing; the wall around it was low enough to allow a rider on horseback to peer inside.

The warden of the Denma Rogoku was a middle-ranking samurai who adopted the hereditary name Ishide Tatewaki. About thirty-eight people were employed by the jail. They were identified by happi coats bearing the character *de* (from Ishide) on their backs. Ironic, perhaps, since the character means to "go out."

Men and women were held separately, and strict class distinctions were maintained among prisoners, with better conditions for samurai, doctors and those of higher social status. Separate jails for farmers and the indigent were eventually built to prevent their mingling with hardened criminals. Prisoners rose at 4 A.M. and bedded down at 8 P.M. Aside from the roll call and the two simple meals, served at around 8 A.M. and 5 P.M., there was little to keep them occupied. Prisoners bathed three times a month in winter, four times a month in the spring and autumn months, and six times a month during the summer.

Prisoners could not have visitors, but were able to receive certain types of provisions, such as dried fish, to supplement the meager diet. For a price, sake and tobacco could be smuggled in. In exchange for added rations, a prisoner could volunteer to stay up all night to shoo rats away from the others while they slept. On hot days, the prisoners lowest in the pecking order were obliged to take turns fanning the head trusty.

The jail had a capacity of around four hundred people, an impressively low figure for a city of one million. When at its most crowded, conditions in the commoners' jail were horrible, with prisoners packed together like the proverbial sardines. By one account, eighteen men were forced to spend the night atop a single *tatami* mat. This was done by making them kneel upright, in two rows of nine facing each other. Knees were fitted between those of the men sitting opposite. Each neighbor's shoulder was used as a pillow.

Historical data shows a direct correlation between overcrowding and prisoner mortality. Disease was a factor, but intolerable conditions occasionally led to murder. After dark, the toughest prisoners would fall upon an unsuspecting victim and smother him or use other ways to kill that left no discernable marks. After several days, a doctor would arrive, give a perfunctory glance, and pronounce the deceased to have expired from disease or "natural causes." Out of a total of 8,604 prisoners incarcerated during the years 1818–20, for example, 620 died. This particularly high rate, about 7.2 percent, resulted mainly from poor rations during a period of food shortages.

When Getting the Truth Really Hurt

The popular period dramas shown on Japanese TV have a finale in which the kneeling villains cringe and squirm as his lordship sternly pronounces judgment. Actually, the judge was normally spared the sight of the accused, or at least of those who committed more serious crimes. The bad news was delivered back at the jail, via an official known as the *Kenshi Yoriki*, who read it from a document folded into seven long vertical sections and opened like an accordion. Punishment then followed swiftly.

The process of arrest and interrogation had begun weeks or months before, when a suspect was delivered to a facility known as an *oban-ya*, which was something like the holding cell in modern police stations. While records and descriptions are sketchy, seven of these oban-ya are believed to have existed in Edo. There, suspects underwent interrogation while constables sought out witnesses and other corroborating evidence.

The most frustrating crime to investigate was said to be arson. Not only did the evidence usually go up in flames, but people often set fires with the specific intention of destroying evidence of crimes such as theft. Moreover, an arson suspect knew that if found guilty, he faced burning at the stake.

The death penalty was frequently handed down as prescribed by law, but this does not mean it was dealt out lightly. As was also the practice in China, death sentences and other heavy punishments such as exile and banishment handed down by the magistrate were subject to review by the Shogun's Council and the shogun himself. If they found extenuating circumstances, they had the power to withhold approval, leading to a retrial. Furthermore, officials found to have forced a false confession faced dismissal or punishment.

Soon after Yoshimune reluctantly became shogun in 1716, he began to impose far-reaching reforms. He realized that when a person forced to confess was convicted and executed and the real criminal apprehended afterwards, the people's faith in the system of justice would be shaken. This led him to launch a series of enlightened political and economic measures known collectively as the Kyoho Reforms. Ooka Tadasuke, appointed as Edo's magistrate-governor the following year, was entrusted to elucidate the law regarding the use of torture to extract confessions. This was fixed in 1722.

Specifically, torture in order to extract a confession could be applied for murder, arson and robbery. From 1740, two additional crimes were added: breach of a barrier checkpoint and treason, the latter either by written correspondence or treasonable conspiracy. The 1722 law also states that "If, while an investigation is proceeding, the commission of some other crime by the accused is clearly ascertained, for which the death penalty can be imposed, he may be tortured."

Unfortunately the law contained a loophole. If, besides the cases specified, there were other instances in which it would be advisable to apply torture, it might be applied after a consultation between the judges of a court. Since torture almost invariably resulted in a conviction, this stipulation essentially meant that the suspect was literally at the mercy of the judge.

Among the reforms were restrictions concerning the degree of grilling permitted at the oban-ya. Police were made liable to disciplinary measures in the event of *tori-chigai* (false arrest).

From the oban-ya, suspects were transferred to the city's main jail in Kodenma-cho, where they remained until trial. Prior to appearing before the magistrate, the accused would be taken to a small auxiliary courtroom called the *sengisho* for preliminary testimony. An uncooperative attitude (i.e., refusal to confess) warranted a trip back to the jail. Here, the suspect was moved to a special shed called the *sensakujo* and a confession was extracted the hard way.

This judicial torture had two categories. The first type, called *romon* ("questioning at the jail"), included whipping, forcing a suspect to kneel on a washboardlike surface while heavy stone slabs were successively piled across his thighs (causing excruciating pain in the shins), and *ebi-zeme* (prawn torture), which consisted of being tied and left for hours in a convoluted position with the torso bent forward to meet the legs.

Specialized forms of torture were used to extract confessions.

The process continued—interrogators changed shifts when they grew tired—until the suspect confessed.

The second, and more severe category, was called *gomon* ("torture"). It was regarded as quite extreme and required prior approval of the judicial board. This usually involved *tsuri seme*, in which the suspect's arms were tied behind his back and he was suspended by ropes from the ceiling.

It did not take much pain to lead most suspects to conclude that holding out wasn't worth it—but not always. In 1833, Edo authorities apprehended a tattooed miscreant known as Irezumi Kichigoro on a

Repeat offenders were tattooed with distinctive markings according to the province where they lived.

charge of theft. He was whipped, stones were piled on his thighs, and he was hog-tied and dangled from the ceiling, all to no avail.

Over a period of one year and nine months, Kichigoro underwent no fewer than forty-four such sessions. His defiance seemed to increase with each session, further confounding the deputies. But they had one last trick up their sleeve: a process called *satto-zume* allowed the court to pass sentence in rare cases when a confession was not forthcoming, provided other compelling evidence of guilt could be produced. This judicial loophole was invoked, and Kichigoro was subsequently beheaded.

Around the mid-1800s, a police official, Sakuma Osahiro, produced a manual entitled *Ginmi Kaitei*, in which he outlined techniques for questioning suspects. Sakuma, clearly a man with keen psychological insights into human nature, was successful in extracting confessions through persistent but gentle persuasion. He would refrain from angry outbursts, speaking quietly and carefully observing the suspect's reaction.

After August 1874, police were officially forbidden to use torture to obtain confessions except when deemed "unavoidable," for which prior permission from the court was required. Even after this ostensible banning of torture, investigators found Sakuma's example too taxing, preferring their own heavy-handed methods.

It is difficult to imagine a female standing up to such mistreatment, yet one woman proved she could take it. Fukui Kane was arrested in 1871 on suspicion of murdering her patron, a government counsellor named Hirosawa, while he slept. Fukui, pregnant at the time of her arrest, was incarcerated from January 1871 to July 1875. During this period of four years and seven months, she endured several dozen torture sessions all the while steadfastly denying her guilt. She was finally released and Hirosawa's murder, for which she was the sole suspect, remained officially unsolved. Fukui's formidable ability to endure such protracted pain and humiliation led some to theorize that she was one of those perverse people who actually enjoyed such abuse.

THE DEATH PENALTY

DURING THE DECADES of civil war prior to the establishment of the Tokugawa regime in 1603, numerous cruel forms of punishment and execution were utilized. These included disfigurement (cutting off of nose and ears); being flayed alive, thrown from a cliff, or pulled apart by oxen; stoning, having the skull crushed by a heavy mallet, boiling to death, being buried alive, and being tied upside down to a cross set in a tidal flat to cause slow drowning by the incoming tide.

The Tokugawa bureaucracy streamlined the death penalty, limiting forms of execution to *zanzai* or *shizai* ("decapitation"), *haritsuke* ("crucifixion"), *hi-aburi* ("burning at the stake") and *nokogiri-biki* (killing by using a saw on the criminal's neck). The crimes to which these punishments applied were clearly spelled out in the *Osadamegaki Hyakkajo*. Judges could also order specific refinements to punishments. After beheading, a criminal could be subject to *gokumon*, the displaying of his severed head on a gibbet exclusively for this purpose, measuring four feet long by three feet five inches. The head, propped up by mounds of clay and impaled on one or more large nails to keep it from rolling off, would be displayed for two nights and three days. At night a wooden bucket would be placed over the head to prevent scavengers from nibbling on it.

Samurai tradition once attached scant concern to the act of lopping off someone's head. By around 1716, however, Yamamoto Tsunetomo,

Gokumon, the display of an offender's severed head on a gibbet, served as a warning.

AEL13.—Japan. Strafrecht.

Shizai (decapitation) was the most common form of execution.

author of the *Hagakure*, was already complaining that the marital spirit that thrived in earlier times had deteriorated. "Last year I went to the Kase Execution Grounds to try my hand at beheading," he wrote in William Scott Wilson's translation, "and I found it to be an extremely good feeling. To think that it is unnerving is a symptom of cowardice."

Another *Hagakure* passage goes, "Yamamoto Kichizaemon was ordered by his father Jin'emon to cut down a dog at the age of five, and at the age of fifteen he was made to execute a criminal. Everyone, by the time they were fourteen or fifteen, was ordered to do a beheading without fail. When Lord Katsushige [the Kyoto shoshidai] was young, he was ordered by Lord Naoshige to practice killing with a sword. It is said at that time he was made to cut down more than ten men successively.

"A long time ago this practice was followed, especially in the upper classes, but today even the children of the lower classes perform no executions, and this is extreme negligence. To say that one can do without this sort of thing, or that there is no merit in killing a condemned man, or that it is a crime, or that it is defiling, is to make excuses. In short, can it not be thought that because a person's martial valor is weak, his attitude is only that of trimming his nails and being attractive?

"If one investigates into the spirit who finds these things disagreeable, one sees that this person gives himself over to cleverness and excuse making not to kill because he feels unnerved. But Naoshige made it his orders exactly because this is something that must be done."

After decades of prolonged peace, however, opportunities for the removal of heads became fewer, and eventually it became necessary to entrust the job to those with expertise. In the cemetery behind the Shoun-ji temple, not far from Ikebukuro Station, stands a stone memorial to the eight generations of men named Yamada Asaemon who were the closest thing that old Edo had to a Lord High Executioner.

In the early years of the Tokugawa regime, the position of Edo's "head-chopper" had been held by a number of people. Beheadings were once carried out by a fellow named Nakagawa Saheita, who died in 1653. By official decree in 1717, Yamano Kanjuro was authorized to combine two tasks, sword tester and head-chopper. He was said to have tried out new blades on more than six thousand corpses before passing away from illness at age seventy.

Yamano's appointed heir, unfortunately, proved incompetent, and by the first decade of the eighteenth century, the work was apportioned among four individuals. In addition to Yamada Asaemon, there were three samurai named Nezu, Matsumoto and Kuramochi. When Kuramochi, last of the three, finally died in 1736, Shogun Yoshimune granted Yamada an exclusive arrangement. The first Yamada was apparently kept quite busy; legend has it he lopped off 999 heads during his illustrious career.

One source says Yamada was descended from a family of fishmongers. That might provide a suggestion as to how he gravitated to this particular profession. In any case, at some point he gained samurai status. Due perhaps to the bloody nature of the job, he and his descendants remained masterless *ronin*. Each Yamada groomed a successor who inherited the same name, a practice that continues in such traditional disciplines as sumo and Kabuki.

Yamada's work as a decapitator was ad-hoc and his engagements depended largely on who was due to lose his head. For samurai and nobles under a sentence of death, no executioner was needed, as they were typically permitted to save face by ritual suicide (*seppuku*). In such cases they designated their own second to perform the customary *kaishaku* (coup de grace). More severe punishments, such as crucifixion and burning at the stake, employed outcasts armed with spears or burning tapers. The most extreme form of punishment, called *nokogiri-biki*, was, in theory at least, open to all comers who could work up the courage. It involved sawing off a criminal's head while he was immobilized in a pit. Saws were supplied at the site.

The task of beheading common criminals was typically delegated to a lower-ranked yoriki posted at the jail. In theory, the job was not especially taxing for any samurai trained in swordsmanship, but many of these men were still young, some in their late teens, and this duty was

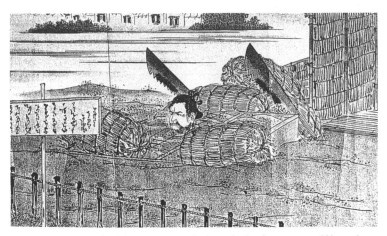

Nokogiribiki was considered the most extreme death penalty, but few citizens could bring themselves to use the saw on a condemned criminal's neck.

not always performed with enthusiasm. Even with a razor-sharp sword, the act of beheading is not as easy as portrayed in TV period dramas, particularly when the sword made solid contact with the vertebrae. While 100 percent fatal, failing to deliver a clean cut on the first swing could be messy, and cause the condemned to suffer unnecessarily.

A beheading needed assistance from two or three hinin, who would tightly grasp the condemned (whose eyes were covered by a paper mask), tug his garment down past his shoulders, and force his upper torso forward over a shallow pit. According to some references, at a sign from the swordsman they gave a hard yank on the condemned's big toes, which caused an involuntary stretching of the neck. Some old illustrations show the swordsman's right leg raised off the ground, like that of a baseball player, in order to get more power into his swing.

When a policeman was not up to the task, Yamada would be summoned from his residence in Hirakawa-cho, just west of Edo castle's inner moat, to do the job. He received a nominal payment for removing a head, but his main source of income was testing and certifying swords, an activity called *tameshi giri*. Good swords did not come cheap,

In *haritsuke*—crucifixion Japanese style—two executioners with spears brought the condemned to an excruciating end. It was said in those times that "even a hardened man could not keep from shuddering at the gruesome sight."

and it made sense to ascertain that the blade was suitably robust. Yamada made sure buyers got what they paid for. To do this, ropes were tied to the wrists and ankles of a headless corpse, which was stretched over wooden sawhorses by two hinin attendants. (It should be noted that only male corpses were utilized for this procedure, the musculature of women not being firm enough to offer suitable resistance.) The corpses had to be in otherwise good condition; those with obvious disfigurements or people below a certain social class were ineligible. Yamada methodically made a prescribed series of slashes across the torso. If the sword performed as expected, Yamada's chop (or signature, if you prefer) went on the document of certification.

The corpse, now in considerably worse condition following this mistreatment, would be wrapped in straw matting and transported to the execution ground for burial. This differed from a simple beheading, in which case the corpse was returned to the family for burial without further indignities. To undergo tameshi-giri after death was regarded as additional punishment—although it could at least be argued that it was painless.

At one time, tameshi-giri was apparently performed on live prisoners, but the process proved a bit messy and it was discontinued.

Another source of Yamada's income involved removing the livers from his victims. These were hung out on strings, dried, ground into pellets called *kimo-maru*, and sold as a remedy for people with diseases such as tuberculosis.

Legends abound regarding the various Yamadas' prowess with the sword. While a hard rain was falling, one story goes, the seventh generation Yamada, first name Yoshitoshi, gripped his sword with only one hand while severing a head, not even bothering to lower his umbrella. His son Yoshifusa proved a worthy successor; he once lopped off nine heads in quick succession without so much as breathing hard.

How did the Yamadas focus mentally while engaged in their gruesome tasks? In his memoirs, Yamada Yoshifusa revealed his family secret: he silently recited four short passages from the "Nehan-kyo" (Sutra of Supreme Enlightenment). Each line was synchronized to a stage of mental and physical preparation. With the completion of the final couplet *"Jyaku-metsu-i-go,"* he swung downwards and lopped off the head.

On January 31, 1879, Yamada Yoshifusa, age twenty-five at the time, conducted Japan's last officially sanctioned decapitation of a woman. She was O-Den Takahashi, a notorious *dokufu* ("she-devil"), alleged poisoner and convicted murderess. Yamada's fumbling of the execution (she moved abruptly and he failed to dispatch her on the first two swings) was instrumental in the decision to adopt hanging as the sole form of the death penalty. Still, Yamada was called back for a few more jobs, perhaps for old time's sake. On July 24, 1881, he performed his last execution, beheading Iwao Takejiro and Kawaguchi Kunitoshi, a pair of thieves who had committed murders in the act of robbery. Legend has it that Yamada performed his first job at age twelve; over a decade and a half, he executed an estimated three hundred people.

Yamada's well-used sword, named "Mago Roku Kengen," is stored in close proximity to the remains of some of his victims at the Eko-in temple, adjacent to the old Kotsukappara execution grounds in Minami Senju.

A Visit to the Boneyard

At the end of October 1998, the metro editions of several vernacular newspapers reported that in Tokyo's Arakawa Ward close to Minami Senju Station, construction workers at a site for a new Japan Railways' Joban line had unearthed 105 human skulls. Blackened from the mud, the skulls had been buried in large barrels.

Police were not summoned to the scene, and in fact, no one appeared the least bit surprised. The location, after all, had once been known as the Kotsukappara Keijo and for over two hundred years served as one of Edo's main execution grounds.

Kotsukappara was just off Oshu Kaido, the "narrow road to the deep north" taken by haiku poet Matsuo Basho on his poetic sojourn. In olden times, travelers passing the spot no doubt kept their eyes turned to the ground and picked up their pace, eager to avoid the grim sight of bloody corpses still tied to crucifixes and severed heads on gibbets—reminders that stern punishment awaited those foolhardy enough to violate the laws in the shogun's capital.

The derivation of Kotsukappara is unknown. Some scholars suggest it was a corruption of *kotsu-ga-hara*, ox-head field, or perhaps field of bones. The latter certainly came to apply. The figure two hundred thousand is commonly given for the number of people executed herein over a period of two centuries. This, however, would seem to contradict historical accounts that most executions took place inside the jail at Kodenma-cho. Then, too, the bodies of some executed criminals were returned to their families for burial. The rest, heads separate from the torsos, were wrapped in straw matting, suspended from poles and transported to Kotsukappara for burial.

Thus the figure two hundred thousand, if correct, would include those put to death on the site, the bodies of criminals who were executed elsewhere, plus condemned criminals who died of disease in jail (or who were murdered by fellow inmates) while awaiting execution.

The graves at Kotsukappara were shallow, and wild dogs would come at night to scavenge on the remains. The euphemism that someone was "even lower than a dog at Kotsukappara" became a colorful part of Edoites' speech.

Edo's public executions were originally carried out at Shinagawa or Asakusa. As Edo's population grew, the original execution grounds, called *shioki-ba*, were relocated to Suzugamori (near Omori on the old Tokaido road) and Senju, but the old names were retained by judges when passing sentence. Therefore, although a judge sentenced a criminal to die at Asakusa or Shinagawa, he (or she) was actually executed at Senju or Suzugamori.

It appears that according to the old system, the choice of execution ground was linked to the criminal's native province. Those whose ancestral villages lay to the north and east of Edo were sent to Senju. Those from the south or west of the city met their end at Suzugamori.

The borders of Kotsukappara originally measured approximately 110 meters in length by 54 meters in width, slightly larger than a football field. Most of the grounds today lie under train tracks, and what remains is a small fragment of the northeast corner, squeezed into a narrow triangle between the Joban Line, a railway freight yard, a stretch of paved road and a pedestrian bridge.

On June 14, 1871, the Ministry of Punishments announced that henceforth the beheadings previously conducted inside the jail would take place at Kotsukappara and the other execution ground at Suzugamori, effectively making executions a public spectacle. Less than a month later, Suzugamori was relieved of this function.

Between 1868 and 1872, an average of 708 executions were performed nationwide each year—roughly two every working day. The figure progressively declined. During 1912, when an amnesty was announced to commemorate the ascension of Emperor Taisho, a remarkably few 16 executions took place.

In 1873, however, there was still plenty of work to keep executioners busy; that year 970 executions were performed. On October 16 , the Japan correspondent for *The Times* went to observe a public execution out of what he describes as "vile curiosity." "I repented of it," he wrote, "but still it was a most extraordinary spectacle, and impressed me very much."

He provided a rather grisly but extremely detailed eyewitness account of the proceedings, which were probably conducted at Kotsu kappara by the penultimate (seventh) Yamada, Yoshitoshi.

"The culprits were eight in number, one being a woman. They were all beheaded with a sword. The operation was performed with wonderful dexterity and coolness, and not one of them, even the woman, showed the slightest symptom of fear.

"On one side of the enclosure were two Japanese officials, in chairs, to see the thing properly conducted. The criminals were placed in a row, on one side of the enclosure, blindfolded with pieces of paper. What struck me most was the horrid coolness of the executioner's assistant, a good-looking lad of 18; he went up to each poor wretch in his turn, gave him a tap on the shoulder, led him up to the mound, and made him kneel on the mat; he then stripped his shoulders, made him stretch out his neck, said 'That will do,' and in a flash the man's head was in the hole in front of him and his bleeding neck was, as it were, staring me in the face. The assistant, still with the same pleasant smile, picked the head up, threw some water on the face to wash off the blood and mud, and presented it to the Japanese officials, who noted and signed to go on with the next; the assistant then gave the corpse a blow between the shoulders to expel the blood, and finally threw the carcase [sic] aside like a log of wood. He then repeated the same pleasant programme with the next.

"I never thought a man's head could come off so easily; it was like chopping cabbages, only accompanied with a peculiar and most horrid sound—that of cutting meat, in fact.

"There was a dense crowd of Japanese present, including many women and even children; these people never ceased to eat, smoke, and chatter the whole time, making remarks on the performance, and even occasionally laughing, just as if they were at a theatre. The executioner poured water on his sword between each decapitation, as one wets a knife in order to cut India rubber."

Soon afterwards executions shifted back to the jail and the Kotsu-kappara execution ground was transformed into the prison cemetery. What remains today has not been preserved with the same loving care and attention devoted to the national historic treasures in Kyoto and Nara, but the site is easy to visit. Leaving by the south exit of Minami Senju Station on the Eidan Hibiya subway line, immediately across the street are two temples. To the right is the Eko-in (built in 1662), to the left, the Enmei-ji. Both are modern concrete buildings that do not fit the typical image of temples. In spite of the area's historic background, most of the graves in their cemeteries are apparently those of ordinary citizens from the local neighborhood. Very few executed criminals warranted grave markers, but there are a few notable exceptions, such as nationalist Yoshida Shoin (executed in 1859) and murderess O-Den Takahashi (1879).

The Enmei-ji, with its 3.6-meter high Kubi-kiri Jizo, is the more photogenic of the two sites. This guardian diety was erected using stones from Akita Prefecture's Hanaoka quarry in 1741. The Jizo was moved several dozen meters to its present location in 1895 to make way for the railroad. A large engraved stone in the foreground bears the cursive characters "*Namu myoho renge kyo*" (Hail, Book of the Lotus of the Good Law), an incantation of the Nichiren sect. This was the only solace available to the condemned, since members of the clergy were not in attendance at the final moment. (The system of using prison chaplains did not begin until 1872. The first was a Buddhist priest named Keitan Ukai, a member of the Otani sect of Nagoya.)

No more than three minutes away from the Kubi-kiri Jizo is the Obana restaurant, which was doing business when the execution ground was still in use. Although Obana's eel dishes are superb, one is moved to think that Edoites must have been a bit callous to enjoy a tasty repast while, within what must have certainly been hearing dis-tance, criminals were suffering excruciating deaths.

FAMOUS ROGUES

"THIEVES EXIST IN a variety of types," Edo-period philosopher Miura Baien (1723–89) once observed. "Some operate by stealth; others force themselves into peoples' homes; and still others lie in ambush beside roads to rob travelers at knife point."

The oldest historical reference to criminal behavior in Japan dates back to the 34th year of the Empress Suiko (554–628). A single line, it reads in its entirety, "Prolonged rains continue, starvation plagues all the provinces, many deaths, and numerous outbreaks of robberies."

By the seventeenth century, historical accounts of crimes had become far more detailed. Surely one of the most famous desperados to ever appear in Edo was a man known as Hirai (or Shirai) Gompachi. As the member of a low-ranking samurai family in Inshu (Tottori Prefecture), he trained in sword fighting and other martial arts as a youth. He was muscular and handsome, but had a hairtrigger temper and often became involved in brawls.

In the autumn of 1673, a fight broke out between dogs owned by Gompachi's father and that of another samurai, Honjo Suketaro. Honjo made an offensive remark, and when the teenaged Gompachi learned of it, he became infuriated, forced his way into Honjo's home and cut him down with his sword. Obliged to flee his home province, Gompachi made his way to Edo and found employment with several powerful samurai families. While employed by the Abe clan, he actually apprehended a thief who struggled violently, injuring five samurai before he could be subdued.

Perhaps his heroic action went to his head, but Gompachi soon discovered the delights of the Yoshiwara, and began spending far beyond his means on wine, women and kimono, for he also had a reputation as a flashy dresser. To fund his wardrobe purchases and nocturnal escapades, he turned to armed robbery.

Edo at this time had been the shogun's capital for less than eight decades, and still offered many isolated areas where thieves could lurk in ambush. Gompachi's main haunts were between Asakusa and the Sumida River, the Shitaya district just north of Ueno, and in Ushigome, near Ichigaya. Over the next three years, he killed as many as 130 people in the course of his robberies, making him truly a world-class felon. Most of his spoils were spent in the brothels of the Yoshiwara, where he procured increasingly high-class courtesans. His favorite was a lady who went by the professional name Komurasaki ("Little Purple"), whose remuneration for an evening's entertainment ran upwards of 10 *ryo* (silver coins).

Gompachi came under suspicion—not for theft, which it was assumed was beneath a samurai's dignity—but for what he claimed were repeated duels of honor, another practice Edo authorities were determined to curb. When things got too hot in Edo, he moved northwest to Kumagaya, where he tied up with a local gang and resumed his career. There, he murdered a wealthy silk merchant and attempted to flee with 300 *ryo*, but was spotted by local farmers, who gave an accurate description of him to the authorities. Soon fliers were posted around northern Kanto requesting people to "be on the lookout for Hirai Gompachi, age 24–25, white complexion, about 5 *shaku* 5 *mon* [about 165cm] in height."

Resigned to his fate, Gompachi sneaked back into Edo. He tearfully confessed his crimes to a Buddhist priest, saying that his only wish was to see his parents once more before turning himself in. He was given sanctuary at several temples and finally in 1678 made his way home, but was distraught to find that both his parents had died. Bowing before their graves, he begged forgiveness. Then in keeping with his promise to the priest, he struck out for Edo but took sick when he reached Osaka and turned himself in to the local magistrate.

Gompachi was transported under heavy guard to Edo. En route, he managed to steal the identity papers of the owner of the inn where he was spending the night and escaped, for a last emotional reunion with his favorite courtesan Little Purple. He then surrendered to the authorities.

At his trial in late 1679, Gompachi admitted to multiple robberies and murders but refused to reveal the names of any of his cohorts. Judge Miyazaki found no grounds for mercy and sentenced him to crucifixion.

Taken from the jail to the Suzugamori execution grounds, Gompachi was bound to crossed beams and hoisted upright. The execution ers crossed their spears before his eyes and awaited the order to thrust them into his torso. Before the sentence was carried out, Gompachi sang "Yae Ume," a song supposedly composed by his beloved, which begins, "I am an azalea that blooms in the wild, if you bend me, my blossoms will never fall. I am a firefly that lives in the wild, flickering like a torch on the bank of a river." He was then put to death and his remains buried in an unmarked grave at the Meguro Fudo temple, before which, legend has it, his lover committed suicide. At the time of his death he was twenty-five.

The Terror of the Tokaido

In late 1746, public signboards in Edo and throughout the provinces began to bear this public notice:

Citizens are requested to be on the lookout for a man who matches the following description:

—Name: Nippon Zaemon, also known as Hamashima Shobei
—Height: around 165 centimeters
—Age 29 years, but 31 or 32 in appearance
—Allows hair on brow to grow out to about 3 centimeters in length
—White, well aligned teeth
—Almond-shaped eyes
—Long, slender nose, slightly elongated face
—Shaves away hair from temples, wears thick topknot
—Right shoulder slumps slightly
—Carries an *inro* [lacquered medicine case] with inlaid bird pattern

Thus did the bandit Hamashima Shobei, also known as Nippon Zaemon, claim the distinction of becoming the first criminal in Japan to be the subject of a nationwide dragnet.

The man who inspired this effort was born in Totomi, present-day Shizuoka Prefecture. Named Tomogoro, he was a clever boy, and proved to be so skillful at the martial arts that he often astonished adults with his agility. He was also handsome and personable. Unfortunately, these qualities led him to shun gainful employment in favor of wine, women and gambling. By age eighteen, he had taken up stealing to support his dissolute tastes. After Tomogoro's father disowned him, he moved to another town and changed his name to Shobei.

Along with his other sterling qualities, Shobei also proved to be a natural leader, and soon found himself the head of a gang of bandits, to whom he proclaimed this business strategy:

"Important townsfolk and rich farmers have extensive holdings. Even though they do nothing, they continue to accumulate wealth. These people are immoral. It is from them we shall steal. We'll share the spoils with the poor and use the rest to have as much pleasure as we can, so we'll never have any regrets."

Shobei and his outfit roamed the countryside, robbing the affluent and holding up medieval Japan's equivalent of the Wells Fargo stagecoach. Their crimes covered parts of present-day Shiga, Mie, Gifu,

Aichi, Shizuoka, Yamanashi and Kanagawa prefectures—regions controlled mainly by *hatamoto*, mid-ranked vassals of the shogun, where law enforcement tended to be sketchy.

Shobei proved a highly competent leader, and his outfit swelled to number over two hundred. His confidants went by names like Gempachi, Kamiarai no Jinbei, Ima Benkei, Akaike Hoin and Onigoroshi ("Devil-killer") Heisuke.

One night, a roving constable caught Shobei's band in an act of thievery and gallantly attempted to arrest them, but found himself overcome by the criminals. Observing the struggle with amusement, Shobei magnanimously told his men, "Hey, this noble cop is even willing to risk his life on the job. Don't hurt him." After binding the policeman with ropes, they made off with their loot, leaving him uninjured.

Such acts of gallantry helped create the legend that Shobei was a "righteous thief." Then temptation got the best of him. In the spring of 1745, an influential landlord named Oikemura no Soemon prepared to fete his son's marriage with a lavish wedding feast. Shobei and a dozen or so of his cohorts crashed the party and made off with the wedding gifts, worth about 1,000 *ryo*. To add insult to injury, Shobei's gang raped all the female guests, including the bride.

This was the second time in two years that Shobei had robbed the unfortunate Oikemura. The rape of his daughter-in-law was the last straw. The injured party appealed directly to the governor-magistrate of Edo's northern court, who agreed that action was warranted. He assigned Tokunoyama Gohei, head of Edo's SWAT team, to organize a posse of twenty men and track Shobei down.

The posse managed to haul in eleven of his partners in crime, but Shobei himself was not among them. Thus the nationwide dragnet was launched, with his description circulated in some sixty districts around the country.

Realizing the trap was closing, Shobei became resigned to his capture. Early in 1747, he surrendered to the judge in Kyoto, ostensibly out of concern for his arrested cohorts.

He was transferred to Edo for his trial. Upon conclusion of the proceedings, governor-magistrate Nose ruled as follows: "The accused entered the provinces of Mino, Owari, Mikawa, Totomi, Suruga, Izu, Omi and Ise, where he used force to steal gold and silver; for these serious crimes, he shall be paraded before the public, after which his head shall be displayed at the Enshu Mitsuke."

On the eleventh day of the third month of 1747, Shobei, bound with ropes, was placed astride a horse and trotted about the city of Edo, after which he was taken back to the city jail in Kodenma-cho and put to death. His head, together with those of his trusted lieutenants Nakamura, Iwabuchi and Nakajima, was displayed for three days at the point on the Tokaido marking the boundary between Kanagawa and Shizuoka Prefectures.

Nezumi Kozo—the Saga of Japan's Not-so-noble Robin Hood

A fairly common sight in Edo times was the public display of criminals, both those who had been sentenced to death and those convicted of lesser crimes. The worst offenders were subjected to a form of display referred to as *hikimawashi* (literally, "to be pulled around"), which could cover a considerable distance.

So it came to pass that on the nineteenth day of the eighth month of 1832, the citizens of Edo got a last look at a thirty-six-year-old rogue named Jirokichi. Crowds lined the streets to watch as the procession, which included a placard announcing his crimes, passed on its way around the city. Jirokichi wore a dark blue hemp garment over a white shift. A string of prayer beads hung from his neck. He was described as small in stature, with a round, slightly chubby face. On his last public appearance he was permitted to apply light cosmetics, a custom among males in those times.

Jirokichi was raised the son of a gatekeeper. Apprenticed to the building trade, his real occupation, for what it's worth, was day laborer; he also belonged to a volunteer fire brigade.

The grave of the legendary thief Nezumi Kozo Jirokichi, executed in 1832. He earned an undeserved reputation as a Robin Hood.

Late one night three months before, Jirokichi had been apprehended in Hama-cho, adjacent to the estate of a member of the powerful Matsudaira clan, blood relatives of the Tokugawa rulers. His arrest came not through any particularly brilliant detective work. He dropped onto the street from the high wall around the premises of his most recent victim, only to encounter a constable named Oyagi Shichihei, who by pure coincidence happened to be passing on patrol. Finding such behavior somewhat suspicious, Oyagi detained the unlucky thief on the spot.

Edo's wealthy merchants made exceptional efforts at guarding their property. The samurai, smug in their position atop the social ladder, apparently did not, so Jirokichi singled them out for his own efforts to redistribute the wealth. His compact physique and ability at surreptitious entry into their sprawling estates earned him the moniker of Nezumi Kozo, which in the vernacular of the American West might be rendered as "Kid Rat." The sobriquet appears to have been synthesized from the names of two other noted thieves who probably inspired his career—one named Konezumi Ichinosuke, the other Inaka Kozo Shinsuke.

According to the laws of the times, theft of 10 ryo was sufficient to warrant the death penalty. By his own confession, Nezumi Kozo had, over the previous fifteen years, plundered the coffers of ninety-nine samurai estates in Edo and made off with loot from at least seventy-six of them, for a grand total of 3,183 ryo, 2 bu (a bu being one-fourth of a ryo) and assorted small change.

In pronouncing sentence, the judge noted sternly that Jirokichi was a repeat offender, who had been granted leniency for a crime he committed ten years earlier. At that time, Jirokichi had been expelled from Edo and his forearm tattooed with a distinctive stripe to mark him as a criminal. In a terse ruling, the judge ordered that Jirokichi be taken from the jail at Kodenma-cho, bound with rope, mounted on the back of a horse, paraded about the city's markets, and then beheaded, after which his head would be displayed on a gibbet for two nights and three days.

Edo's common folk had no great love of their samurai overlords, and Nezumi Kozo's exploits soon became, if not exactly a role model, something of a legend. Among the posthumous embellishments of his story was that he magnanimously shared his booty with the poor. Alas, any acts of philanthropy on his part were no more than wishful thinking. The funds he looted made it possible for him to marry four women (serving girls from teahouses) and have numerous mistresses. But most of it went to gambling, an activity to which he was hopelessly addicted. He was, nevertheless, smart enough to keep a low profile, and avoided undue suspicion by living a simple life and not flaunting his illegally acquired wealth. His career as a thief may have also been prolonged because his victims, perhaps out of embarrassment, chose not to report their losses to the city tribunal.

Not long after his execution, Nezumi Kozo was revived, so to speak, in songs, folk tales and stage dramas. He became a leading character in a well-known Kyogen drama in the 1850s, and in the twentieth century was the protagonist in the short story "Nezumi Kozo Jirokichi" by Ryunosuke Akutagawa.

While accounts vary as to where his execution took place, Nezumi

Kozo has the distinction of having stone memorials at both Eko-in cemeteries, in Ryogoku and Senju. The one at the latter boasts a protective covering of chicken wire, for it seems that when some people visit, it is not for the purpose of paying their respects to the departed but to chip off a fragment for good luck at gambling. When Nezumi Kozo's own luck ran out, alas, he paid the ultimate price.

When Outlaws Roamed the Kanto Plains

Following the disastrous failure of the Tempo Reforms in the early 1840s, the Tokugawa regime gradually began coming apart at the seams. One sure symptom of this meltdown was the appearance of armed bandits and brigands who roamed over large areas in the present-day prefectures of Gumma, Nagano, Tochigi, Tokyo, Saitama, Chiba, Kanagawa and Shizuoka.

While primarily made up of ex-farmers, these groups of the dispossessed also included masterless samurai, former sumo wrestlers and a few men who claimed to be physicians. Those from the lower classes were typically referred to as *mushuku*, meaning of no fixed abode, i.e., vagrants. Some eked out a living as *bakuto*, professional gamblers who were the forerunners of the yakuza. Armed with swords, spears and firearms, they swooped down from mountain hideouts to rob wealthy merchants and farmers. They were not the least bit intimidated by the rural samurai, who were too widely dispersed to mount a strong defense.

A chronicle from the period noted that in Gumma, when rumors began to fly that armed desperados had abducted an imperial princess who was en route from Kyoto to Edo, the local lords put their troops on high alert.

One of the more notorious gangs was headed by a thirty-two-year-old rogue from Shimousa (northern Chiba) by the name of Seiriki Tomigoro, a.k.a. Sasuke. He reputedly maintained a private arsenal that included an 80cm-long sword, two short swords, a bow and arrows, four spears and four matchlock rifles.

To subdue this Japanese Pancho Villa, in the early summer of 1849 the shogun's forces mobilized a posse of over 2,500 men. They combed the Chiba countryside and conducted house-to-house searches. Even then, Seiriki led them on a merry chase for fifty days before he was finally cornered at Mt. Konpira. As his pursuers closed in, he shot it out with them, killing several. When capture became imminent, he and a trusted lieutenant disemboweled themselves. Another fourteen members of his gang, ranging in age from eighteen to fifty-five, were bound in ropes and marched past large crowds to the Edo jail.

Seiriki was able to hold out as long as he did thanks to support from sympathetic local farmers and villagers, who like Edoites had no great love for their samurai overlords and assisted the fugitives in eluding their pursuers. The Chinese adventure novel *Shui Hu Chuan* is believed to have exerted a strong influence on these events. This famous Ming-period epic (rendered in English as "All Men Are Brothers") tells the story of righteous guerrillas who rebelled against the country's corrupt and decadent rulers.

A portion of the book was translated into Japanese in the 1720s. Extrapolated by Japanese authors, woodblock artists and dramatists, *Suikoden* had become part of popular folklore by the early nineteenth century. Much like the Chinese, downtrodden Japanese came to regard these men as chivalrous outlaws who stood up for the poor and oppressed. This was mostly wishful thinking, of course, but after nearly 250 years of stability under the Tokugawa's ironfisted rule, people were clearly starting to get bored.

Other troublemakers roamed the provinces, seemingly at will. Not long after the death of Seiriki, one armed gang of gamblers headed by a certain Kojiro clashed at Shimada, a post station on the Tokaido, with a rival gang. Both sides suffered heavy casualties. Kojiro, a tall, heavy-set rascal, had already terrorized Kumagaya, Chichibu and other parts of Saitama, stealing gold and raiding armories.

Another celebrated brigand extolled years later in books and on stage was Kunisada Chuji, the son of a Gumma farmer. At age seven-

A weakened Kunisada Chuji about to be captured, after twenty-four years on the run.

teen he killed a man in an altercation, and to prevent reprisals against his family and village became a fugitive. In Kawagoe (Saitama) he came under the wing of a powerful gambler named Omaeda and proved such an apt pupil he soon started his own franchise.

In 1836, on his way to Shinano province (Nagano), Kunisada and some twenty cohorts fought their way through a barrier checkpoint, driving the guards to flight, and by so doing making himself one of the country's most wanted fugitives. For more than a dozen years, he managed to elude the authorities by constantly shifting his base of operations through the Northern Kanto, Hokuriku and Tohoku regions. The fugitive lifestyle took a hard toll and his vigor gradually waned.

Perhaps out of a desire to see his old home one last time, he crept back to Kozuke (Gumma) in 1849, where he suffered a stroke. Too weak to flee, he was captured the following summer and taken to Edo, where he was sentenced to death by crucifixion at the scene of his crime, the barrier checkpoint between Gumma and Nagano.

The execution was carried out on a winter morning in early 1851. Kunisada, then forty-one, had been on the run for nearly twenty-four years—more than half his life.

CRIMINAL WOMEN COURTED CRUEL FATES

WHEN A WOMAN went before a judge in the Edo period, a common pronouncement from the bench was, "*Onna no gi nite waki-mae korenaku*." (You have forgotten your obligation as a woman to comport yourself with humility and restraint.)

Thanks to the Confucianist social hierarchy that accorded women a lowlier status than men, women who committed minor offenses were generally regarded as being less responsible than males and as such, the courts tended to be more lenient when meting out punishment. Whenever possible, women were spared tattooing and flogging, and let off merely with *kitto shikari*—a severe scolding—administered while they knelt before the bench, head bowed (if they knew what was good for them) in contrition. Although the woman would be released afterward, her offense and punishment remained on the judicial record.

More serious crimes, including the theft of more than 10 ryo, arson and murder warranted the death penalty. *Mittsu* ("adultery") was also regarded as a serious threat to social stability and punished severely when discovered. In 1720, a woman who conducted an affair with a man indentured to her husband appeared before Ooka Tadasuke and was sentenced to death by decapitation. Her lover was paraded about the city on horseback before the death sentence was carried out, and his severed head was displayed on a gibbet.

Love suicides were also a crime, and a couple that botched the effort would receive harsh treatment. Typical punishment would call for their being put on public display side by side for between one and three days at the *sarashi-ba*, a shed beside the Nihombashi bridge. Afterwards, they could also be subjected to *hinin deka*, demotion to the bottom rung of the social order.

Those who succeeded in a love suicide were denied funeral rites. If one partner died and the other survived, the survivor was beheaded, usually within the same year the crime occurred.

Women were not entirely without rights, but life was never easy. Men could annul a marriage with a simple writ of divorce, called a *rien-jo*, popularly referred to as *mikudari-han* (literally, "three and a half lines"). The letter's prescribed length was at least three and a half lines, and this made its intent readily apparent regardless of the contents. This format may have originated in the Nara period (710–94), when a divorce document had to state seven reasons. By the Edo period, seven was deemed too long, so the figure was halved. Another theory suggests that the customary Chinese divorce document, as mentioned in several Ming-period literary works, ran to three and a half lines, and this system was adopted in Japan as well.

According to one source, an illiterate man could divorce his wife by taking a brush to paper and simply inscribing the prescribed number of solid lines.

The document did not mince words, and its brevity left little room for details, although some did cite specific complaints. A typical example might have read: "To my worthless disobedient (obstinate, unruly, disrespectful, incorrigible, etc.) wife _____ (name). I hereby divorce you for reasons of my own. I don't care if you marry someone else in the future."

In addition to the criminal code, a system of *shikei* (private punishments) allowed people in positions of authority to apply creative and exceptionally cruel measures apart from the judicial process. A commoner could legally punish his wife by forcing her to work at what effectively amounted to slavery in a samurai household or a brothel. A lighter punishment was shaving her head—regarded as a great humiliation that prevented her from appearing in public—and sending her home to her family. Unable to bear the indignity, some women would enter a Buddhist nunnery, remaining there until their hair grew back.

Some of those who dispensed such punishments may have had more on their minds than simple administration of justice; they probably found it sexually stimulating. Some of the more exotic, sadistic practices included *hebi-zeme* (torture with live snakes); *yuki-zeme* (being dangled naked from a tree in the falling snow); and *kusuguri-zeme* (merciless tickling). Another interesting torture was known as *gochiso-zeme*. This involved withholding food for a considerable length of time, after which the person was tied up and placed in front of a sumptuous meal, which she could not reach to eat.

Of course, torture also took place in order to extract confessions. A "special investigator" by the name of Ishigo Kamenosuke supposedly produced a manual that contained special precautions to be taken into consideration when torturing women. The book, entitled *Onna no Semekata Kokoroe-gaki*, does exist, although Ishigo apparently did not. An interesting facet of its contents involved advice to avoid letting the torture victim's hairdo come undone. An excerpt reads, "The method of torture to be applied to a woman varies according to her hair style . . . Women from samurai families tend to use a lot of hair ointment to hold their coiffure together . . . Attention should be given to this."

During the Taisho period (1912–26), an artist named Seiu Ito became fascinated with these traditional torture techniques. He used his young wife as a model to experiment with some of the tortures outlined in Ishigo's manual, photographing her nude body in sessions that lasted as long as three hours. Mrs. Ito reportedly even took part in some sessions while pregnant.

Ito became quite famous in his day for his portrayals of this particular genre. The June 1924 issue of *Sunday Mainichi* magazine featured a visit to his studio. As can be seen in adult bookstores and on the Internet, Ito's legacy lives on today among fans of Japanese S/M.

Seiu Ito's rendition of courtesans being tied up and suspended for breaking the pleasure quarter's rules, along with a male customer confined in an overturned bathtub for his wrongdoings.

Rough Times for Female Criminals

Nothing served better to underscore the lowly status of women in feudal Japan than did the mistreatment meted out to prostitutes in brothels. Those who failed to ply their trade enthusiastically enough were denied meals or stipends. Punishments included being made to clean toilets or, in extreme cases, to take on a succession of clients who paid as little as 2 *bu*, 5 *rin*—the equivalent of the price of a bowl of noodles in today's money—for a few minutes of the woman's company.

Not surprisingly, some made desperate attempts to flee from the "life of shame." Few succeeded. After being captured and returned to their employers, they were subjected to the indignity of being bound hand and foot and left tied overnight to one of the large stone lanterns flanking the entrance to the Yoshiwara or other licensed pleasure quarters. Once back at work, further abuse awaited them.

If convicted of a serious crime not warranting the death penalty, a woman might be sentenced to *ento*, banishment to a distant island, which for Edo residents usually meant the seven islands of Izu. Harsh conditions prevailed, and their property was typically confiscated by the state.

The departures of exile ships were infrequent, which meant lingering for several months in the overcrowded and filthy conditions of the jail at Kodenma-cho. The ships displayed a banner with the words *runin-sen* (a ship carrying people into exile), and left from a pier at either Eitaibashi, in Tokyo's present-day Chuo Ward, or Kanasugibashi in Minato Ward, depending, respectively, on whether the exile was to be permanent or temporary. As in the jail, women were confined to their own section of the ship.

Juvenile offenders age fifteen and under were not regarded as responsible for their actions and were usually consigned to the care of a parent or guardian, but if an adult female was convicted of a serious crime, neither pregnancy nor motherhood gave any assurance of leniency. Nursing mothers unable to find a wet nurse brought their infants into the jail with them. Like the mother, the baby underwent a careful inspection upon admission to prevent smuggling of contraband. (The smuggling of money concealed in bodily orifices was usually overlooked, as the jailers profited from bribes.) Pregnant women gave birth inside the jail, assisted in delivery by the wife of the jailer or an attendant. Prior to 1790, pregnancy was not considered grounds to postpone an execution. After that date, the execution was delayed until the condemned woman gave birth. No specific duration appears to have been stipulated between birth (the child's) and death (the mother's), but it must be assumed that parent and child were not accorded much quality time before permanent separation was enforced.

The most common form of execution for men and women alike was decapitation, called *geshunin* or *zanzai*, which took place not at the execution grounds, but in a corner of the jail. Old illustrations show that unlike condemned males, who were forced into an almost horizontal position over the shallow pit into which their severed head was to drop, women were beheaded while in a seated position or leaning forward. Their slimmer, less muscular necks apparently gave little resistance to a firm whack from the executioner's sword.

The Edo period produced few women thieves of great notoriety, although it did have its share of murderesses and arsonists. When the supreme penalty was warranted, they were not spared from more drastic public executions—crucifixion or burning at the stake—although in the case of the former, the procedure differed slightly from males. Women met their end bound to the cross in the shape of a T, with legs together (perhaps for reasons of modesty), whereas men had both arms and legs extended so they formed the shape of an X.

One of the most famous women in Japanese history to lose her head was from Kyoto and about fifty years old when executed in March 1771. She remains known only as "Aocha Baba," or Green-tea Granny. At Kotsukappara her headless body underwent *fu-wake* (internal organ separation, i.e., autopsy) at the request of Sugita Gempaku, Maeno Ryotaku and other physicians. For centuries, Japan's traditional medicine was based on non-invasive treatment as developed in China, so doctors had no experience dissecting bodies. For the cutting job, they employed an elderly man who belonged to the class of outcasts that was employed to butcher livestock and tan hides.

The doctors present at Aocha Baba's autopsy were astonished to see that the position of her internal organs matched the illustrations in the Dutch-language reference work *Tafel Anatomia*, which they immediately set out to translate. They worked mostly from educated guesses and conjecture, taking about three years to finish. The five volumes they produced became known as the *Kaitai Shinsho*.

This shocking encounter with the scientific method as practiced in the West stirred a desire for new knowledge among Japanese intellectuals. It was to play a key role in nudging Japan out of its 250 years of isolation.

Fighting Fire with Fire

In Tokyo's Shinagawa Ward, a small triangle of greenery forms a V between National Highway 1 and a street marked as a remnant of the old Tokaido. Located close to the site of a World War II POW camp subsequently named Heiwajima—"peace island"—this is all that remains of the old Suzugamori execution ground. In its heyday, Suzugamori's area measured slightly larger than a football field.

Suzugamori is well maintained and identified by signs as a Tokyo historic landmark. Among the relics on display are two square stone slabs, measuring slightly less than one meter on each side. The one on the left has a circular hole to support a wooden post used for burning at the stake. Its companion has a square hole, which supported the cross-beams used for crucifixion.

With closely concentrated neighborhoods built of wood and paper, Edo and other cities were tinderboxes, especially on dry winter nights when winds blew strongly. The Yoshiwara pleasure quarter alone suffered over twenty-three major conflagrations during its history. Most fires were accidental, but when an arsonist was caught in the act, the prescribed punishment was to be burned at the stake.

Hinin employed for this job first tied the condemned to the stake with hands bound behind his or her back. A framework of strong but flexible bamboo strips was looped around the stake, supporting the canopy of straw which took the shape of an Indian tepee, rendering the condemned invisible. Several dozen bundles of firewood and more straw were stacked at the foot of the stake. At a signal from the presiding official, several hinin lit the pyre.

If the condemned was fortunate, the fire consumed the oxygen inside and swiftly rendered him or her unconscious, making death less painful. Some accounts, however, record that screams were audible as far away as eight kilometers.

A few references indicate that the condemned was put to death before the fire was ignited, and this may well have been the case for some. While torture was used to extract confessions, Tokugawa law in general eschewed executions that involved lingering death (crucifixions, for example, were excruciating, but usually ended in a few minutes). As previously noted, during the many decades of Japan's civil wars, executions were indeed protracted affairs, and numerous cruel variations—such as boiling alive, slow drowning, etc.—were practiced. Following unification of the country under Tokugawa rule, the policy gradually became more humane, not necessarily in terms of sparing lives, but at least in terms of not prolonging the agony. To some degree, it is likely these attitudes arose out of consideration for the sensibilities of the officials who supervised the executions. In other words, with the bureaucratization of samurai authority, those directly involved in the work of executions sought to make their tasks a little less unpleasant, and whenever practical, delegate the most distasteful work to others beneath them on the social ladder.

As with other forms of the death penalty, further "punishment" was meted out following death. In this particular case, once the fire had burned itself out, the corpse was made to suffer *todome-bi*, in which a burning taper was held against the charred corpse's nose and genital area (for males) or nose and breasts (for females). The remains were displayed for two nights and three days, with a placard giving the name of the criminal and his or her offense. Scavengers paid nocturnal visits to nibble on the remains.

Old records show that outcasts acted as subcontractors in hi-aburi executions, procuring the rope, straw, firewood and other materials, for which they submitted a meticulously itemized bill to the city authorities.

This form of punishment was one of the first to be outlawed under the new Meiji government, being abolished in 1869.

Which brings us to the famous tale of the teenage firebug known as Yaoya no O-Shichi. She was the daughter of a dispossessed samurai who became a greengrocer in Komagome. When a fire broke out at the end of 1682, O-Shichi and her family evacuated to temporary quarters at the Enjo-ji, the family temple. There she caught the eye of a novice priest, and romance blossomed.

Thinking perhaps that another fire in the neighborhood would allow her to enjoy a repeat encounter with her cloistered paramour, she attempted to set fire to her own house, but was caught red-handed and charged with arson. Having not yet turned sixteen, O-Shichi should have been tried as a juvenile, which would have reduced her sentence by one degree, to exile on one of the Izu islands. The love-struck teenager, deciding that death would be preferable to permanent separation from her beloved, inflated her age by one year and suffered the consequences.

Justice came swiftly. On the eighteenth day of the third month of 1683, she and five other arsonists were bound, set atop horses, and led in a procession though Kanda, Asakusa, Yotsuya, Shiba and Nihombashi. A sympathetic bystander is said to have thrust a sprig of late-blooming cherry blossoms into her hand, one of the many romantic stories spun following her death. Her execution at Suzugamori came two days later.

And the novice priest? Whether out of deep remorse or simply in shock over the whole affair, he took a vow of celibacy. In one version, he became a wandering mendicant, erecting Jizo statues at roadsides. His name was never really ascertained; some versions give it as Onogawa, others as Ikuta and still others as Yamada.

O-Shichi's crime was not unique. A woman named O-Hara, also sixteen, was executed for the same offense just one month earlier. O-Shichi's enduring popularity must be credited to sensational coverage in *kawara-ban* (Edo's rudimentary tabloids) and *Five Women Who Loved Love*, Ihara Saikaku's 1686 bestseller, which appeared three years after her death.

Saikaku's popularity is easy to understand. He not only spins a good story, but concludes his tales with sensible, if somewhat ironic, advice: "In this world we cannot afford to be careless. When traveling keep . . . money . . . out of sight. Do not display your wife to a drunkard, and don't show your daughter to a monk, even if he seems to have given up the world."

Femmes Fatales of Legendary Notoriety

An old Japanese saying goes, *Oni no nyobo ni, kijin ga naru*. Kenkyusha's dictionary renders this as "like attracts like," but elsewhere I have seen it more creatively rendered as "The devil's wife is worse than the devil."

Kijin, written with two characters meaning "devil god," might be idiomatically translated as "the essence of evil." This implicit meaning is fitting for the name Kijin no O-Matsu, who was perhaps Japan's most frightening female criminal of all time. Fortunately, she is no more than a colorful legend.

O-Matsu's modus operandi was certainly scary enough. Stunningly attractive, she would wait along the bank in the lower reaches of the Oiwase River in Aomori Prefecture where it flows into Lake Towada, and accost samurai traveling alone. Claiming to have a stomach ailment, she would implore the samurai to carry her across the shallow rapids.

Agreeing, the doomed man would gallantly invite her to climb on his back. She would wrap her legs around his torso and extend her arms around his neck. Stepping carefully to maintain his footing on the slippery river bottom, the samurai was no doubt further distracted by the sensation of warmth from her slim, young body and voluptuous curves. And thus paid little attention to the other movements she made—right up to the time she pulled a knife from her bodice and, with a bloodcurdling scream, slit his throat. She would then steal whatever funds he carried and allow the rushing waters to sweep away the corpse.

O-Matsu was supposed to have used this ruse to kill forty-eight men before potential victim No. 49 sensed something suspicious. He reacted before she could use her knife and promptly dispatched the homicidal female with his sword.

Some say O-Matsu was a man-hater motivated by revenge; others, that sexual frustration drove her over the edge of sanity; still others, that "she" was actually a male bandit in drag. The legend does appear have some basis in fact. Back in the 1780s, a real woman named O-Matsu, the widow of a samurai, robbed and murdered travelers in the region around Sendai.

Edo had no shortage of genuine female criminals. One of the most colorful was a young woman named Shirokoya no O-Kuma. She was the daughter of Shosaburo, an elderly lumber merchant, and his young, attractive and bored wife O-Tsune. This story is a familiar one: O-Tsune was not only self-indulgent, she was also promiscuous, regularly sneaking away afternoons for romantic trysts with her hairdresser, a chap named Kiyosaburo.

O-Kuma grew up in her mother's spitting image. She was spoiled, irresponsible, and a wanton. It soon came time for her to get married, and in the spring of 1724 her father arranged for her betrothal to Matashichi, the son of a well-to-do landowner in the neighborhood.

Matashichi sent O-Kuma's family a generous wedding gift of 500 ryo, but when it came time to consummate the marriage, O-Kuma kept making excuses to avoid him. Actually she had her own lover, Tadahachi, and was in no rush to settle down to a life of domestic drudgery. By this time, O-Kuma and her mother had already spent all of Matashichi's money on wine, men and song. Rather than request annulment of the marriage contract—which would have obliged them to repay the funds—they conspired with their two paramours, Kiyosaburo and Tadahachi, to kill the groom.

In their first attempt, they poisoned Matashichi's dinner; he survived. They then arranged to have him attacked by a robber, with the same lack of results. Finally, O-Tsune ordered her maidservant, a wench named O-Kiku, to sneak into Matashichi's room while he slept, cut him with a knife, and concoct the story that he had coerced her to join him in an illegal love suicide. This last tactic got the entire crowd hauled before Ooka Tadasuke, Edo's most astute judge. Adultery itself was illegal, but the great judge took an especially stern view of those who attempted to get out of a marriage contract through murder.

In 1727, Ooka sentenced O-Kuma and Tadahachi to be led around

Edo on horseback, after which they were decapitated and their heads displayed on a gibbet. The maid, O-Kiku, was beheaded, but without the previous refinement. O-Tsune was exiled to the Izu islands. Her lover Kiyosaburo fled town, but was tracked down, arrested and sentenced to death. Finally, Judge Ooka sentenced Shosaburo, the husband and father of the two wayward females, to be banished from Edo. His crime? Gross negligence in controlling the scheming, outrageous behavior of the women in his household.

En route to her execution, O-Kuma wore a kimono of checkered yellowish silk. It is said that particular style promptly went out of fashion, and remained unpopular for quite some time afterwards.

EXILE AND REHABILITATION

ALTHOUGH IN FEUDAL Japan a word existed for a life sentence (*eiro*, literally "permanent jail"), the length of stay was generally of short duration. After the death penalty itself, the harshest punishment was considered to be the sentence of exile, known as *ento* (literally, "distant island"), also called *ruzai* in common parlance. The system dates back at least to the eighth century Nara period and continued until the modern penal system was adopted from 1871.

Exile was applied to those guilty of involuntary homicide, as well as to those judged to be accessories to a crime. It was also used to punish Buddhist priests, who were generally exempted from execution for religious reasons, and to deal with political offenders and their retainers.

For residents of Edo, exile usually meant the seven islands of Izu. Miyakejima was considered the best of the lot, with Oshima and Hachijojima, the closest and most distant islands from the mainland, also affording limited creature comforts. Much harsher conditions prevailed on the smaller islands of Toshima, Kozushima and particularly Mikurajima.

According to historical records, a majority of the convicts were vagrants, petty thieves and other social misfits. By type of offense, illegal gamblers with repeated offenses topped the list, followed by Buddhist priests who failed to uphold vows of celibacy. When a person was

An exile ship sails from port.

sentenced to exile, his land, house and other property was confiscated by the state. Until their ship sailed, convicts remained incarcerated. They were informed of their final destination only on the evening prior to departure.

As in the jail, women were confined to their own section of the *runin-sen*, the ship that carried them into exile. After leaving port in Edo, an exile ship would spend three days anchored offshore, during which time relatives could supply the departing prisoners with provisions and receive letters from them in return. The ship then docked once at Shinagawa, set sail again, and made a final stop in Uraga, on the Miura peninsula, to pick up more passengers. Sailings from Edo and stops at ports and islands en route could be considerably delayed, sometimes for weeks, by adverse weather.

From 1610 to 1866, which basically corresponds to the entire Tokugawa period, a total of 1,823 people were exiled on Hachijojima. At any given time, the island was home to perhaps 200 exiles, who represented 5 to 10 percent of the total population. From such small numbers, it is clear that exile was a quintessentially lonely and wretched existence. A few of the more fortunate received provisions from their families to help tide them over. Those with knowledge of farming, or with useful skills such as carpentry or weaving, made the best of it. Island women who lacked better prospects often moved in with male convicts. Referred to as *mizu-kumi onna*, or "women who draw water," they were instrumental in helping many exiles survive.

Upon arrival, an exile was assigned to a group of five, who were made responsible for each other's behavior. Whether serving a life sentence or a fixed term, an exile's life was precarious even in the best of times. An old saying went, "The life of an exile is as fragile as a sheet of paper." Rice was a rare treat; the staple foods were millet, barley and, from the nineteenth century, sweet potatoes. These were supplemented by barter and scavenging. Famines occurred, and convicts who resorted to theft out of desperation could be chained inside their huts and allowed to die from lack of sustenance.

In addition to attempted escape, the death penalty could be meted out for even minor infractions. Convicts were typically bound and tossed from a high cliff, beheaded by axe, garotted, bludgeoned with an iron bar or shot with a gun. In 1845, a former Yoshiwara prostitute named Toyokiku, exiled to Hachijojima for arson, had a vicious run-in with a younger female rival. Toyokiku persuaded six male convicts to steal a boat and attempt escape. The men were shot or drowned offshore; she met the firing squad. Her last words before she died were, "After I'm dead, I'll come back as an insect and ravage your crops." A pest that infested the island's sugarcane fields was subsequently named *toyomushi* in her honor.

Hachijojima's local headman once submitted a report to the authorities about executions on his island. "Here," he wrote, "we have no jail. If necessary, we keep criminals in a hut modified for that purpose. Since the shedding of blood is distasteful, executions are usually carried out by throwing the condemned from a high place. The proceedings are observed by a person of authority, but since we lack an official executioner, local farmers are ordered to carry it out."

With the increasing presence of foreign ships in Japanese waters from the mid-nineteenth century, authorities became concerned that exiles in Izu might find an opportunity to escape. In 1862, the exiles were placed under the control of the governor-magistrate of Hakodate, to effect their transfer to confinement in Hokkaido. This policy proved impractical and was abandoned about a year later.

In September 1870, as part of a general amnesty for rebels who took part in the Boshin Civil War leading to the overthrow on the shogunate, sentences were reduced to exile in the Izu islands.

As prisons came into existence in the early years of the Meiji period, the practice of exile was halted. At least one attempt to restore it was made by an official who proposed to use convicts to toil in the fields. This was abandoned when the local residents voiced strong opposition.

From Punishment to Rehabilitation

Following the violent eruption of the Mt. Asama volcano in Nagano in 1780, crops failed and famine spread throughout eastern Japan. From 1783 to 1787, desperate country people flowed into Edo, swelling its already congested streets with hungry and miserable vagrants.

These were indeed the worst of times. Rather than endure slow starvation, some people took their own lives by jumping into the Sumida River. Others, accusing merchants of holding back stores of rice to force up prices, formed mobs and marched on the city's granaries.

During crises, when ordinary police lacked the manpower to suppress riots and uprisings, the shogun's government was not without a modicum of crisis management. When the going got rough, it could call upon the assistance of a special brigade of samurai, numbering some sixty men, who were essentially a military troop. Unlike the civil police, they were not confined to any particular jurisdiction, so, for example, an offender could not obtain sanctuary by hiding out on the grounds of a temple or in a samurai's mansion. The brigade could be quickly mobilized with orders to quell the rebellions at any cost, if necessary even by enforcing the samurai's right to perform *kirisute gomen*—cutting down unruly commoners on the spot.

The men who headed this SWAT team of yore, which existed until 1866, bore the title *hitsuke tozoku aratame chokan* ("leader of the group to subdue arsonists and bandits"). One of them, Hasegawa Heizo, came to be known as "Onihei" ("Hei the Demon") by criminals for his ability to bring down troublemakers. The eldest son of a middle-ranking samurai family from Chiba, Hasegawa took on the job in the footsteps of his father. He died of illness in 1795, and his story might have lapsed into obscurity had it had not been for novelist Shotaro Ikenami, a man whose passion for writing about samurai adventures was fully matched by his knowledge of Edo period history. In 1967, Ikenami began writing stories under the title *Onihei Hankacho* (The Case Book of Hei the Demon) and turned out more than 130 of them before passing away in 1990.

While "Demon" Hasegawa proved reasonably proficient at dealing harshly with serious offenders, in the final years of his career he helped bring Japan's criminal justice system out of the dark ages. Indeed, his true claim to fame may be for his humanitarian work in overseeing the creation of the *ninsoku yoseba*, a vocational institution aimed at social rehabilitation and training rather than punishment.

Although a few experiments had been conducted in other parts of the country, most notably on Sado Island, the first attempt to rehabilitate the indigent in Edo took place in the Fukagawa district in 1780. It closed in mid-1786, but the situation began to worsen by the following year, and Matsudaira Sadanobu, in name a member of the governing council of elders but effectively the country's ruler, sought out solutions. He first proposed shipping the indigent to the northern Tohoku region, where they could be put to work clearing land for farming, but this idea met with opposition from the local lords.

Finally, Hasegawa Heizo was entrusted with the establishment of a vocational institution on a triangular strip of reclaimed land between the islands of Ishikawajima and Tsukudajima, where the Sumida

River meets Tokyo Bay in what is now part of Tokyo's Chuo Ward.

At the yoseba, as many as six hundred prisoners were taught skills that ran the gamut of everything from carpentry, shoemaking, blacksmithing, stonemasonry, charcoal- and paper-making, hair grooming and other tonsorial skills, to the carving of false teeth, which in those days were made of wood. Blind indigents learned massage. Those with limited dexterity but strong backs put in long hours pressing lamp oil from beans.

Harsh punishments were dealt to inhabitants caught stealing or gambling, but while life was regimented, treatment was reasonably humane, and Japan can take pride in the fact that it was one of the first countries in the world to rehabilitate prisoners through vocational training. Inmates worked from around 8 A.M. to 4 P.M. They were allowed three days off per month and had hot water for bathing every other day. They also had access to medical care. Women worked in the kitchens, and in addition to preparing the regular fare, served up special dishes at the New Year and other holidays. Wages were paid every ten days, with one-third of their earnings being held back and given to them in a lump sum upon their release, typically after three or more years.

Even more to the credit of its founders, the ninsoku yoseba did not drain the government's coffers, and actually may have earned it money. Well-behaved prisoners, recognizable by their polka-dotted *happi* coats, could be seen in the city markets selling lamp oil and other products. Additional income was earned from leasing part of its land to store building materials.

The success of the ninsoku yoseba led to the establishment of similar facilities in other areas under direct Tokugawa control: Ibaraki, Hakodate, Yokosuka and Nagasaki. Edo's lasted around eighty years; no trace remains of the site today.

QUACKS, PHONIES AND OTHER
CON ARTISTS OF YORE

IN 1982, TOKYO POLICE arrested a young acupuncturist from Kyushu on charges of selling spurious medication. The main ingredients in his miracle elixir, called "Almighty Medicine," were tangerine peels in an alcohol solution. After three weeks in jail, the man was ordered to pay a token fine, a fraction of what he had taken from his mostly elderly victims.

Discouraged from further ventures into the pharmaceuticals business, young Chizuo Matsumoto decided that religion offered the potential for greater profits at far less risk. As "guru" Shoko Asahara of the AUM Supreme Truth cult, Matsumoto is, at the time of this writing, on trial for multiple felony charges including two counts of inciting mass murder by toxic nerve gas.

Had Matsumoto plied his trade in the Edo period, it is unlikely his career would have fared nearly as well, or for as long. Those found guilty of peddling spurious medications literally lost their heads. Article 66 of the *Osadamegaki Hyakkajo* states: "The person found guilty of selling spurious remedies will be put on public display and then executed by decapitation."

In 1803 such a fate befell a man named Kichiemon, whom Osaka authorities arrested on the charge of selling a quack remedy. The real medicine, known as *usaikaku* (literally, "black rhinoceros horn"), was produced not from rhino but from ground water buffalo horn. Unlike the real McCoy, which was quite expensive, the preparation Kichiemon offered was suspiciously affordable, and tests performed by a local pharmacist determined it to be spurious. Kichiemon, a druggist by profession who certainly knew better, forfeited his life in the manner prescribed above.

That same year, 1803, another man named Kisuke was arrested in Edo for selling a concoction of camphor pellets and small stones, which he claimed would help to ensure safe childbirth, help women become pregnant and even cure seriously ill children. Kisuke managed to convince at least some gullible people that his prayers had miraculous healing powers. He would mix his medication in a large ceramic bowl with salt, light it ablaze and begin muttering incantations.

"It's working, I can feel it," he would exclaim to the family of the ailing person. "Drop a gold or silver coin into the bowl. Go on, just drop it in."

After they did so, Kisuke resumed his chants. Then by a clever sleight of hand, he would sneak the precious metals out, leaving stones in their place, rattling the bowl as if the precious articles were still inside. He usually accepted articles of clothing as his payment, but naturally held onto the coins as well.

Soon after his scam was exposed, Kisuke lost his head.

Medieval fraudsters adopted a number of strategems. While not a particularly common occurrence, some criminals went to quite a bit of effort to impersonate officers of the law. In Joshu province (Gumma) in 1814, a robber named Ichiroemon and five cohorts masqueraded as a police official and his assistants. They made a paper lantern bearing the word *goyo* ("official business"). Not having a real sword, they carried tree branches in a cloth sack. Fire tongs were modified to resemble a truncheon, and kite string was twisted to produce a facsimile of the distinctive *torinawa* ropes used to restrain criminals. The band would pounce upon unsuspecting locals and relieve them of their money. Once the authorities got wind of his activities and tracked him down,

Ichiroemon's head did not remain attached to his torso for very long.

A few incidents were almost comical. In 1812, a smooth talking man who claimed to be related the local lord in Yamanashi commandeered a *kago* ("palanquin") and bearers for an "official trip" down the coast to Shizuoka. Actually, he was an unemployed farmer named Shosuke, but his masquerade was thoroughly convincing, and he managed to run up a hefty tab for meals and accommodations at inns along the route. At one post station he encountered a female pilgrim who had lost her way. "Oh, I know your husband," said Shosuke, the consummate phony. "Just hop in the kago with me. I'll take care of everything." It's not hard to imagine what transpired between the two afterwards.

The outcome in Shosuke's case was not quite as grim as one might expect. One interesting aspect of Tokugawa law was that victims of theft or fraud were at least partially held accountable for not exercising greater caution. Shosuke was merely banished to a distant province.

Article 67 of the *Osadamegaki Hyakkajo* prescribes punishments for a variety of frauds. Currency counterfeiters were subjected to death by crucifixion. The penalty for use of fraudulent scales or measures of volume was decapitation, with the head displayed in public. Forgery of an official seal on a document earned the offender confiscation of his property and banishment. Merchants caught dealing in false goods were tattooed to mark them as criminals and banished. Habitual swindlers lost their heads, irrespective of the amount they swindled. In the view of historian Haruo Okubo, the number of violations and punishments included in the law suggests that criminal fraud must have been rampant in Edo times.

Perhaps the most outrageous fraud of all was a semi-legendary pretender to the Tokugawa shogunate named Ten'ichi-bo. He supposedly hailed from the same town in Kii province (Wakayama), as a son born to a woman made pregnant by Shogun Yoshimune. Mother and child subsequently died, but years later Ten'ichi-bo obtained Yoshimune's document and a short sword from the woman's mother, and bided his

Fraudster Ten'ichi-bo, who claimed to be Shogun Yoshimune's son and therefore potential heir to the Tokugawa dynasty, was eventually exposed and executed.

time until he could concoct an elaborate scheme to claim he was Yoshimune's son. He enlisted supporters, traveled to Edo and made his pitch before the authorities, who either uncovered, or chose to ignore, his ruse. He was beheaded in 1627.

The story may have some basis in fact, but was greatly embellished in 1882 with the publication of *Ooka Seidan*, the fictionalized accounts of the great judge Ooka Echizen.

Gamblers and Peddlers—Roots of the Yakuza

The inhabitants of the Japanese archipelago have long possessed a great affinity for games of chance. The earliest reference to gambling, in the *Nihon Shoki*, states that in 685 no less a figure than Emperor Temmu indulged in a game played with dice known as *sugo-roku* (double sixes). After his successor, Empress Jito, assumed the throne, however, the pastime was banned.

This set the stage for what would become a 1,400-year-long running battle with the law. Historical accounts of life in twelfth century Heian-kyo (Kyoto) included details of brawls, killings and robberies involving gamblers, spurring increasingly strict measures to repress their activities.

In the *Buke Shohatto* (laws governing the samurai) issued by Shogun Tokugawa Hidetada in 1615, the second article pronounced, "Drinking parties and gaming amusements must be kept within due bounds. To be addicted to venery and to make a pursuit of gambling is the first step toward the loss of one's domain (*'baku wo gyo suru mono wa kore bokoku no moto nari'*)." While samurai were thus merely discouraged from gambling, it is noteworthy that the law prescribed no specific penalties, leading more than a few to revel in the so-called three depravities: *nomu, utsu, kau* (drinking, gambling and whoring).

The law applying to commoners was less ambiguous. Enforcement was strictest in the early years of the Edo period, with offenders sentenced to floggings, exile or even death. A *kosatsu* ("notice board," upon which edicts were published) was issued in 1711 under Shogun Ienobu. The fourth article states, simply, "Gambling of every description is strictly prohibited." During the rule of Shogun Yoshimune (1716–45), gamblers were punished by heavy fines. Losers could bring suit against gamblers in court, and if they won, could claim reimbursement for their losses.

A key event occurred in 1718, when authorities made an official distinction between light betting (wagers of under 50 *mon*) and larger bets. Petty gambling, such as lotteries, came to be tolerated as a means of controlling the populace, but the move also reflected the inability to halt the practice. Indeed, as soon as one game was banned, new ones were promptly devised to circumvent the laws. By around 1784, one type of dice game had become so popular that a strip of gambling sheds called *chohan'ya choboichi* ran for an entire *ri* (3.75 kilometers) along the road from Asakusa to Senju. Asakusa was to remain the center for Edo's gamblers and other roughnecks well into modern times.

As samurai power began to wane in the nineteenth century, gambling, which had largely been confined to the townspeople, became

A dice game in progress.

widespread in rural areas, leading to running battles between authorities and heavily armed gangs.

Many games used *karuta* (orig. Portuguese *carta*), small cards with multicolored patterns that had been introduced in the sixteenth century. In the game of "three-card," each card was assigned a numerical value between 1 and 9. The strength of a player's hand was determined by the sum total of the cards. A winning score could be 9, 19, 29, etc., but the next number, ending in zero, was worthless. In gambling patois, the losing numbers 10, 20 and 30 were called *buta*. One combination of a losing hand were cards worth 8, 9 and 3—pronounced *yatsu*, *ku* and *san*, totalling 20—and abbreviated to *ya-ku-sa*. Thus *yakusa no buta* came to mean something totally worthless, a loser. Written with different characters and pronounced *yakuza*, it also carried the meaning of an outsider or unlucky person. In either case it came to reflect the bravado that gamblers assumed to promote their business. Yakuza only came into use to refer to organized crime syndicates and their members after World War II.

Modern-day gangs also owe their origins to a rough-and-tumble group of street peddlers called *tekiya*. Spreading out their goods at temple and shrine festivals (where they could sidestep the jurisdiction of civil courts), the tekiya combined showmanship and business, selling shoddy merchandise and quack remedies to the gullible. The name is a corruption of *yashi*, originally a peddler of medical remedies. The forerunners of tekiya were once under the control of the head of Edo's outcasts, who also oversaw the activities of beggars, fortune tellers, sideshows, street performers and actors. Through a series of petitions they gained their independence, which soon led to fragmentation and turf battles.

From the yakuza's humble origins, their evolution into modern crime syndicates stands out as a remarkable study in business diversification. The list below, by no means all inclusive, gives some typical sources of revenues. It does *not*, however, imply that all individuals who engage in such businesses are necessarily yakuza.

"Legitimate" enterprises: Construction, earth grading, real estate, finance, food and beverages, love hotels, pachinko parlors, game arcades, entertainment, leasing.

Illegal activities: Gambling, bookmaking, narcotics, drug smuggling, racketeering, loan-sharking, prostitution, protection, money laundering, gunrunning, securities extortion (better known as *sokaiya*), intimidation, debt collection, illegal marriage brokering, ticket scalping and others.

While gambler- or tekiya-related gangs did not evolve from Edo times in a linear manner, vestiges of old customs and traditions have remained, such as their hierarchial organizations, colorful jargon, the custom of severing a finger in apology for one's acts and body tattooing. The sole common thread would seem to be that their ranks have almost without exception been filled by the economically disadvantaged. As postwar crime historian Kata Koji observed, "Nobody ever set out in life with the ambition of becoming a yakuza."

Slight Mercy for Wayward Clergy

Throughout most of its history, the Tokugawa regime went to great extremes to root out the practice of Christianity. Like despotic governments at other times and in other lands, it kept a close eye on religion in general. Essentially, the legal code as applied to religion sought to maintain the status quo. Article 53 of the *Osadamegaki Hyakkajo* specifically protected established religions from any new upstarts. Those found guilty of introducing "novelties in the worship of the gods or into Buddhist observances," or anyone who proclaimed "mysterious heresies" and attracted crowds "with the intention of founding a new sect" were expelled from Edo.

Long before the *Osadamegaki Hyakkajo*, one Buddhist group called Fuju-fuze, an offshoot of the Nichiren sect, was regarded as so radical it was banned in 1614, the same time as was Christianity.

Because Buddhist temples typically conducted funerals and burials, occasions arose where priests were bribed to overlook an accidental or suspicious death. To discourage this, the law provided for fifty days of house arrest, probably a rather light penalty for covering up a murder.

The jisha bugyo or ecclesiastical magistrates (three officials whose duties rotated every ten days) had charge over Buddhist and Shinto priests, temples and their properties, and rituals and ceremonies, among other things. If the magistrate found a member of the clergy guilty of a crime, he usually turned him over to the leaders of his sect, who would mete out the appropriate punishment. These fell into four main categories: being put on public display for a specified duration, being expelled from the temple, being expelled from the order, and being expelled from the sect.

Along with abstention from alcohol and the ways of the world, members of the Buddhist priesthood took vows to forego sex. When they succumbed to temptation and broke their vows of celibacy, they were guilty of *nyobon*—"woman-crime," i.e., fornication—a punishable offense under Article 51 of the legal code. After 1742, priests found to have committed adultery with a married woman were beheaded. (It should be noted, on the other hand, that homosexuality between priests was practiced quite openly.)

Prior to excommunication, a priest found guilty of nyobon might find himself subjected to a particularly humiliating form of punishment known as *inu-barai*, (literally, "driving away the dog"). The priest would be stripped naked and a rough straw rope tied around his neck; he was then obliged to crawl on his hands and knees, while being pulled along at the end of a rope leash, around the circumference of his temple grounds. To add insult to injury, he was forced to carry a dried fish in his mouth—the message here being that his behavior was regarded as that of beasts, not humans. After making three full circuits of the temple, he was given a garment to cover himself and sent packing.

Priests engaged in lecherous behavior so frequently that considerable efforts had to be devoted to discourage them. In 1671, one underwent crucifixion in Edo for cavorting with a nun. In Hyogo in 1718, another was beheaded for a similar offense. The above apparently failed to prove an effective deterrent. In 1841, some forty-eight priests found guilty of violating their vows of celibacy were put on public display en mass.

In 1803, a sixty-six-year-old resident priest named Ryugon at the Nichiren sect's Enmei-in temple in Yanaka (in present-day Taito Ward) was discovered to be regularly engaging in sexual depravity at the nearby Yoshiwara. His partner: a lively granny in her mid-fifties. His venerable age notwithstanding, he was expelled from the priesthood.

Even worse than fornication itself was the selling off of holy relics and other temple property and using the proceeds to fund one's sex activities. Such a case was tried in 1797, when a priest named Mitsumon pilfered his temple's copy of the Sutra of Great Wisdom and forged a document stating that the temple had authorized him to conduct the sale. A dealer in manuscripts paid him 12 ryo, with which he intended to fund further escapades.

The punishment for document forgery was being paraded around Edo on horseback and then having one's head displayed on a gibbet. Any theft valued at 10 ryo or more was punishable by simple decapitation. The judge was mulling over which of the two Mitsumon deserved (he decided to show a modicum of mercy and opted for the latter) when the priest fell ill and died before sentence could be carried out.

One of the strangest oddities of Edo times was how religion and sex were combined as a business through women known as *bikuni*. In the original meaning of the term, *bikuni* were Buddhist nuns who strived to attain virtue through obeisance of 348 canons. The phony bikuni adopted an appearance similar to nuns, but actually worked as low-class prostitutes. Several hundred plied their trade in Fukagawa (the present Koto Ward). Their customers, apparently, were not the least bit repelled by women who lacked not only adornment, but hair as well.

Morals, Obscenity and Censorship

In Edo times certain topics were banned outright from appearing in print. These included anything to do with the dissemination of Christianity; writings disparaging the government or which criticized court judgments; writings that showed "disrespect" toward the Tokugawa clan; and works disseminating deliberate falsehoods, such as one in 1648 that told people they could protect themselves from cholera by drinking a boiled concoction of nandin nuts and *umeboshi* (pickled plums).

With the country at peace and enjoying improved living standards, Japan's literacy rate climbed to include over one-third of the population. By the end of the seventeenth century, people were enjoying shocking and sensational stories by Kabuki dramatist Chikamatsu Monzaemon, and the tales of Ihara Saikaku, whose *Diary of an Amorous Man* and *Five Women Who Loved Love* became instant bestsellers.

As the public's hunger for sexy dramas, writings, and illustrations developed, so did publishing technology and distribution. The government reacted with renewed efforts to suppress vulgar works. In 1723, the *Shuppan-Rei* (publishing edict) came into effect. Among other things, it specifically forbade ideas contrary to established Confucian, Shinto and Buddhist doctrine. It ordered all existing *koshoku-bon* (books whose contents ran from love stories to outright pornography) off the market. It provided for strict investigation into claims of libel. And it required printed matter to carry the names of authors and publishers.

In 1758, a storyteller and encyclopedist named Baba Bunko found out the hard way that the authorities meant business; he was executed for writing and speaking out on forbidden historical and political topics. By 1771, the government had issued a list of 122 banned titles; the reprinting of another 51 works was prohibited.

The intelligentsia being suitably intimidated, the government then turned to more lowbrow works. In 1790, an edict banned *share-bon* (novelettes, often about life in the red-light district). The following year, Santo Kyoden, author of such steamy best sellers as "Behind the Brocade" and "The Prostitute's Silk Sieve," achieved the distinction of being the first writer put under house arrest and forced to wear *tegusari* (iron handcuffs) for fifty days.

By the early nineteenth century, authorities turned an increasingly jaundiced eye toward works that pandered to people's emotions or libidos. Strict punishments awaited those who got caught writing, printing and selling smut: closure of their businesses, time in jail, banishment from Edo, or house arrest. Among those who fell victim to this official prudery were the author Ryutei Tanehiko and the woodblock artist Kitagawa Utamaro, famous for his spectacularly erotic *shunga* prints.

In 1834, Mizuno Tadakuni, the gaunt forty-one-year-old lord of Hamamatsu, was appointed to the shogun's council. Mizuno fared poorly in his efforts to control inflation and enact land reforms. Deciding that life was perhaps a little too pleasant for city dwellers, the dour Mizuno decided to add a modicum of misery.

Named head of the council in 1839, Mizuno began to consolidate his power. In 1841, this culminated in a series of strict edicts that became known as the Tempo Reforms. Publications depicting Kabuki actors or prostitutes were banned. The front and back covers of publications could not use bright colors, and the only illustrations of women permitted were those of small girls and infants.

That year, police constables tracked down and arrested Tamenaga Shunsui, the author, under a pseudonym, of several wildly popular romantic novels that were even read by the shogun's concubines. Tamenega was put under house arrest and forced to wear handcuffs for fifty days. The ordeal left him so upset he went on a drinking binge from which he never recovered, passing away the following year at age fifty-three.

By New Year's 1843, only seven new book titles made their appearance, and the covers of reprints of extant works had been toned down to either solid black or indigo blue.

Eager to gain favor with Mizuno, certain members of the police and judiciary cooperated wholeheartedly. The worst was the magistrate of Edo's Southern Court, Torii Yozo. Devious and unprincipled, Torii delighted in enforcing the Tempo blue laws and engaged in subterfuge to force out more tolerant officials, such as Toyama Kinshiro.

So unpopular was Mizuno that, at one point, a mob of infuriated townspeople marched on his residence and pelted it with stones. Resistance also took more sophisticated forms. In 1843, woodblock artist Kuniyoshi caricatured Mizuno in a series of grotesque cartoons depicting an infestation of *tsuchigumo* (legendary cave dwellers). Authorities rushed to snatch up copies but pirated versions were passed from hand to hand.

Upon hearing the news of Mizuno's dismissal, an ecstatic populace spilled into the streets and posted graffiti in celebration. One "author" aptly summed up the public's scorn, writing, "The triangular Lord tried to force his square mold on a round world. Good riddance."

SCARY TIMES FOR FOREIGNERS

"THE JAPANESE had a way of cutting a man to pieces rather than leave any life in him. This had a most powerful effect on the minds of Europeans, who came to look on every two-sworded man as a probable assassin, and if they met one in the street thanked God as soon as they had passed him and found themselves in safety."

The writer of the above, a young British diplomat named Ernest M. Satow, arrived in Japan in September 1862 fully acquainted with the risks to life and limb a foreigner's presence here entailed. Naturally, he took precautions. As he noted in his diary, "I bought a revolver . . . powder, bullets and caps. The trade to Japan in these weapons must have been very great in those days, as everyone wore a pistol . . . and constantly slept with one under his pillow. . . ."

Satow's fears, unfortunately, were well founded. After Japan's rulers were forced by the U.S. and European powers to open ports and conduct trade, many samurai deeply resented the unequal treaty provisions. The issue was eventually to become a rallying point for overthrow of the Tokugawa shogunate and restoration of the emperor, so in a sense, foreigners were not-so-innocent bystanders in disputes between rival camps of Japanese.

Even before the emergence of the xenophobic ideology embodied in

Foreigners witnessed the December 16, 1864, execution of Seiji Shimizu and his cohorts for the murder of two British officers in Kamakura.

the slogan *sonno-joi* ("revere the emperor, expel the barbarians"), hostile samurai struck out at foreigners, often without warning or provocation. In August 1859, a Russian ship captain named Popov and a British ship officer named Moffett were cut down on the street in Yokohama.

Whatever their motive, the assassins were remarkably impartial in their xenophobia. In November 1859, an unfortunate Chinese employed by the French legation in Yokohama, who was in the habit of dressing in Western garb, was apparently mistaken for a European and murdered. Early in 1860 a Japanese known as "Dan," who served as an interpreter for British Counsel General Rutherford Alcock, was murdered. In the ensuing months, two Dutch merchant captains and an Italian were cut down.

Deadly assaults continued sporadically. Henry Heusken, the Dutch interpreter for U.S. Counsel Townsend Harris, ignored the authorities' warnings that foreigners should avoid the streets of Edo at night. On January 14, 1861, he was attacked by a group of samurai at Azabu Nakanohashi, not far from the present-day Tokyo Tower. Literally eviscerated by a razor-sharp sword, Heusken was carried to the nearby U.S. legation, where he expired the next morning.

Rumors flew of impending attacks, which the authorities appeared to be unable to prevent. *The Times* of April 22, 1861, reported that "the foreign Ministers were informed by the Japanese Government that there were some 500 or 600 Zoonines [i.e., *ronin*] mediating a general massacre of the foreigners at Yokuhama [sic], the burning and pillaging of all their property, the murder of the consuls at Kanagawa, and the total annihilation of the various legations at Yeddo, with their inmates."

Things never got that far, but a troop of samurai from Mito, one of the domains in open rebellion against the shogun, did assault the British Legation at Takanawa on July 5, 1861, causing injuries but no deaths. The foreign legations in Edo took the hint and decided to withdraw to the safety of Yokohama, where their warships were reassuringly anchored offshore. Only the Americans stayed behind.

Satow described the ambivalent feelings of resident foreigners when he wrote, "The general belief in the bloodthirsty character [of the samurai] . . . was to a very great extent without foundation." But he qualified this by remarking, "It must be admitted that whenever a Japanese made up his mind to shed the blood of a foreigner, he took care to do his business pretty effectually."

Just *how* effectually was demonstrated once again on October 14, 1863, when a French lieutenant named Camus set out for a ride from the Yokohama settlement. Satow's account of the fate that befell him reads like a forensic pathologist's report.

"His right arm was found at a little distance from his body, still clutching the bridle of his pony. There was a cut down one side of the face, one through the nose, a third across the chin, the right jugular vein was severed by a slash in the throat, and the vertebral column was completely divided. The left arm was hanging on by a piece of skin and the left side laid open to the heart. All the wounds were perfectly clean, thus showing what a terrible weapon the Japanese *katana* was in the hands of a skillful swordsman. No clue to the perpetrators of this horrible assassination was ever discovered . . ."

The foreign powers became increasingly assertive in their demands for reparations and the punishment of perpetrators. This came to a climax with the killing of British merchant Charles Lenox Richardson on September 14, 1862, which occurred at Namamugi, a small village astride the old Tokaido close to where Yokohama borders on the present-day city of Kawasaki.

Richardson, a thiry-eight-year old Shanghai merchant, had stopped in Japan en route to England. Earlier that day, he set off for some sightseeing along the Tokaido—referred to by local foreigners as "The Avenue"—with three compatriots: Messrs. W. Clarke and W. Marshall, and a Mrs. Borradaile, another tourist.

The four picked an inauspicious time for sightseeing. Japanese authorities had issued an advisory warning foreigners to stay off the roads that day because feudal lords and their retainers were in the process of their periodic *sankin kotai* rotation, an obligation to spend alternate years in Edo in effect since 1635, and were "unaccustomed" to the sight of foreigners. Alas, relations between the diplomats and merchants in the British community were not particularly good (Consul General Alcock had once referred to them in rather undiplomatic terms as the "scum of Europe"). The warning was either not convincingly relayed, or perhaps it was disregarded. Whichever the case, it was to cost Richardson his life.

It was early afternoon. An entourage of some one thousand men from the powerful Satsuma domain reached a narrow section of the Tokaido. The Satsuma samurai, accustomed to being treated with extreme deference, were supremely annoyed by the sight of four barbarians peering down at them from astride their mounts.

Accounts differ as to what transpired next. The samurai may have demanded that the foreigners dismount or move aside, and when the

The slaying of Englishman Charles Richardson at Namamugi, which led to the Royal Navy's attack on the port of Kagoshima.

four failed to respond, attacked them for their impudence. In another version, the woman's horse got spooked and galloped into a ditch. Richardson's mount then bolted into the midst of the procession, upon which a headman named Narahara Kisaemon unsheathed his sword and struck the Briton a fearsome blow. Others waded in using swords and spears. The two other Britons received serious wounds; the terrified woman, left unharmed, galloped frantically back to Kanagawa for help.

Mortally wounded, Richardson fled a short distance with the samurai in hot pursuit. He fell from his horse near a tea house and by one account pleaded for water; instead, he was dragged into a small garden and given the coup de grace.

As a news report from the time related, "Passing for a mile along the ranks of the men whose swords were reeking with the blood of Englishmen . . . [Dr. Willis] proceeded onwards to Namamugi, where poor Richardson's corpse was found under the shade of a tree by the roadside. His throat had been cut as he was lying there wounded and helpless. The body was covered with sword cuts, any one of which was sufficient to cause death. It was carried thence to the American Consulate in Kanagawa."

Richardson was interred in Yokohama's foreign cemetery.

Eight foreign warships were anchored offshore at the time, and the British military commander briefly considered an attack on the killers, who bedded down for the night not far away, but decided to let the diplomats have first crack at resolving the issue. Besides, he reasoned, if the conflict widened it would put the civilians in the settlement at risk.

The diplomats may have held the merchants in contempt, but could not very well ignore the cold-blooded murder of one of Her Majesty's subjects. Jingoistic English publications clamored for "a war of just retribution." After conferring with the Foreign Office, Britain demanded that Japan punish Richardson's killers and pay a heavy indemnity of 100,000 pounds. It demanded an additional 25,000 pounds restitution from the ruler of Satsuma.

Fearing a complete breakdown in relations, foreign merchants closed their stores and made plans to leave. During those tense months, the *North-China Herald* reported that the foreign residents who stayed behind felt "considerable apprehension" for their safety.

"It appears that every foreigner goes about armed with a weapon of some description; and as they pass the two-sworded 'yaconins' [*yakunin*, i.e., officials] in the street, the fellows frequently touch their hilts, as if about to draw, when the handle of a revolver is grasped in return . . . . which generally causes these 'Swash-bucklers' . . . to make off speedily."

When Japan delayed its response to Britain's ultimatum, a Royal Navy flotilla of seven warships under Vice-Admiral Augustus L. Kuper embarked on a punitive expedition. On August 12, 1963, the squadron blasted ships and fortifications in Kagoshima harbor and then laid waste to undefended parts of the city, displacing some 180,000 people. The British incurred few casualties. Although Satsuma capitulated and agreed to pay the indemnity, the drain on its treasury was minimal; it apparently borrowed the money from the shogunate and never paid it back.

The *New York Times* denounced the bombardment as "British Barbarity," saying, "There is no more reason to suppose Kagoshima had anything to do with Mr. Richardson's murder than San Francisco. And if the English were obliged to obtain satisfaction . . . the burning of [Satsuma's] navy was surely enough."

Reflecting on the tragic chain of events that led to Richardson's slaying, some British newspapers expressed sympathy for the Japanese. The *London and China Telegraph* remarked, "One cannot regret . . . that [the incident] should have originated in the arrogance and disregard for national customs of a party of our own countrymen, who . . . deliberately rushed on their own destruction."

Other notable events followed, including the murders of two British officers in Kamakura on November 20, 1864, a run-in between foreign troops and samurai in Kobe (the Bizen Incident of February 4, 1868) and, one month later, the Sakai Massacre, in which eleven French sailors were slain by Tosa samurai.

In punishment, twenty Tosa men were ordered to commit seppuku. The first is said to have attempted to tear out his intestines and fling them at the French commander before his assistant could cut off his head. The suicides by ritual disembowelment continued, but after the figure reached eleven, the French captain decided he had seen enough blood and insisted that the lives of the remaining nine be spared.

Satow, England's intrepid diarist, was indignant. "The twenty were all equally guilty," he wrote, "and requiring a life for life of the eleven Frenchmen looked more like revenge than justice."

Following the sporadic incidents in which xenophobic samurai attacked foreigners, the former were increasingly ordered to commit seppuku. An early eyewitness account was provided by Lord Redesdale, who recorded it in his book *Tales of Old Japan*. It took place in

February 1868, and involved the seppuku of a Bizen official named Taki Zenzaburo. "It was horrible," wrote Redesdale.

Indeed, some foreigners questioned the propriety of diplomats' attendance at such spectacles. Charles Rickerby, the owner-editor of the original *Japan Times* of Yokohama, pronounced it "disgraceful" for Christians to attend executions, and went so far as to express his hope that the Japanese, if they ever took revenge for such "judicial murders," would turn their swords on the diplomats.

Clearly irritated by Rickerby's editorializing, Satow countered, "As for being ashamed of having been present at a *harakiri* on the ground that it was a disgusting exhibition, I was proud to feel that I had not shrunk from witnessing a punishment which I did my best to bring about. It was no disgusting exhibition, but a most decent and decorous ceremony, and far more respectable than what our own countrymen were in the habit of producing for the entertainment of the public in the front of Newgate prison."

To put a halt to further bloodshed, in March 1868 the new imperial government issued an edict that sternly pronounced ". . . All persons . . . guilty of murdering foreigners . . . will be acting in opposition to Our express orders . . . [and] shall be punished in proportion to the gravity of the crime." The edict had its intended effect. The emperor was clearly in control.

MEIJI
PERIOD

1868–1912

EARLY MEIJI TIMES

THE OVERTHROW of the Tokugawa shogunate in 1868 and restoration of imperial rule came about through the Boshin civil war (1868–69). People flowed out of and into Tokyo, and during this period of confusion, the new Meiji government ordered the military to maintain order. But it was clear that a new police organization would be needed to replace the teetering machi bugyo system of feudal times.

The provinces of Satsuma (Kagoshima), Choshu (Yamaguchi) and Tosa (Kochi), which had supported overthrow of the Tokugawa regime, were requested to dispatch samurai for police duties in Tokyo. These men were initially known as *torishimari-gumi* (group of controlling officers). Satsuma furnished the largest contingent, of about one thousand men. Even 130 years on, vestiges of this regional flavor are said to influence the police organization.

Japan began to modernize its judiciary, police, civil and criminal codes, and penal system. The government requested educator Yukichi Fukuzawa, who had travelled extensively outside Japan, to provide details about police systems in the West. The first punishments to be abolished, from 1869, were crucifixion and burning at the stake. The practice of tattooing habitual criminals was halted in 1870. Judicial torture to extract confessions under most circumstances was officially phased out in 1874.

Tokyo's police came briefly under the jurisdiction of the Justice Ministry, but in 1873, a military officer from Kagoshima named Toshiyoshi Kawaji was appointed the first superintendent general of Tokyo's Metropolitan Police Department. In preparation for his post, Kawaji had traveled to Europe in 1872 to study judicial systems. He was most impressed by the French system, which led to Japan's adoption of many of its salient characteristics. While on a second trip to France in 1879, Kawaji fell ill and died at age forty-five. His contributions to the modernization of Japan's police have not been forgotten, and he is regarded as the "father" of the Japanese police system.

Foreigners were involved at many levels. French law professor Gustave Emile Boissonade, employed by the Japanese government for over two decades from the early 1870s, left an indelible stamp on the legal system. The Foreign Ministry employed a German, Hermann Roesler, from 1878 to advise it on international law and the constitution. Ottmar von Mohl of Prussia advised Japan on imperial court etiquette and the police system. Another Prussian, Wilhelm Hoehn, trained police officers and is credited with proposing the system of small substations that became the forerunner of today's *koban*.

In spite of the thin distinction between the Japanese police and military, this does not mean the two groups got along. Nineteenth-century Tokyo was full of military posts and barracks, and run-ins with the cops were common. In June 1874, police arrested three soldiers in Tokyo's Atago district (present-day Minato Ward) for noisy carousing. When their comrades learned of the arrest, they formed a mob outside the police station, pelting it with rocks and overturning wagons. Following another altercation in Ueno the following April, a regulation was enforced confining garrison troops to their camps without passes.

Meanwhile Yokohama, being a city with a large foreign population, had promulgated an ordinance back in 1868 prohibiting males from relieving themselves in public. The ordinance stated: "In places lacking urinals, the act of urination in view of others is hereby illegal,

and as it is particularly shameful when done before foreigners, it is prohibited. Violators will be arrested."

This ordinance was adopted with varying degrees of success by
Tokyo and other cities. It also led to several notorious incidents between
cops and soldiers that became known as *Honyo Ranto Jiken*—literally
the "urination riots."

The first melee occurred on January 18, 1874, at Hongo Sanchome
(near present-day Tokyo University), when a policeman observed a soldier leisurely relieving himself and ordered him to halt forthwith. The
soldier, being quite inebriated, comported himself in a disrespectful
manner. The policeman tried to apprehend him and the soldier fought
back. His comrades in arms came to assist him, and before long they
grew in to an angry mob of over fifty men. The soldiers began beating
the policemen with sticks until the curfew was sounded and they
returned to their barracks. One corporal was later arrested and court-
martialled.

Another "urination riot" occurred in Osaka on January 5, 1878,
when about eighteen members of an engineer detachment based in the
city were marching across the Umemoto bridge and several of them
decided it would be a good place to take a leak. When a policeman
ordered them to halt, they responded by tossing him into the river they
had just polluted. A free-for-all ensued, although no permanent injuries
seem to have resulted.

It was altercations such as these that led to the *Kempei Jorei* of
March 1881 that established the Military Police, and made the military
responsible for the conduct of its own soldiers.

That did not mean the end of the piss riots, however. On January 3,
1884, about twenty soldiers were partying in an upstairs room in Osaka's
Matsushima pleasure quarter, when a soldier opened the window and
began urinating onto the street below. His mischief was spotted by a
cop, whose order to desist was rudely ignored. Insisting that the slight
was intentional the officer rushed upstairs, only to be given a sound
whipping. He returned to the station and summoned reinforcements.

Things were about to turn really nasty, until a police supervisor named Oura, who also happened to be a lieutenant in the army reserves on duty that day, quickly exchanged his army garb for a police uniform and ordered the cops to stand down until he could summon the MPs. Oura's quick thinking in preventing a full-scale riot earned him the everlasting gratitude of the people in the neighborhood.

Japan's First Gallows

No doubt partially due to Western influences at the time, the nation's leaders sought to make a clean break with the past. And since the samurai class was in the process of being phased out, the sword's aesthetic appeal began to decline.

New judicial guidelines introduced in December 1870 provided for adoption of a "strangulation pillar," a variation of the Spanish garotte. The condemned would be seated in a contraption with his back against a wooden pillar through which a rope was looped. A heavy weight (or two if needed) was attached to the other end of the rope. The loop was placed around the neck of the condemned, and at a signal, the executioner allowed the weight to drop, leading to slow strangulation.

But not always. In the city of Matsuyama late in 1872, a man named Tanaka Tosaku was to be executed for inciting a public disturbance. After appearing to have expired, he recovered consciousness. This was perceived by authorities as a "sign from heaven" and he was absolved. (In present-day Japan, the law would require the executioner to keep at it until he finished the job.)

The pillar usually achieved its desired function, but the sight and sounds emanating from the condemned proved extremely unpleasant to the officials who served as eyewitnesses, and its use was dropped within two years.

Hanging as a form of execution is believed to have originated in Persia. It was adopted in England from the twelfth century and refined through the years. James Berry, Yorkshire's executioner from 1884 to

1892, calculated a table of body weights that determined the falling distance (i.e., the distance it took for the rope to be made taut by the falling body) of from one to ten feet. This system, described by one member of a Royal Commission as "quicker than shooting and cleaner," was designed to fracture the cervical vertebrae (usually the fourth and fifth), rupturing the spinal cord and causing almost instantaneous death.

After observing the "long drop" gallows in the British colonies of Hong Kong and Singapore, the Japanese became convinced hanging offered a swift and more humane means of execution. On February 20, 1873, government Decree No. 65 prescribed the adoption of a gallows. Plans called for it to stand 3 meters in height with a hinged platform measuring 2.6 by 2 meters.

Armed with sketches from which a blueprint was produced, Japan's Ministry of Punishments invited bidders to build the nation's first gallows. A carpenter named Hasegawa, who had performed construction jobs for the Home Ministry, reluctantly placed his bid.

"I thought I could probably do the whole job for 25 yen or so," Hasegawa recalled to a chronicler of contemporary events. "But it seemed rather distasteful work and I bid 120 yen, thinking I would hardly land the job at that price. But I guess the other carpenters were thinking the same as me; they bid even higher, some as much as 150 or even 300 yen. Being the cheapest, I got stuck with the job.

"Anyway, I figured there would be enough money left over afterwards for a night out on the town.

"They told me they didn't want the neck to be scarred," he continued, "so we wrapped hairs around the rope at the point where it made contact with the neck, and on top of that we stitched a cover of deerskin. The rope was looped through a copper ring and secured to another ring on one of the pillars."

Skeptical about whether the ring would support the weight, an official named Iso Mataemon tested it on himself with a counterweight of 15 *monme*. He almost strangled, and his assistant was obliged to force warm water down his throat and pound vigorously on his boss's back until he revived. Insisting he was all right, Mataemon repeated the test, but this time using only 13 *monme*.

Decapitation by sword continued to be carried out concurrently with hangings through the 1870s. A clear disadvantage of the former was that it required the condemned to cooperate by remaining stationary as the sword descended. This failed to happen at the execution of murderess O-Den Takahashi in January 1879. Her final moments were so distressing for the witnessing officials, the episode was to spell the end of the decapitation of women. It continued a few more years for males, but was halted in favor of hanging.

The Woeful Fate of a Poisonous Wife

Poison is so associated with women who kill that Japanese commonly refer to a murderess with the sobriquet *dokufu* (poisonous wife). Perhaps the best known murdress of Meiji times was O-Den Takahashi. Born in Gumma Prefecture in the waning years of the Edo Period, she was the daughter of a soldier. By her early teens, O-Den had a lovely fair complexion and was quite attractive. At age fourteen, she was betrothed to a youth in her village named Yojiro, but the two did not get along and divorced after less than two years. She subsequently remarried, to a handsome fellow named Naminosuke. The newlyweds developed a mutual fondness for gambling, and after squandering their assets left town for the big city in 1871.

Naminosuke subsequently fell ill with what turned out to be leprosy. In the futile hope of finding a cure, O-Den arranged for her husband to be examined by an American missionary doctor in Yokohama, and to pay for his treatment sold her body to foreigners around the port. But his condition continued to deteriorate. One version of the story has it that she used poison to euthanize him, but there is little evidence to support this.

Now a young widow whose sole livelihood was prostitution, she fell in with a low-life named Ichitaro Ogawa and planned to rob one of her customers, a wealthy used clothing merchant named Goto, and use the funds to get out of the life.

On August 27, 1876, she slit his throat with a straight razor while he slept, then was dismayed to find only 26 yen on his person.

To throw the police off her track, O-Den left a note beside Goto's corpse that read, "Five years ago, this man was responsible for the death of my elder sister. After reporting my actions at her grave, I intend to take my own life. (Signed) Matsu."

Based on witness descriptions, police had little difficulty in tracking her down. At her trial, her crime was judged to have been vicious and premeditated, warranting the maximum punishment.

Ever after hanging became the method of execution, the practice of decapitation was perhaps viewed as a deterrent and lingered for a few more years. The unfortunate O-Den was the last female in Japan to be executed by sword. The order to proceed with her execution was issued, and on January 31, 1879, O-Den and a male prisoner named Inosuke Yasukawa were taken from their cells to a corner of the city's new jail at Tomihisa-cho, near Ichigaya. The various accounts of her execution are remarkably consistent. Watching the condemned Yasukawa trem-

Murderess O-Den Takahashi, the last woman to be executed by decapitation.

bling with fear, she harangued him by remarking caustically, "Isn't it just like a man to be so cowardly! Watch how I go!"

When her moment came, however, she lost her nerve. She begged the jail officials for one last meeting with her beloved Ichitaro. No doubt eager to be rid of the brazen woman, Warden Yasumura refused, and nodded to executioner Yamada to get on with the job. Yamada raised his sword above the slender neck of the ranting woman and swung—just as she moved. The razor-sharp blade struck the back of her head, leaving her dazed and flopping about in her own blood, repeatedly murmuring "Ichitaro, Ichitaro . . ." Unnerved, Yamada's second pass also failed to complete the task. Finally, he was forced to hack though her neck "like cutting a *daikon* ('giant radish') " as she lay semiconscious on the ground.

No records remain of how the man she had harangued a few moments before reacted to the spectacle. Still, it was enough to convince any remaining skeptics that hanging was less prone to error, if not cleaner, and Yamada found considerably less demand for his business, although he did perform beheadings on a few more males over the next two years and afterwards earned a livelihood from certifying newly made swords.

Only a few months after her execution, her story, with the name altered to "O-Den Tamahashi," became a Kyogen play performed by Kikugoro V at the Tokyo Shintomiza theater.

Following O-Den's execution, her corpse underwent autopsy at the army medical school and her reproductive apparatus was preserved in formaldehyde. Shortly after the World War II, the Ministries of Health and Welfare, Labor, and Education, the Japan Teachers' Union and the Tokyo Metropolitan Government staged a joint exhibition at a department store in Asakusa. There, among the other curiosities on display, was the preserved portion of her anatomy.

A small stone memorial to O-Den can be found beside rat burglar Nezumi Kozo at the Eko-in cemetery in Minami Senju and a more elaborate one in the Yanaka cemetery near Nippori. The latter, erected in 1881 with funds collected by writers, is engraved with her *jisei*, her parting words prior to her execution, which begin, "I no longer wish to be part of this hapless world . . ."

To this day, her name remains a household word among educated Japanese.

THE MID-MEIJI PERIOD

IN THE AUTUMN of 1542 or 1543, three Portuguese traders accidentally became the first Europeans to arrive in Japan. While traveling aboard a Chinese ship from Macao to a port further north, perhaps Ningbo, Zhejiang Province, they were blown off course by a powerful typhoon, taking them hundreds of kilometers north to the southern tip of Tanegashima island. Using sticks to scratch mutually intelligible Chinese characters into the sand on the beach, the Chinese explained to the Japanese that their European passengers were *Nambanjin* or "Southern Barbarians."

As a way of demonstrating their peaceable intentions to Tokitaka, the island's titular head, the three Portuguese used their firearms to give an impressive demonstration of marksmanship. Tokitaka immediately grasped the significance. By fortuitous coincidence, his island was home to skilled metalworkers, high-quality iron sand and other materials needed to manufacture guns and ammunition—except sulfur for gunpowder, which could be obtained from nearby Yakushima island.

The Tanegashima smiths attempted to produce imitations but were unable to comprehend the intricacies of the gun's mechanism. According to one account, as an incentive for revealing this secret, the blacksmith made a barter agreement: Portuguese gun technology in exchange for his teenage daughter.

Japan was in the midst of prolonged civil war, and the introduction of firearms, by this time referred to as *Tanegashima teppo*, eventually played a decisive role in pacifying the country.

To maintain control over the populace, Tokugawa rulers adhered to the doctrine of *Iri-deppo, de-onna* (Keep the guns from coming in and the women from leaving). The manufacture of all guns in the country came under control of a special government bureau called the Teppo Bugyo. The sole mention of guns in the Tokugawa criminal code, in Article 21, relates mainly to prohibiting their use within a 10 *ri* (about 40km) radius of Edo. Anyone who turned in an armed poacher received 20 silver coins in reward.

By the late Edo period, a small number of guns managed to find their way into the hands of groups of outlaws who roamed the countryside. Nevertheless guns have never developed into a serious problem, partially due to a cultural aversion to weapons firing projectiles, known as *tobi-dogu*, the use of which samurai regarded as cowardly.

From the 1850s, foreign civilians in Yokohama and other settlements argued vociferously over their right to bear arms, and had occasional disputes with the shogunate authorities when they embarked on hunting expeditions in the districts of Sagami (Kanagawa Prefecture) where travel was permitted. After the law banning the carrying of swords in public was issued on March 28, 1876, handguns were widely advertised as a means of self-protection. But gun crime in Meiji times remained a comparatively rare phenomenon.

One notable exception was Sadakichi Shimizu. The eldest son of a Buddhist priest, he was a bright lad and initially showed promise of following in his father's footsteps. Then from around age fifteen he underwent an abrupt change and fell into wayward behavior. He entered a dojo to study martial arts, which proved useful when he began what was to become an eighteen-year career of robbery and intimidation.

Shimizu was clearly not an ordinary hood. He took the trouble to learn acupuncture and massage. Having married and become a father, it is possible that he intended to give up his larcenous ways and go straight, but the thrill of crime proved addictive.

Assuming the name Kiyoyuki Ota, Shimizu adopted the guise of a blind masseur, advertising his services by tooting out characteristic notes on his flute while roving neighborhoods in eastern Tokyo. Once inside people's homes, he would surreptitiously survey their possessions and, if the pickings looked good, return to rob them at knife point.

From around 1880 Shimizu refined his robbery techniques by arming himself with a pistol. In those days handguns were not especially difficult to obtain; they were even advertised in vernacular newspapers as a means of self-protection. In 1881, Shimizu used his weapon to rob the home of a pawnbroker named Matsuda in Okachi-machi. After wounding the watchman, he tied up eleven family members and domestics and spent the rest of the evening hauling out booty.

The police, well aware that masseurs were often summoned to public baths, inns, brothels and pawn shops, used them as informers to report on goings-on in the neighborhood. Having been recruited for this purpose, Shimizu/Ota was made party to inside information on police activities that allowed him to stay one jump ahead of his pursuers, who had organized a special task force to hunt him down.

Shimizu became increasingly bold. During one of his robberies, a sixty-six-year-old woman heard a noise and went to investigate. He shot her in cold blood and made off with 3 yen.

On December 3, 1886, Shimizu forced his way into the home of a merchant in Bakuro-cho, Nihombashi, and demanded money. His knife failing to impress his intended victims, he discharged his handgun. This produced some loot, which he promptly grabbed before dashing off. A jinrikisha puller heard the gunshot and summoned a patrolman, Takichiro Ogawa. When Shimizu reached a nearby intersection, Ogawa accosted him with the authoritarian "*Oi, kora*" ("Hey, you") by which citizens were once typically addressed by police. Shimizu pulled out his gun and got off a shot at Ogawa. He missed. Police officers did not carry firearms, so Ogawa engaged the felon in a fierce struggle. Shimizu used his knife to stab the cop, who, although seriously wounded, managed to summon reinforcements who apprehended Shimizu.

In August 1887, Shimizu was found guilty of having committed six murders and more than thirty armed robberies. (He is believed to have committed as many as fifty other robberies, but was not charged due to the statute of limitations.)

Shimizu went to the Ichigaya Prison gallows on September 7, 1887. The official police version puts his age as forty-five; other writers give it as forty-nine. In the end, he proved rather fastidious. Aware that death by hanging results in the condemned soiling themselves, he reportedly embarked on a fast two days before his excecution.

Upon Ogawa's discharge from the hospital in February 1887, he returned to duty and received a special promotion for his heroism in helping bring Tokyo's most notorious robber to justice. His condition continued to deteriorate, and he died on April 26 at the age of twenty-four. His death was treated the same as if he had been killed outright in the line of duty, allowing him to be be buried with full honors in the special section of Aoyama Cemetery reserved for policemen.

The Fugitive Who Became a Judge

In a rigidly traditional society such as Japan's, it was difficult, but by no means impossible, for fugitives to elude the authorities. Jailbreaks used to be a fairly common occurrence.

The tale of Sakigake Watanabe, however, is right out of a Victor Hugo novel. It is not his escape that fascinates so much as the life he assumed afterwards. Watanabe did not merely go on the lam; after assuming a new identity, he passed the civil service examination, and when police finally tracked him down, he was presiding over a rural Nagasaki court, handing down sentences on criminals!

Sakigake Watanabe was born in Edo in 1859, the eldest son of a samurai family from the domain of Shimabara in Nagasaki. After studying at the School of Commerce (the forerunner of Hitotsubashi University) he returned to Nagasaki and was hired by Mitsui Bussan, a major business concern. At age twenty-two, Watanabe became infatuated with a lovely geisha and, to support her expensive tastes, embezzled a considerable sum of money. His pilferage was discovered and in July 1880 he was sentenced to life at hard labor.

As one of the few literate men in the prison population, Watanabe was assigned to perform rather light work. He showed his appreciation for this privileged treatment by joining three other felons in a failed escape attempt. This earned him a transfer to the Miike coal mine, where prisoners labored under horrendous conditions; fatalities were a frequent occurrence.

The second year into his sentence, Watanabe managed to evade prison guards by hiding in a toilet. He made his way to his father, who, through his position as a low-ranking justice official, helped create the false identity of a man named Kota Tsujimura. With this, Watanabe was able to establish the *koseki* (family registration) needed to obtain legitimate status. His next move was to pass the civil service examination; he then commenced work collecting taxes for the Oita prefectural government. He soon moved up the ladder to take the position of judicial clerk, at a salary that allowed him to marry into an influential family.

A judge took close note of Tsujimura's acumen and advised him to take the examination to become a judge. In late 1887, he passed with a high score, and the following year was appointed an assistant judge with the princely monthly salary of 25 yen. He was also transferred back to Fukue island in his home prefecture of Nagasaki. Realizing his presence so close to home raised the risk of discovery, he considered resigning but finally decided the position was too attractive to turn down.

Tsujimura proved highly capable in ruling on civil matters, and within three years was promoted to full judge, which meant he would also hear criminal cases—thereby increasing the chances of encountering the very type of people who, a decade earlier, had arrested and prosecuted him for embezzlement. This in fact finally came to pass; on

February 19, 1891, he was approached by a Nagasaki prosecutor named Uehara.

"Your honor," said Uehara, "I wonder if you remember me. I believe your real name is Sakigake Watanabe. I investigated your case when you forged exchange documents at Mitsui Bussan."

"Why, why, this is an outrage," the judge sputtered. "Actually, I do happen to be Sakigake Watanabe's younger brother. But I am not the same man."

A policeman then read out the warrant for Watanabe's arrest.

Judge Tsujimura spent that night in a cell at the police station and the following day was transported to the local jail, where he spent the next four days. All the while, he continued to deny being Watanabe. Finally, when confronted by the Nagasaki prosecutor, he broke down in tears and confessed.

Watanabe's father was also arrested on the charge of document forgery and was sentenced to eighteen months in jail, with an additional six months probation.

Watanabe, by this time thirty-three years old, was ordered to return to the coal mines to serve out his life sentence. Perhaps because theft was punished with less severity by that time (or, perhaps, owing to his exemplary record as a judge), he received a pardon and was released in the autumn of 1892. Returning to his home town of Shimabara, this real life Jean Valjean went into business, carving seals, making signs and working as a paperhanger. The remainder of his life was otherwise uneventful until his death in 1922 at age sixty-four.

Arise, Ye Wretched of Saitama

After Emperor Napoleon III of France surrendered to the Prussians at the Battle of Sedan, the Republicans of Paris staged a bloodless revolution and proclaimed a republic. In 1871, Paris capitulated to the Prussians after a four-month siege, and France elected members to a National Assembly to vote on whether to make peace with Prussia.

The Republicans of Paris established a *Commune* in the city. The National Assembly ordered in troops, leading to a full-fledged civil war. During May 21–28, 1871—remembered as "Bloody Week"—savage fighting raged, and by the time the Commune fell on May 28, parts of Paris were in ruins and an estimated eighteen thousand people killed.

A month after the fall of the Paris Commune, Eugene Pottier, who had been sentenced to death in absentia, wrote the stirring lyrics of *The Internationale*, which begins (in its American version):

> Arise you prisoners of starvation,
> Arise, you wretched of the earth!
> For justice thunders condemnation.
> A better world's in birth.

Even if the farmers in the mountainous western Saitama region centered around Chichibu had known about these momentous events, it is doubtful they could have imagined that, a decade hence, they would rise up in a similar fashion. They kept occupied cultivating their silkworms, as had their ancestors since ancient times, and managed to earn a respectable livelihood from it.

To curb inflation at home, the Japanese government cut the money supply, leading to higher interest rates and deflation. By 1881, the price of silk began to plummet, in spite of lower production. France, which fought a war with China in 1884, ironically became a catalyst in further depressing silk prices to around one third the level of 1881.

As their debts grew, Chichibu's farmers were driven to moneylenders, who charged them rates as high as 150 percent per year. On top of the interest burden, the farmers were taxed on their landholdings, and when they couldn't pay, they forfeited ownership.

Taking a cue from newfangled liberal views that pushed for a less authoritarian government—giving people more rights and a greater voice in the way things were run—Chichibu farmers and their supporters banded together to present the government with a list of demands: a ten-year moratorium on outstanding loans and repayment in installments; a three-year suspension on compulsory schooling (in order to let children work during the busy months); tax cuts; and reduction in expenditures by local officials.

When the government proved unsympathetic, farmers began to hold secret meetings. By late summer 1884 they had named their group the *Konmin-to* (Party of Destitutes), with Eisuke Tashiro as the party secretary. The group had planned to hold a rally in November, but on October 31, a farmer hailing from Fuppu, a nearby village, decided to jump the gun and began going from door to door calling for armed rebellion.

The man's call to arms went something like this: "I'm amazed to hear this myself, but we're rising up against His Majesty. Please join us." Hardly as arousing as Paul Revere's words, but it somehow worked. Farmers in Saitama, Nagano and Gumma prefectures streamed out of their homes and formed angry mobs, pouncing on moneylenders, trashing their IOUs and overwhelming police sent to quell the disturbance.

Later in the day, some three thousand farmers converged at the Muku shrine in Yoshida village, waving swords and clubs. These men formed the core of the "Poor People's Army" whose "revolutionary headquarters" was meticulously organized. Kampei Kikuchi of Nagano served as chief of staff, overseeing brigade commanders, a quartermaster, paymaster, armorers, and a transport and signal corps.

To enforce discipline and prevent mayhem, the "army" posted five regulations, infractions of which were punishable by death. These applied to those caught looting, committing rape, carousing, committing arson or acts of violence to the detriment of the party, and failure to obey orders.

The "army" then marched off, capturing the town of Ogano and burning down the houses of moneylenders and profiteers. On November 2, the group captured Omiya, now part of Chichibu City. Since police and government officials had fled the town, the rebels marched in unopposed. Once again, the moneylenders bore the brunt of their fury, and the group's success attracted new recruits.

Eighty kilometers away in Tokyo, the Minister of Home Affairs was in no mood for compromises. He ordered crack army troops to quell the rebellion. Bad luck struck when the rebels' top commander was fatally wounded by one of the policeman being held prisoner. The high command collapsed and although some farmers harassed the army with guerilla tactics, the uprising was crushed in a final shootout near Karuizawa.

In all, 380 men were arrested, and another 3,238 turned themselves in. The 11 principal leaders received the death sentence in February 1885 and were executed in May. Party treasurer Denzo Inoue, a Yoshida merchant who sympathized deeply with the farmers' plight, was sentenced to death in absentia. Inoue hid in a friend's storehouse for two years and then vanished, but the prayers of the people of Chichibu must have sustained him through some rough times. During his years on the run, he staved off homesickness by contributing poetry to literary magazines under a pseudonym. He materialized on his deathbed in a remote Hokkaido village thirty-two years later under the name Fusajiro Ito. Inoue finally did come home; his grave can be found in his hometown.

Kashiro Shimazaki, twenty-six at the time of the rebellion, fled to Kofu in Yamanashi Prefecture. He lived an unassuming life as a livery under the name of Senno, and passed away in 1919, one year after Inoue. It was not until 1983 that a historian, working with a local newspaper, established his identity.

In his book *The Chichibu Incident and the Paris Commune*, Albert Corvaisier wrote, "Although their scale was different, both . . . ended in suppression by the government . . . now over a century later, they remind us that without peace and democracy, 'freedom' and 'justice' are merely empty concepts . . ."

FOREIGNERS IN JAPAN

FRIDAY, APRIL 4, 1890, marked two singular events involving foreigners in Japan. The first was the arrival of Irish-Greek-American author Lafcadio Hearn, who, over the next fourteen years, would distinguish himself as a prolific writer on the subject of things Japanese. Particularly violent and ghoulish stories.

There is perhaps an irony to this, because on the evening of the same day Hearn disembarked from the *Abyssinia* at Yokohama port, Reverend Thomas Alfred Large, the thirty-one-year old Canadian principal of the Toyo Eiwa school for girls in Azabu, was murdered in his own residence.

The present-day Toyo Eiwa Jogakuin was founded in 1884 by Martha J. Cartmell, the first female missionary sent to Japan by Canada's Methodist Church. Cartmell was succeeded by Eliza Spencer, who wed Large in 1887. He then took on responsibility for running the school. The young couple was soon blessed with a daughter.

On the evening of April 4, the Large family returned from a holiday trip to Hakone. They retired around 10. About one hour later, two men forced their way into the house, overpowered the night watchman, and tied his hands behind his back. They then forced him at sword point to guide them to the Large residence upstairs.

Hearing a commotion outside, Mrs. Large opened the door and

found herself confronting one of two men, who brandished his weapon. She screamed, bringing her husband running. He lashed out at one of the intruders with a stick, but the other assaulted him from behind, stabbing him. The second joined in, and Large went down gasping with wounds that proved to be fatal. Mrs. Large tried to intervene but was knocked unconscious.

The watchman escaped and ran shouting for help. By the time police arrived, the criminals had vanished into the night. They left behind several pieces of evidence, including a tobacco pouch. It was found to contain a substance at first suspected of being a "powerful drug"; it turned out to be a cold remedy.

Initially, the Japanese government's first concern was the political implications of the slaying. If the assailants had acted out of anti-foreign or anti-Christian motives, some feared the Western powers might reject Japan's ongoing efforts to renegotiate unequal treaties.

A substantial reward was posted for information leading to the killers' apprehension.

The killers' motive was almost certainly apolitical. In those times, burglars had no apprehensions about robbing foreigners. The *Japan Weekly Mail* of April 26 observed, "Without some hypothesis, it appeared difficult to imagine that the onslaught . . . could have been incidental to a mere burglary. But several Japanese . . . say it is the habit of sword-carrying burglars in this country to . . . simply kill or maim the obstructionist, and then proceed with their thieving work. . . ."

While newspaper reports of the crime itself were sensationalized and full of inaccuracies, public opinion was uniformly sympathetic toward the Large family. The vernacular *Hochi Shimbun* editorialized, ". . . the victim was a foreigner who had come here from a distant land, and was engaged in teaching Japanese students. There is something sad about the fate of a man who dies far away from the land of his birth . . . How much sadder is the lot of one who falls under the weapons of common burglars in a foreign country. Such a fate should move everyone to pity . . . We trust, however, that the foreign public will not judge Japan by this catastrophe."

In remarks that would apply equally well in the present times, the *Japan Weekly Mail* astutely observed that "the police are working very secretly in this matter. If they have any clue, we may be tolerably sure that nothing will be known as to its nature or their manner of using it, until all fear of failure is at an end."

The police failed to apprehend Large's killers. The Metropolitan Police Department had just recently undergone reorganization in the wake of a scandal, and confusion in the ranks may have been one factor in the failure. While no arrest was ever made for the Large murder, the identity of the killers was eventually discovered. In fact, they had been briefly detained during the investigation. They were a former soldier, Shigesue Ogasawara (thirty-nine at the time of the crime), and Tsune-hachi Baba (fifty-seven), a professional gambler. Both had turned to robbery after running up heavy gambling debts.

The two men were eventually nabbed in 1893 on suspicion of committing over a dozen similar robberies. Baba, sentenced to fourteen years, died in prison in November 1896. Ogasawara received a thir teen-year sentence but was released after serving nine years and nine months as part of an imperial amnesty to commemorate the death of the Empress Dowager in 1898. When Ogasawara's involvement in the crime was revealed, the statute of limitations had expired one month earlier. When questioned, he of course blamed his confederate. And dead men, as the saying goes in Japanese, have no mouths.

Reverend Large was buried in the foreigner's section of Aoyama Cemetery. Beneath his name the inscription reads, "This stone erected by Japanese friends."

Berserk Cop's Legacy a Scarred Czar

In May 1891, a deranged policeman named Sanzo Tsuda came close to assassinating Nicholas Romanov, heir to the throne of Imperial Russia, in Otsu City.

Czarevitch Nicholas Romanov in Nagasaki. While riding in a similar jinrikisha in Otsu he narrowly survived an assassination attempt.

Russia's handsome, mustachioed czarevitch had embarked from St. Petersburg the previous November to lay the eastern cornerstone of the Trans-Siberian Railway. En route he toured Asia with his younger brother Georgy and a cousin, Prince George of Greece, visiting India, Siam, Singapore, Java, French Indo-China, Hong Kong and China.

Upon arrival at Nagasaki on April 27, the twenty-three-year-old Nicholas was deferentially welcomed and enjoyed a nine-day sojourn, during which he purchased an astonishing assortment of local handicrafts: ceramics, ivory carvings, Japanese dolls, screens, lacquerware and lamp stands.

Nicholas also showed his generosity to the city's inhabitants. Impressed by a night school where day workers sought to improve their lot, he bestowed a magnanimous gift of 1,000 yen in silver.

After a brief visit to Kagoshima, Nicholas' ship docked at Kobe. Following a tour of Kyoto he headed to Otsu City, on the shore of Lake Biwa. On May 11, he lunched with Shiga's prefectural governor in Otsu. His party, traveling by jinrikisha, then headed back to Kyoto. At 1:50 P.M., the procession turned down a street lined with shops.

Uniformed police were posted along the route at intervals of eighteen meters. As Nicholas, riding in the fifth jinrikisha, passed close to a policeman, the cop suddenly brandished his police saber, shouted, and swung his weapon against the right side of the czarevitch's head, above the ear. Stunned but alert, Nicholas attempted to flee his assailant, pressing against the wound to stem the bleeding. The policeman set off in pursuit.

The Japanese hosts looked on, frozen in horror. Fastest to respond was Prince George, in the next jinrikisha, who joined the pursuit and began thrashing the policeman with a bamboo cane. A pair of quick-thinking jinrikisha pullers then tackled the assailant and bloodied him with his own saber.

Nicholas, bleeding copiously from the head wound, was taken into a nearby kimono shop and treated for a nasty gash, about 7 centimeters long, that had penetrated all the way to the bone.

His would-be assassin, patrolman Sanzo Tsuda, age thirty-eight, was not your everyday criminal. A native of Tokyo, he distinguished himself as a soldier in the seven-month-long Seinan War of 1877 and was decorated for bravery. Unfortunately, mental illness ran in Tsuda's family; both his father and older brother had suffered from spells of eccentric behavior.

What apparently set Tsuda off was a bizarre rumor that rebel leader Saigo Takamori (who committed ritual suicide on September 24, 1877, after defeat of his forces by government troops) had survived the Seinan War and spent the ensuing years secretly exiled in Russia. The czarevitch having earlier visited Kagoshima, Tsuda somehow came under the delusion that Saigo had been clandestinely smuggled back into Japan by the Russian prince. The idea was too much for him to handle; at the sight of the czarevitch he snapped.

Aghast at the news, Emperor Meiji took it upon himself to apologize in person. Clad in military uniform, he departed Tokyo's Shimbashi Station early on May 12 and called on Nicholas's hotel the following morning. He remained with the czarevitch until May 19, seeing off his ship, the *Souvenir de l'Azow*, at Kobe.

The *North-China Herald* of May 15 reported, "Japan has received a blow from which it will take a long time to recover," gravely adding, "There is no fear, of course, of Russia exacting reprisals from the country; but the blow to Japan's self-respect is a very serious thing."

A grateful Nicholas arranged for the two jinrikisha pullers to receive generous cash rewards and lifetime annuities. One returned to his home town in Ishikawa Prefecture and went into politics, becoming a councillor in the local assembly. The second blew his money on wine, women and song. Both lost their pensions when Japan and Russia went to war in 1904.

At least one of Emperor Meiji's subjects could not bear the shame of seeing a visiting royal receive such dreadful treatment. On May 20, a twenty-five-year-old divorcee named Yuko Hatakeyama, carrying a letter of apology, slashed her throat in front of the Kyoto prefectural office.

Authorities had hoped to put Tsuda to death for high treason, but found to their chagrin that the applicable statute applied to Japan's own royals, but not to those of other countries. Tsuda was indicted on the lesser charge of attempted homicide.

His trial, held on May 27 at the Shiga District Court, lasted one full afternoon. He was sentenced to life imprisonment at Kushiro, Hokkaido. Mercifully, perhaps, his sojourn barely lasted until cold weather set in. On September 27, 1891, he died of pneumonia.

Nicholas, who loved uniforms and the military, became czar in 1894. After Russia was bled white by wars with Japan (1904) and Germany (1914), his countrymen deposed him in a bloody revolution. He was executed with his entire family in 1918.

It is hypothetical of course, but had Tsuda's assassination attempt succeeded, the twentieth century might have turned out differently. Possibly even worse.

A Suspicious Death in Yokohama

The Siege of Krishnapur, J.G. Farrell's award-winning 1973 novel set in nineteenth-century colonial India, contains this observation: "As silkworms secrete silk, so human beings secrete sin. There is a normal quantity of sin which . . . any community of erring humans cannot help spinning in the course of their lives."

The above would have certainly applied to the Yokohama foreign settlement in the autumn of 1896, when Edith Carew was put on trial for murdering her husband.

Walter Carew, forty-three, a stocky, hard-drinking man with a walrus moustache, managed the Yokohama United Club. At age twenty-eight, Edith, nee Pouch, was fifteen years younger than her husband. She had a reputation for being flirtatious, which did not exactly endear her to other wives in the settlement.

Edith received an annuity from an inheritance, and Walter entertained the notion of using his wife's money to set himself up as a silk trader. Then in October 1896, Walter, who had been under the care of a Dr. Wheeler, suddenly began to sink rapidly. He was admitted to the local hospital, where he died on October 22.

Dr. Wheeler received an anonymous note that read, "Three bottles of solution of arsenic a week." It may have been written by the Carews' English governess, Mary Jacobs, who had a reputation as a gossip. In any event, the note prompted a forensic autopsy, and sure enough, Walter's mortal remains were loaded with toxic substances.

After hearing testimony from twenty witnesses at the inquest, the British court moved to indict Mrs. Carew for having ". . . willfully and with malice aforethought . . . killed Walter Carew . . . against the peace of Our Lady the Queen, her Crown and dignity."

The shocking news spread, and wherever English expatriates gathered in their far-flung Asian communities, men and women shook their heads in disapproval.

The prosecution's case was by no means cut and dried. Walter Carew was in the habit of taking large quantities of Dr. Fowler's Solution, a popular medication containing potassium arsenate (which was, in the days before antibiotics, used to treat a variety of ailments). Carew made no secret of his arsenic dependence. A year before his death, he had boasted while in his cups that he "took enough poison to kill six men," adding he was "obliged" to do so.

Dr. Wheeler reluctantly testified at the inquest that Carew suffered from a chronically inflamed bladder, possibly caused by venereal disease, although he avoided mention of the specific malady. Edith, who suffered from malaria, also regularly ingested arsenic.

In a gothic twist right out of a Mary Shelly novel, it was learned that twelve days before Carew met his maker, a mysterious woman named Annie Luke, veiled and dressed in black, appeared at the Carew home in Yokohama and demanded an audience with Walter. Annie subsequently penned a message to Edith that threatened, "Beware! Dare to speak one word of the truth and you shall never leave Japan alive."

Shortly after Walter's death, Annie Luke disappeared. Although a large reward was offered for information leading to her whereabouts, her involvement, if any, remained a mystery.

Edith was tried before a jury of five men. A stir was caused when an "indiscreet" letter to her from a local banker (referred to only as "Mr. X") was introduced into the proceedings, raising suspicions of infidelity. Suddenly, the letter disappeared from the courtroom's evidence table. Mrs. Carew was searched by a matron and found to have concealed it on her person, leading one of her attorneys to resign in a huff.

This suspicious behavior perhaps removed any doubts the all-male jury entertained concerning her guilt. After twenty-one days of testimony, they needed only twenty-five minutes to reach their verdict, and Edith was sentenced to hang.

Edith's sympathizers immediately raised questions over the trial procedure. Reluctant to risk hanging an attractive young widow whose guilt was by no means certain, diplomat Ernest Satow had her sentence commuted to life at hard labor. She was transferred to a prison in Hong Kong, but her malaria recurred and she was once again moved, to Aylesbury, England. She was paroled in 1910 after thirteen years behind bars. The rest of her life was otherwise uneventful; she passed away in 1958 at age ninety.

Carew's tombstone in the Yokohama Foreign Cemetery reads:

Walter Raymond Hallowell Carew
In Loving Memory
of
My Husband
Who Died October 22nd 1896 aged 43 years

Beneath this is a slightly revised passage from Tennyson's "Crossing the Bar" that reads:

> Twilight and evening star
> And one clear call for me
> And may there be no moaning of the bar
> When I put out to sea.

Some believe it was Edith's subtle way of thumbing her nose at the court (the bar) when she eluded the hangman's noose and sailed away from Japan.

It would be nearly three more years before the foreign powers would sign away their rights to try their own nationals suspected of committing crimes in Japan, but for once at least, the Japanese were probably relieved they were not obliged to oversee the young widow's arrest and trial. The case had more turns than a corkscrew, and to this day is remembered for its enigmatic circumstances.

The definitive work on the Carew incident, published in 1990, is in Japanese. Author Takao Tokuoka, a former *Mainichi Shimbun* journalist, concludes that Mrs. Carew had the opportunity, a means (the arsenic) and most important, a motive to poison her husband. But did she? We'll never know for sure.

The First to Hang

During the nineteenth century, Japan, China and other Asian countries that had not been colonized were forced to conclude unequal treaties with the Western powers. One of the salient features of such pacts was the principle of extraterritoriality. (Referred to colloquially as "ex'trality.") When a crime or other legal matter involving their nationals occurred on Japanese soil, the signatory countries reserved the right to try such a person under their own jurisdiction.

In other words, if an American killed a Japanese on Japanese soil, he would be tried by an American judge, usually a consular official, in accordance with American law. If found guilty, he would be transported to the closest U.S. federal prison.

The Western powers justified their insistence on "ex'trality" by claiming a lack of confidence that their citizens could obtain a fair trial under Japan's feudal legal system, in which suspects were tortured until they confessed and in which the accused criminals had no right to legal representation. Moreover, the sentences meted out were final: no appeals.

The British government took the law quite seriously, going so far as to establish a branch of Her Majesty's Supreme Court of China in Yokohama in 1865, although most countries used diplomats to conduct trials, and the system was full of loopholes. A foreigner arrested for a crime, for instance, might refuse to state his nationality if he thought a Japanese court would be more lenient. This supposedly once led to a fugitive from Germany arguing before a Japanese court against his own release!

Needless to say, Japan found such arrangements humiliating, but it took several decades to bring its legal system up to the standards demanded by the powers. Finally Foreign Minister Shigenobu Okuma proposed a plan to hire Western justices at what was then called the Great Court of Cassation (the present Supreme Court) to try their own nationals. The proposal was accepted by the U.S., which signed a revised treaty in February 1899. Other powers agreed, and "ex'trality" was abolished.

The new treaty came into effect on July 16, 1899. It did not take long before the law was tested. As fate would have it, an American seaman, Robert Miller, was implicated in a triple slaying the very next day. The crime took place at a saloon called The Rising Sun in what is now Yokohama's Chinatown. Miller, who was later to claim in his defense that he had been drinking heavily, used a straight razor and claw hammer to murder an American named W. Nelson Ward; the saloon's female proprietor, Suye Tonokura (age twenty-four); and an employee, Aki Suzuki (age nineteen).

The next morning a maid found the three mangled bodies. Her screams soon brought the police, who began a search of the neighborhood. A gatekeeper at the settlement said he saw Miller leaving The Rising Sun a little before 7 A.M. Miller stopped to wash his blood-stained hands at a hydrant. He then entered a saloon operated by James Curtis located a few doors away and demanded a drink—threatening to shoot Curtis if he did not comply.

About 11 A.M., police went to the saloon and found Miller snoring away in an upstairs room. They shook him awake and arrested him.

Miller, age forty-nine, told his interrogators he had parted company with his ship the previous April, due to what he claimed was mistreatment by the captain and mate that had cost him partial use of his right arm. With $60 in gold and another 100 yen from his ship, he found a room in Chinatown. He performed a few odd jobs in the Honmoku shipyard but began spending a good deal of time imbibing whiskey at The Rising Sun.

Miller and Ward, another sleazy character, had apparently been competing for the affections of Ms. Tonokura, both hoping to conclude a marriage with her and take over control of the saloon. Miller had followed his rival into the saloon, killed him with the razor, and then "in a fit of mad rage and jealousy" murdered the two women.

The public procurator, a judge of the Yokohama District Court, and a court-appointed doctor held an inquest. Among other things, they heard one witness relate that a Japanese gambler named Ishikura was seen leaving The Rising Sun shortly before or after Miller. This raised the possibility that Miller had an accomplice, but nothing ever came of this account.

By afternoon, the American consul had been notified and an official named Scidmore came to identify Ward's body. Miller, bound in handcuffs, was taken to the Public Procurator's Office at 5 P.M. At a preliminary examination on July 18, he reportedly confessed to the crime. The same day, all three of his victims were cremated.

After Miller's indictment, the *Yorozu Choho* newspaper reported he was incarcerated in one of the cells that had been newly prepared to accommodate foreign prisoners, a four-and-one-half-mat room with a table and chair. In those times, 20 *sen* a day was budgeted for a prisoner's meals, consisting of bread and sliced beef on a tin plate and barley tea.

"When a warder or inspector comes in . . . [Miller] rises and salutes him," the newspaper reported. "Undoubtedly he has a large [sic] experience of prison life."

The trial convened at 9:20 A.M. on Monday, August 7, with attorney Genzo Akiyama, a former jurist, representing the defendant. "He is a man of low type," was the way the *Japan Weekly Mail* described Miller as he stood in the dock, "with the dull eye and flabby cheek of an habitual drinker, a drooping moustache, and a beard of several days' growth. He has, however, the air of slouching self-assurance and slovenly smartness common to so many men of his type. He . . . seemed less interested in the case than many of the spectators."

Miller claimed there were extenuating circumstances to his homicidal behavior, which resulted, he insisted rather incredibly, from his having been served an inferior Japanese whiskey. His lawyer went so far as to apply for laboratory analysis of the hootch Miller imbibed just before his crime, to see if he might be able to claim temporary insanity brought on by the Japanese product.

On August 19, the court found Miller guilty of having murdered three persons and sentenced him to death. In a lengthy statement, the judges ruled, "It is the benevolent desire of His Imperial Majesty the

Emperor that all strangers within our Empire should be treated with magnanimity, and it is also the wish of our people to extend kindness and hospitality to aliens resident in this land.

"At this juncture, when Japan has taken her place among the community of nations, and her legal autonomy has been restored, it is most distressing to the judicial officials to be placed under the painful necessity of sentencing a citizen of one of the Treaty Powers to death.

"The Court deems it most regrettable that in the pleading of the accused and the earnest arguments of his counsel, it is unable to discover any adequate grounds for defense."

While awaiting execution, Miller received weekly visits from a pastor named Charles H. Evans. In a letter to the *Japan Weekly Mail*, Evans later wrote, "I was with [Miller] at the last . . . For a man whose life had been stained by almost every sin . . . and for one who had never known the meaning of religion, the sentiments uttered by him in the latter days of his life seem to show a great measure of repentance, with a true sorrow for his sins."

The Supreme Court rejected the condemned man's final appeal. Miller's lawyer then petitioned the emperor for leniency. This drew an angry response from *The Eastern World*, which editorialized, "The petition asks the Emperor to sanction the slaughter of women who are not virtuous as they might be . . . [If] one little step from the narrow path of virtue may make a woman an outlaw whom anyone may slay . . . where is the line to be drawn?"

The appeal was disregarded and on the morning of January 12, 1900, while the world's attention was focused on the Boer War and depredations of the Boxers in China, Robert Miller consumed a hearty breakfast. He thanked the staff of the prison for their kindness and then requested a last drink of alcohol, which was refused. Permission to smoke a last cigar was granted, however. The chaplain drew one from his pocket, and Miller lit up and took several contented puffs.

"When the cigar was only half smoked," wrote Harold S. Williams in *Tales of the Foreign Settlements in Japan,* "the Governor announced that time was up. The hood was pulled over Miller's head. His arms and feet were bound and the noose tightened around his neck. The trap was sprung and . . . precisely eight minutes later the doctor declared him dead."

No one claimed his body, and he was buried in an unmarked grave in Tokyo's Zoshigaya cemetery.

Japanese criminal courts have considered the death penalty for Westerners on only a few occasions since then. One was super-spy Richard Sorge, whose reports to Moscow on Japan's decision not to engage the Soviet Army in 1941 played a major part in the outcome of World War II.

THE TRIPLE MURDER IN CHINA TOWN.

——

SENTENCE OF DEATH ON MILLER.

——

In the Yokohama Chiho Saibansho to-day, the verdict and sentence of the Court was delivered on Robert Miller, charged with the murder of W. Nelson Ward, an American citizen, and two Japanese women named Tonooka Suye, and Suzuki Aki, in the Rising Sun saloon, China town, on the morning of the 17th July last.

The Court, consisting of Chief Judge Sato Hakuai and Associate Judges Shigara and Morii, in a very lengthy judgment, found the prisoner guilty of the premeditated murder of the three persons named and under Article 292 of the Criminal Code, sentenced him to death; five days being allowed for appeal against the decision.

Mr. Akiyama, on prisoner's behalf, gave notice of appeal, and the Court rose.

——

The Eastern World (August 19, 1899) reporting on Robert Miller's death sentence.

THE LATE MEIJI PERIOD

THE JAPANESE WORD *ryoki hanzai*, meaning abnormal or bizarre crimes, is written with characters that mean "hunting the strange." One such crime came to light in late March 1902, when the parents of an eleven-year old Tokyo boy summoned the police and told them their son had failed to return from the public bath. A search was mounted, and the boy's body was found in a vacant lot near Yotsuya Station.

An autopsy determined the boy had been smothered. In those times, the science of forensic psychology was still in its infancy and homicide detectives had yet to develop sophisticated methods for investigating strange crimes driven by passions not easily understood. To them, it was all very simple: murder was murder. Besides, they had no pat explanation for the 18cm by 14cm strip of flesh missing from the dead boy's left buttock.

The *Jiji Shimbun* newspaper speculated that the killing was an "extreme action," perhaps linked to some sort of superstition.

While human flesh does not, as a general rule, find its way into Japanese cuisine, a number of old wives' tales relate to its use for treatment of disease. Human liver, for example, offers supposedly beneficial properties for the eyes. The blood of newborn infants was also believed to remedy certain otherwise incurable diseases. In this particular case, a foreign angle surfaced, as it was noted that an old Korean folk remedy for leprosy called for soup using flesh taken from the buttocks of a young child.

Among those the police encountered in the course of their investigation was Osaburo Noguchi, a recent university dropout with aspirations of becoming a Russian-language interpreter. Although he presented a handsome figure, people in the neighborhood considered him somewhat "strange."

Originally surnamed Tatebayashi, Noguchi had come to Tokyo from Osaka in 1898, where he was taken under the wing of Neisai Noguchi, a traditional poet of some renown. As was the practice in families without sons, Osaburo adopted the Noguchi family name.

It may have been coincidental, but Noguchi's mentor happened to be suffering from leprosy. It was never determined if the elder Noguchi was actually served this grisly therapy, but relations between the two men continued to sour. Osaburo later eloped with Noguchi's daughter O-Soe. He appeared to have been a devoted husband and father, but not long afterwards, on May 12, 1905, his father-in-law died suddenly under "suspicious" circumstances.

Then on May 25, the corpse of Tomitaro Tsuzuki, a twenty-three-year-old pharmacist from the neighborhood, was found in a thicket near Yoyogi. The cause of death was determined to be poisoning. Suicide was initially suspected, but large funds turned out to be missing from Tsuzuki's shop. Investigators also learned that one of his close friends was Osaburo Noguchi.

On the evening of May 28 Noguchi was arrested at Iidabashi Station. Over 270 yen was found on his person, a hefty sum in those days, particularly for an unemployed man.

Noguchi was charged with murder for the purpose of robbery. He also came under suspicion of the death of his father-in-law, whose body was exhumed. The autopsy determined he had been murdered by asphyxiation. Meanwhile, the father of the dead boy claimed that his son had been acquainted with Noguchi, leading that as yet unsolved case to be reopened as well.

Under heavy interrogation, Noguchi confessed to the slaying of Tsuzuki but continued to deny any part in the other two murders. While he was prosecuted for only one crime, the media sensationalized the cannibalism angle and trial sessions attracted hordes of curious spectators. Based on the evidence and his confession (which some maintained was coerced), he was sentenced to death.

Socialist and anarchist Sakae Osugi met Noguchi while serving a sentence in Ichigaya Prison.

"We prisoners waited for visitors in a cubicle called the 'cockpit,' " Osugi wrote in his autobiography. "Somebody had used his fingernails to scrape into the wood, 'That beast Osaburo ought to be promptly executed.' "

The Great Court refused to hear Noguchi's appeal, and he went to the gallows on July 3, 1908, at the age of thirty-one.

Before the noose was placed over his head, Noguchi's lawyer asked him if he had any last words. The condemned man turned to him and stammered, "From a long time ago . . ." Seven or eight minutes passed while the prison officials fidgeted impatiently for him to finish his statement. He never did.

"Debakame," Japan's Most Famous Peeping Tom

Although the English term "Peeping Tom" can only be traced back as far as 1796, oral tradition ascribes it to a tailor in the town of Coventry, England, who was supposedly struck blind after sneaking a peek at Lady Godiva when she took her famous nude ride in 1040.

Japanese have an equally colorful, if somewhat more recent, term for voyeurs. It is derived from Kametaro Ikeda, who got himself in deep trouble for peeping at women in the public bath. To this day, the epithet *debakame* ("buck-toothed turtle") is attached to individuals with a propensity for voyeurism.

On the evening of March 22, 1908, O-En Koda, the twenty-seven-year old wife of a telephone company employee, was reported missing in Okubo, now in present-day Shinjuku Ward. After mounting a search, police found O-En in a vacant lot, propped against a tree and very dead. She had been at the public bath. Her soap box and a jar containing face powder had been placed neatly beside her body. The cause of death was her towel, which had been thrust down her throat. She had been five months pregnant.

Okubo was still largely rural in those days, and armed robberies had been known to occur even in the daytime. Other attacks had been reported on women walking alone in the area. One victim told reporters that the previous November a man attacked her from behind and attempted to strangle her. Only days before O-En's murder, the wife of a physician fought off a male attacker in nearby Hyakunin-cho.

The criminal, if it was the same man, had crossed the line from assault to murder and the police were now doubly concerned. They set up a task force and within three days had thirteen suspects under scrutiny. Several women were recruited to assist the police by canvassing residents of the neighborhood, marking what was perhaps the first time Japanese authorities utilized females in a felony investigation (policewomen only began serving from 1946).

The crimes continued. On the morning of April 2, a thirty-year-old woman named Ota was assaulted. Police arrested a twenty-three-year old charcoal maker named Yokogawa, who lacked an alibi for some of the crimes, but he did not match the descriptions provided by the victims. Meanwhile, an informer tipped off police that a thirty-five-year-old gardener and steeplejack named Kametaro Ikeda was in the habit of peering through knotholes at the local public bath. He had been seen following some of these women home, and, most important, he appeared to have no alibi for the evening of O-En's murder.

On March 31, Ikeda was taken to the Shinjuku police station on suspicion of performing obscene acts. Under questioning, he admitted to his peeping activities, and the police detained him for ten days. On the fifth day of his confinement, Ikeda tearfully confessed to murdering O-En. By his account, he had seen her voluptuous body in the bath, and felt the urge to possess her. He accosted her on the street and when she cried out, he thrust her wet towel into her mouth, not realizing that she would suffocate.

Ikeda was charged with murder. The newspapers went wild, referring to the case as the "Buck-toothed Turtle Incident." (The *kame* in Kametaro means turtle.) Fanned by the media, the term spread like wildfire and soon became part of the modern Japanese lexicon.

Ikeda stood about 160cm in height, stocky, with a swarthy complexion and bushy eyebrows. While an old photograph shows he suffered from a pronounced overbite, it is possible that rather than "buck-toothed," the term may have derived from *debaru*, meaning to go out on assignment. (In this case, an "assignment" to peep at unclad females.)

Ikeda's trial began on June 12. The Tokyo District Court was mobbed with curious citizens, including members of the peerage, vying for seats in the spectators' gallery. Through his attorney, Ikeda recanted his confession. The defense alleged the confession had been extracted under physical duress (which the police of course denied). Witnesses were produced who could give Ikeda an alibi for the time of the murder, but their testimony, along with other compelling evidence of innocence, was declared inadmissible by the court; in those days, a confession alone was enough to convict.

On August 10, 1908, the court found Ikeda guilty of homicide without premeditation. The following June, having exhausted all appeals, he began serving a thirteen-year sentence.

After his release, Ikeda went back to his old trade of gardening, but that was not the final word. On May 5, 1933, the *Asahi Shimbun* reported that Kametaro Ikeda, then age fifty-nine, had been detained for three days at the Waseda Police Station. Ikeda hotly denied he had been peeping into a women's bathhouse. This time, the elderly recidivist was allowed to return home without any charges being filed.

Japan's Guy Fawkes

Every schoolchild in Britain learns that on November 5, 1605, a man named Guy Fawkes was thwarted in his attempt to set off explosives and kill King James I as he convened Parliament.

Fawkes's motive in the so-called Gunpowder Plot was to avenge the persecution of Roman Catholics in England. After being tortured to reveal the names of his confederates, he was hanged, drawn and quartered on January 30, 1606.

Earlier this century, a small group of Japanese anarchists conspired to attack key government functions with bombs. They had hoped to draw attention to their cause, perhaps even spur a general uprising. The date planned for their assault was November 3, 1910—two days removed from Guy Fawkes' Day. November 3 was picked to launch their attacks because it coincided with the holiday known as *Tenchosetsu*, the birthday of Emperor Meiji, and a day when the emperor would appear in public.

The Japanese conspirators who hatched the plan had probably never heard of Guy Fawkes, but there is no doubt they were in full agreement with a statement attributed to him: "A desperate disease requires a dangerous remedy."

The alleged instigator of the plot, who suggested such action would spur the country's downtrodden masses to rise up and overthrow the corrupt, self-serving leadership, was a forty-year-old, self-proclaimed anarchist from Kochi Prefecture by the name of Denjiro (a.k.a. Shusui) Kotoku.

Educated in the Chinese Confucianist classics, which exhort the downtrodden to be content with their lot, Kotoku made a radical turn to the left upon reaching adulthood and eventually gained a reputation as one of the nation's peskiest political gadflies, publishing various socialist tracts under the nom de plume of Shusui Kotoku .

From the 1890s, Kotoku had been occupied in espousing increasingly radical politics. Writing for the popular *Yorozu Choho* newspaper and later founding his own journal, the *Heimin Shimbun* (People's Daily), he agitated against a notorious copper mine in Tochigi Prefecture that caused severe pollution and economic hardship throughout the northern part of the Kanto region. He won the hatred of militarists by exposing acts of looting by high-ranking Japanese military officers in the wake of China's Boxer Rebellion. He also vocally opposed Japan's involvement in the Russo-Japanese War of 1904–05, which earned him a five-month term in prison.

After gaining release in 1906, the diminutive, mustachioed Kotoku, a dandy whose wardrobe often mixed formal kimono with a bowler hat, traveled to San Francisco, where he spent half a year exchanging ideas with radical thinkers of all persuasions. He returned from his U.S. sojourn a confirmed anarchist.

The authorities did not care a whit for this radical little popinjay from the remote countryside. The political parties that he and his colleagues formed were ordered disbanded, usually within a day or so of their founding. His more radical publications were shut down. He was slapped with heavy fines. Police detectives tailed his movements.

A less obstinate man would have got the message and acquiesced. But Kotoku hailed from Kochi, and the men of the former province of Tosa had a well-earned reputation for independence and stubbornness.

Kotoku also kept some bad company, which led to his undoing. Suga Kanno, a woman who had a brief fling as Kotoku's mistress, was rabidly radical in her politics. She fell in with a small cell of like-minded revolutionaries, who started plotting the assassination of the emperor.

The anarchists' plan was to add some drama to the emperor's birthday celebration on November 3, 1910. As Japan's monarch rode through the streets of Tokyo in a horse-drawn procession, the group's sole female member, Suga Kanno, was to bolt past the guards and present him with an explosive device.

Unbeknownst to the conspirators, the police were keeping a close watch. In May 1910, a cop in Matsumoto City, Nagano Prefecture, reported to his superiors that Takichi Miyashita had obtained a suspiciously large number of tin cans. Police raided Miyashita's place of employment and discovered bomb-making implements. He was arrested on May 17.

Anarchist Denjiro Kotoku and his mistress Suga Kanno were among twelve "conspirators" executed for plotting the assassination of Emperor Meiji in 1910.

A nationwide sweep of radicals ensued, and Kotoku was among those rounded up.

At one time Kotoku, a prolific writer and one of the country's most outspoken leftists, had indeed been bold enough to suggest that the emperor's assassination might be a good idea. In practice, he had abandoned this idea some time before. He was not initially implicated in the plot, but he was regarded as the group's ideological leader, and he had made enough enemies in high places to come under the scrutiny of the Ministry of Justice.

Kotoku, who had been sickly from childhood, had been diagnosed with intestinal tuberculosis. He had been recuperating at the hot springs in Yugawara, southwest of Tokyo, and was arrested as he prepared to board a train to return to the capital on May 28. The charge: high treason.

Specifically, he was accused of violating Article 73 of the revised Criminal Code of 1908, which stipulated that "a person who inflicts, or attempts to inflict, an injury on the Emperor [and members of the imperial household] . . . shall be punished with death." "Attempts to inflict" included conspiracies, instigation of others and complicity.

Kotoku and his cohorts were found guilty of the treasonous crime of plotting the assassination of Emperor Meiji, who, in the constitution of 1889, was officially deified as a "sacred and inviolable being" and who from 1908 was protected by the aforementioned special law designed to deal harshly with anyone bold enough to wish him harm.

As the law stipulated, the conspirators were tried by special session of the nation's highest court, the Great Court of Cassation. The only possible sentence if found guilty was death, with no chance of appeal.

The authorities muzzled the media from reporting the incident for nearly eight months, until the trial began in mid-December. The defendants were brought from their prison cells to attend seventeen closed sessions. Their defense team was essentially hamstrung as it was not allowed to call witnesses for the defense.

Kotoku was well known among radicals in Europe and North America, and when news of the trial spread overseas, angry crowds of anarchists organized demonstrations outside Japanese embassies and consulates in London, Paris, New York and other cities.

It came as no surprise when the court pronounced Kotoku and twenty-three of his colleagues guilty, and sentenced them to death. One day later, twelve defendants had their sentences commuted to life imprisonment.

The executions were carried out with astonishing swiftness; eleven men went to the Ichigaya Prison gallows on January 24, 1911, only five days after the judgment. Ms. Kanno, who was executed the following day, remained an incorrigible anarchist to the very end.

In a remarkably astute analysis filed the day after the executions, the *New York Times* of January 25, 1911, reported:

"Few Governments other than that of Japan would have ventured, in these days, to put to death twelve persons for participation in a murder conspiracy that not only resulted in nothing, but did not lead to the commission of any overt acts proving a real determination to kill. DEN-JIRO KOTOKU and his associated Anarchists were presumably a bad lot, engaged in a bad business, and there is no particular excuse for doubting the legality of their trial or of their condemnation. Still, they hadn't killed anybody, or, so far as known, even come very near carrying out their plan, whatever it was, and, that being so, the cutting off of a dozen heads [sic], one of them a woman's, is more than a little trying to delicate Occidental sensibilities, long unaccustomed to the exercise of such severity.

"Underlying and explaining Japan's stern treatment of these plotters is presumably the fact that the Emperor of that country is still, theoretically, something more and higher than a man, and that to kill him would be sacrilege as well as murder . . .

"So DENJIRO and all of his closer companions had to die."

All official transcripts and records of the trial vanished, probably destroyed in an concerted effort to sweep the incident under the rug. Ministry of Foreign Affairs Archives made public in 1993 uncovered cables from Japanese diplomatic missions abroad, voicing concerns that foreign reaction over the sentencing would continue to build. This is believed to have moved the authorities to execute the twelve as expeditiously as possible.

"Through this affair," wrote legal scholar Kichisaburo Nakamura in *The Formation of Modern Japan* (1962), "the Emperor or the Emperor system became completely taboo . . . Thus, under such circumstances, the people gradually lost the courage to insist on their rights, the power to stand up against the authorities, and the spirit of resistance. They became obedient servants."

Kotoku's remains were interred at his home town of Nakamura in Kochi Prefecture. Undeterred by the fact that its most famous native son was executed for treason, the city operates a small museum housing Kotoku's writings and other personal artifacts.

The High Treason Incident of 1910 marked the beginning of the end of socialism in Japan. Its advocates were driven into overseas exile, hounded, imprisoned, and even murdered. With dissent stifled by the judiciary itself, Japan's experiment in democracy never really had a chance. The rightists and militarists assumed control, and by August 1945 those consequences were fully evident.

Legal scholars today are in general agreement that Kotoku's execution was a gross miscarriage of justice. In 1964, the Japan Bar Association went so far as to erect a stone monument to him and the other eleven victims on the former site of the Ichigaya Prison gallows.

After World War II, one of the few survivors of the twenty-four who were sentenced in 1911, Seima Sakamoto, petitioned the Supreme Court to reverse his guilty verdict and compensate him for twenty-three years imprisonment. The court threw out his case in 1972 on the grounds that the law under which he was convicted no longer existed. Sakamoto passed away in 1975 at age eighty-nine, seeking a pardon to the very end.

Another of the conspirators was Setsudo Mineo, a priest of the Rinsai Buddhist sect with socialist leanings. He died of illness in 1919 while incarcerated in Chiba Prison. At the time of the incident, the Rinsai headquarters in Kyoto excommunicated Mineo for his involvement in the incident. Some seventy-nine years later (October 1996) the sect announced it had decided to posthumously restore Mineo's status. "The principles of socialism," the sect stated, "are by no means incompatible with the tenets of Buddhism."

In *The Nobility of Failure: Tragic Heroes in the History of Japan*, Ivan Morris introduces the most spectacular losers in Japanese history, men he describes as representing "the very antithesis of an ethos of accomplishment."

". . . [His] single-minded sincerity," Morris wrote, "will not allow him to make the maneuvers and compromises . . . needed for mundane success. During the early years, his courage and verve may propel him rapidly upwards, but he is wedded to the losing side and will ineluctably be cast down . . . His death . . . represents an irrevocable collapse of the cause that he has championed."

Although not mentioned in the book, Shusui Kotoku fit Morris's description to a T.

TAISHO PERIOD

1912–26

THE EARLY TAISHO PERIOD

THE TAISHO PERIOD spanned fifteen years and five months, from the death of Emperor Meiji on July 30, 1912, to Christmas Day 1926. Physically frail from childhood, Emperor Taisho suffered a complete physical and mental breakdown shortly after the ritual *Daijosai* investiture. He has been compared by some to Edward VIII of Great Britain, who abdicated just eleven months after his coronation in January 1936. Taisho left little impact on the era that carried his name, which is remembered as a *kurai jidai* ("dark era"), the most notable incidents of which included World War I, the rice riots of July 1918, the Great Kanto Earthquake of September 1923, and an attempt on the life of Prince Regent Hirohito in December of the same year.

Several events during the twilight years of the Meiji period set the stage for troubles to come. One repercussion of the notorious High Treason Incident occurred soon after its anarchist instigators went to the gallows in January 1911. By August, the "Special High-class Section" of the Tokyo Metropolitan Police, whose task was to monitor activities by socialists and other radical dissidents, became an independent entity. Operating under the authority of the Home Ministry, the *Tokko* extended its branches nationwide and energetically repressed political movements, effectively stifling efforts to establish a rudimentary democracy.

Foreigners were also treated with suspicion. A Japanese columnist, Ketsu Kiyosawa, wrote in the *Tokyo Central Review* in 1920 that a Berlin magazine had contained the following passage.

"Japan is a police country. As soon as you cross its borders, detectives are at your heels wherever you go. They will endeavor to grap an opportunity for entering into conversation with you. They will sit near you in the train and ask you questions in wretched English. If you are a diplomat travelling in Japan, the Foreign Office in Tokyo will telegraph from station to station to let them know where you are."

A decade later, American novelist John P. Marquand is said to have drawn on a similar experience when in Japan to serve as the inspiration for his fictitious secret agent, Mr. Moto.

An amnesty announced after Emperor Meiji's death resulted in the parole from prison of 25,984 individuals. To smooth their return to society and ensure their good behavior, parole organizations, called *hogo dantai*, were established. By the end of 1912, more than two thousand such organizations had been designated, many of them affiliated with religious groups, such as Buddhist sects and the Salvation Army.

By the first decade of the twentieth century, Japan suddenly found itself having to deal with increasing crime by minors. A Taisho-period police report noted Tokyo was home to several dozen youth gangs. The oldest, the Kanda based "Toro Club," had been formed around 1898, and at one time boasted some three hundred members. Others, sporting such names as the "Tiger Club" of Shinjuku, the "Blood Pavilion Righteous Group" of Fukagawa, and the "Free Spirits under Heaven" in Asakusa, created headaches for the authorities.

In August 1914, a man named Kosuke Tomeoka set up a training school and farm in Hokkaido to reform delinquent youths. Juvenile offenders continued to increase, and new facilities had to be built to detain them separately from the adult criminal population. In 1922, six juvenile detention facilities were designated in Kawagoe, Himeji, Nagoya, Iwakuni, Fukuoka and Morioka. The following year, ground was broken for a juvenile reformatory in western Tokyo. A long overdue law to prohibit consumption of alcohol by minors finally went into effect in April 1922.

If there was any question over the cinema's power to influence criminal behavior, Japanese were convinced after a silent film series imported from France, featuring a phantom criminal genius known as Zigomar, premiered at the Kinryukan theater in Asakusa in November 1911. Playing to full houses, the films soon began inspiring local criminals to lurk in the dark and attempt similarly brazen acts. By October of the following year, the authorities moved to ban the films outright.

In 1912, the Tokyo Metropolitan Police Department (MPD) acquired their first two police dogs, a Scotch collie and a mixed breed, both males. The dogs, used to head off criminals who might await the police in ambush, were said to be highly intelligent, understanding about 130 separate commands in Japanese.

Among the most notorious criminals of the period was a man named Ryuun Oyone. In July 1915, he broke into a Buddhist convent in Tokyo's Asagaya district, raping and then robbing a sixty-nine-year-old Buddhist nun of 5 yen. Police immediately recognized the modus operandi, as about eight months earlier, a man answering to a similar description (about age forty, 157cm tall, light complexion, nose with virtually no bridge) was suspected of having robbed and strangled a seventy-two-year-old nun in Shinjuku.

Alerted by the Tokyo report, police in nearby Kamakura recognized an earlier murder-robbery at a convent as likely to have been the work of the same felon. The manhunt intensified. After running down several false leads, MPD detectives Kawauchi and Umeno were told that a used clothing dealer had purchased robes stolen from the convent from a man going by the name of Shiro Matsumoto, who, it was learned, had just departed from Shimbashi Station on a train bound for Hakata with about fourteen items of baggage. The police in Kyushu were quickly notified, and on August 8, 1915, were waiting on the platform to intercept Matsumoto, together with a female companion, when his train arrived in Hakata. The man, whose real name turned out to be Ryuun Oyone, was apprehended with a large number of stolen items. He was ultimately charged with 1 murder, 5 murder-robberies, 138 armed robberies and 100 burglaries. Oyone went to the Tokyo prison gallows on June 26, 1916.

During Taisho, Japan's overall crime rates continued to decline from Meiji times (they were to fall even further after World War II). The crime most representative of the period was not violent: it was arson. Incendiary crimes reached their peak in 1913. In olden times, arson was usually a crime of passion, but Japan's modern firebugs were also motivated by insurance fraud. Love suicides (an offense under the criminal code when the instigator survived) occurred fairly frequently; these peaked in the early 1930s.

By Taisho, more efforts were being devoted to delve more deeply into criminal psychology. Studies were published on how the prevalence of certain crimes changed according to season—like the topics of haiku. Rapes, for example, were more frequent in autumn, while murders tended to occur more in spring. In a 1921 work on criminal behavior, Anko Takada, a physician, noted the similarities of several murders in which the perpetrators used baseball bats, leading him to conclude with confidence that "a majority of crimes are copycat crimes," an observation frequently cited well into the 1990s.

"Intellectual" crimes such as counterfeiting, fraud, forgery and embezzlement began to proliferate. Insurance was now widely available and promoted as a means of savings; it provided a motive for modern murderers. The most notorious insurance murderer was Tadashi Kawamoto, who early in 1920 took out two policies valued at 5,000 yen on his twenty-six-year-old common-law wife, O-Hama. Two months later, she expired from what was diagnosed as acute meningitis. Shortly thereafter Kawamoto began living with O-Fumi, a nineteen-year-old woman who became pregnant with his child. Since a pregnant woman could not apply for life insurance, Kawamoto substituted the late O-Hama's younger sister Kanako and signed up for policies with several companies amounting to 40,000 yen—equivalent to several million dollars at today's rates. He murdered O-Fumi and paid a doctor to issue a death certificate without confirming the cause of death.

Both women were believed to have been poisoned, in the views of the police covering the case, by strychnine. Kawamoto, a medical school dropout who practiced medicine without a license, put his training to use in a nefarious manner. He was sentenced to death in May 1922.

The serial murderer who made his mark in Taisho times was a thirty-four-year-old laborer, Sataro Fukiage. In April 1922, Fukiage assaulted and attempted to rape a ten-year-old Tokyo girl, but was not officially charged. As is often the case, the police came to regret their leniency. Over a period of one month during 1922, Fukiage committed thirteen rape-murders of young women in Tokyo and nearby prefectures.

Fukiage's photo was circulated and a man closely matching his description was detained for questioning in Tokyo. The man insisted his name was Kimura, but when he started to sign the interrogation document, he inadvertently began to write "Fukiage" before halting in midstroke. A sharp-eyed cop named Arai spotted the blunder and kept the man in custody until his identity was confirmed. Fukiage was hanged in September 1926.

Taisho's most shocking crime story surely ranks as one of the century's most bizarre: a deranged serial killer who confined his victims entirely to newborn infants.

On November 12, 1922, a Shibuya tailor named Uchida reported to police that he had found the corpse of a newborn infant outside his shop. Uchida told the police that the same day the infant's corpse was found, a man named Takebei Yamanoi had called on the shop during his absence. Yamanoi was an ex-convict who had served time for fraud and embezzlement. To direct him towards a more honest livelihood, the prison had taught him tailoring, and Tamanoi had worked for Uchida briefly following release from prison.

Subsequent inquiries determined that Yamanoi had paid 20 yen to a midwife in Hongo for an infant born to a young nurse two days earlier. Under questioning, Yamanoi readily admitted that he had told the midwife he intended to raise the child as his own, but then strangled it and discarded the body at Uchida's residence. Under further encouragement, Yamanoi's story gradually came out. After leaving prison, he had gone on one of the most bizarre killing sprees in history.

Yamanoi's modus operandi was to make contact with students or salaried workers who faced imminent fatherhood, but who clearly lacked the means to support their illegitimate offspring. By offering to "adopt" these infants born out of wedlock, he collected a total of 800 yen from the fathers. A portion of the money was used to purchase the infants from the midwives at between 30 and 50 yen each, thus leaving him a handy profit.

This modern-day Moloch confessed to strangling a total of 21 infants. His record was to stand for only two decades. Over a span of five years beginning in 1944, a couple who operated the Kotobuki midwife clinic in Tokyo abandoned some 103 newborn to die by exposure and/or starvation.

The Shocking "Electric Wire Murder Case"

The word *shock*, meaning "to astound, stun or surprise," derives from the French *choc* via *choquer*, meaning "to collide with." Entomologists believe it may have come from the Old French *chuquier*, or possibly from an older term of Germanic origin. In present usage, of course, it is also applied to those who make uncomfortable—or worse—contacts with an electric current.

Death from electric shock results either from paralysis of the brain's breathing center, heart paralysis or ventricular fibrillation, a rapid twitching of the heart muscle. The latter tends to be the most common cause of death. When American inventor Thomas Alva Edison realized that alternating current could easily be fatal under the wrong circumstances, he sought a method of dramatizing his warnings, mainly in the hope of discrediting his business rival George Westinghouse.

Edison sold the state of New York on the idea of an electric chair and on August 6, 1890, a death row inmate at Auburn State Prison, William Kemmler, became the first man to sit in it. The chair succeeded in its intended purpose, but the executioner bungled the job; Kemmler took eleven minutes to die.

Edison's scheme backfired. Newspaper accounts of the execution horrified readers worldwide. The *New York Globe* editorialized that "Manufactured lightning to take the place of the hangman's rope for dispatching of condemned murderers cannot be said to be satisfactory."

On July 7, 1891, five murderers, all male, were executed by the electric chair in New York's Sing Sing Prison. One of them was a Japanese. Historical records mangle his name horribly into "Schichiok Jugigo," but *Nihon no Shikei* gives the name as Jujiro Shibuya, who went to the chair at age thirty-five for the crime of murder in Manhattan.

According to news reports, while awaiting execution Shibuya had apparently been hospitalized due to a hunger strike.

Jujiro Shibuya was executed by electric chair in New York's Sing Sing prison in 1891.

The *Democratic Register* of July 11 reported that Shibuya had always preferred to sit and sleep on the floor of his cell, in the Japanese manner.

Shibuya was the fourth of the five to go to the chair that day. On this particular day, when each of the condemned was pronounced dead, the prison raised a flag of different colored bunting to signal to reporters standing outside that the job was complete. For Joseph Wood, a Negro, a black flag was used. For Harris A. Smiler, a former member of the Salvation Army executed that day, the flag was blue. For former baseball player James J. Slocum, a white flag was raised. And when Shibuya was pronounced dead a flag of red bunting was raised.

Although the sight of death by electrocution proved quite horrifying to behold, some physicians believe that the first jolt of electricity shatters the nervous system instantaneously and beyond recall, thus making it more humane and less painful than hanging. Although largely supplanted today by lethal injection, as many as twenty-four U.S. states and two other countries (the Philippines and the Republic of China) have utilized "Old Sparky."

In the annals of crime, it is almost unheard of for criminals to return the favor by electrocuting a cop. One exception was a truly "shocking" crime that occurred in the Kameido district of Tokyo in 1913.

Around 2 A.M. on April 4, 1913, Mrs. Misao Igarashi arose from sleep to relieve herself. On her way to the outhouse, she heard an odd sound from the lane outside, perhaps a large object flopping in the wind. Thinking it might be an amorous cat, she slid apart the shutters for a look. The view brought forth a scream of horror. This awakened her husband, Kiichi, who, after seeing the cause of the disturbance, set off for the nearby police box at Kameido Tenjinbashi. He was knocked flat by something, as was his father, Tokutaro, who followed in his wake. By this time, people were shouting "Murderer!" and "Fire!" arousing the entire neighborhood.

Those who approached the prostrate bodies saw sparks emanating from two wires running beneath them. One led down from the power line connected to the neighboring house. The other was strung across the lane and wound around the bars on the outhouse window.

A neighbor in the construction trade used a bamboo pole to push away the live wires and three bodies were taken to a nearby hospital. Kiichi Igarashi was unconscious and in critical condition with severe burns on his lower body. Tokutaro Igarashi suffered burns to his right hand, but soon regained consciousness. An MPD patrolman named Shingai got the worst of it; a terrible burn to the head. He was pronounced dead on arrival due to electrical shock.

Forensic investigators determined that the killer had devised an insidious "murder weapon" by removing a switch from a 3,000-volt high-voltage line, stripping off the insulation, and then attaching a length of unshielded wire, which he strung across the street at about shoulder height, winding the other end around the bars on the outhouse. It was clearly a case of premeditation to do harm, employing a means without precedent.

The killer left behind a pair of pliers and a candle. While police found it hard to believe the act to be indiscriminate, the motive for the crime was not immediately evident.

The owner of a hardware store in nearby Honjo told police he had sold the pliers to a young man wearing laborer's clothes, who he estimated to be about twenty years old, the day before the incident.

Police extended their dragnet and soon a man matching the description was traced to a used clothing shop in Asakusa, where he had sold apparel stolen from the neighborhood.

On April 6, police detained one Anjiro Sakamoto, age thirty-four. Sakamoto was known to be familiar with electricity and his wife had dealings with the Igarashi family. Eager to pronounce the case solved, the police issued an arrest warrant.

Fortuitous coincidence intervened to get Sakamoto off the hook. In the early hours of April 14, a cop patrolling the Yurakucho district detained a young man behaving in a suspicious manner. The man, who identified himself as Akira Yamamoto, a twenty-year-old day laborer, had items in his possession that proved to be stolen and he was placed under arrest. Yamamoto had several priors for theft and had served time in a youth reformatory. Under questioning, he eventually confessed to seventeen incidents of theft, one of which was the previous month's infamous "electric wire murder case."

Yamamoto told police he had devised the trap in the hopes of facilitating his getaway. He had attempted to rig a similar device a second time, fortunately without incident. With only a superficial familiarity with electricity, Yamamoto was quite lucky not to have electrocuted himself.

Records about the criminal's fate are a bit sketchy, but it appears he was not executed, by electric chair or any other means.

Author Yasuo Nagayama points out two salient characteristics of this particular case. It encouraged the police to improve their knowledge of scientific matters. It also set the stage for the pattern of so-called urban crimes, in which criminals took advantage of the anonymity afforded by large cities and were generally not personally recognized by their victims.

The Better to Cut and Burn You With, My Dear

The Taisho period was not without its share of strange events. This one, fully deserving of the newly coined term *ero-guro* ("erotic and grotesque"), left authorities shaking their heads in bewilderment.

On March 2, 1917, Dr. Jungo Suehiro was summoned from his clinic at Ryusenji-cho in Tokyo's Shitaya district to treat an emergency. Black bag in hand, Dr. Suehiro arrived at the home of a wooden clog maker and was led to the rental flat on the second floor. He entered a small room and saw a man of about age thirty kneeling beside an unconscious woman, massaging her chest.

As the doctor knelt beside her futon, he was repulsed by a foul smell. Pulling back the blankets, he gasped in horror.

"The woman had gone into spasms," the doctor later related to newsmen. "I gave her an injection of camphor to relieve the pain, but she was in agony from what appeared to be sulfuric acid burns. Some writing had been branded into her flesh. Several fingers and toes had been severed. She was a dreadful sight."

Suehiro promptly notified the police. A detective was dispatched to the scene together with a police physician. The man found at the scene was taken into custody and investigators bagged the evidence they collected.

By around eight o'clock that evening, the woman was dead.

The odd couple turned out to be Matsukichi Oguchi, a twenty-nine-year-old carpenter, and his common-law wife, Yone Yahagi, twenty-three.

Oguchi was described as singularly unattractive. In addition to having below-average intelligence, he was lazy, but his roguish personality endeared him to females, and he apparently never lacked for companionship. At the time he first met Yone in the nearby Yoshiwara (where she worked as a maid in a brothel) he was dividing his affections between two other women. He promptly dumped both and Yone moved in.

While Oguchi was out on occasional jobs, Yone began a sexual liaison with the couple's neighbor, a Yoshiwara pimp named Yamagishi. When Oguchi discovered her infidelity, he gave Yamagishi a severe drubbing, smacking Yone around a few times for good measure. Then he apologized to both, giving the pimp 10 yen (a generous sum in those days) for "get well" money. The couple then moved to new lodgings in mid-January.

The police naturally assumed Oguchi's sadistic actions were spurred by rage over Yone's infidelity. He was indicted on March 3 on the charge of homicide.

When the particulars of Yone's autopsy were reported in detail, the public was not disappointed. Freshly branded on Yone's back, pathologists noted, were the words, "Wife of Matsukichi Oguchi." Both arms bore the same message, which had been crudely tattooed using a needle and ink. Her left ring finger, right little finger, fourth left toe, and right little and third toes had been severed by a sharp instrument, either at the second joint or at the base. The severe burns on her inner thighs and torso had been caused not by acid, but by branding with hot objects. Neither her face nor genitals bore signs of injury.

The cause of Yone's death was ascribed to "autotoxemic shock."

When interviewed by the doctors, Oguchi's account refuted media reports portraying him as a depraved sadist. According to him, Yone had not only been fully aware of the abuse being administered to her, but had actually spurred him on. The dim-witted Oguchi, perhaps out of morbid curiosity, had obliged.

"When I cut off her fingers and toes, she said she felt no pain," Oguchi told the doctors. "She told me it was her way of apologizing. I was afraid she would leave me if I refused, so I went along. I tied threads around the fingers and toes so they wouldn't bleed, and when I cut them—*pon*—they popped right off."

The action subsequently intensified with the searing and branding, some of which Yone apparently inflicted on herself.

Yone, born and raised in the Yoshiwara, was probably aware that tattooing or branding a paramour's name, severing digits, and other forms of self-mutilation (a custom known as *shinju-date*) was sometimes practiced in the Edo period as a pledge between courtesans and patrons, and other lovers.

Oguchi was nonetheless held responsible for her death and sentenced to twelve years in prison. While his case was still under appeal, he died of illness, from what was believed to be tuberculosis.

A photo of Yone's nude corpse, outside what appears to be the morgue entrance, shows her lying atop a wide wooden board, or perhaps a door removed from its hinges. She faces the camera, her eyes partially closed. The burn wounds are clearly visible. Even after such an excruciating death, it is still evident she had been a lovely young woman. Her face appears to be wreathed in a cryptic smile.

An Open-and-shut Case

In the language of jurisprudence, *corpus delicti* refers to the material evidence in a homicide—the victim's corpse —which serves as incontrovertible evidence that murder was committed.

Killers determined to evade the consequences of their act have employed a variety of concealment techniques. In addition to burial, these methods include dismemberment, encasement in cement, decomposition using acid and immersion in deep water. But as J.H.H. Gaute and Robin Odell note in *Murder 'What Dunit'* (1982), ". . . the human body is surprisingly durable and its destruction without trace is difficult."

Placing your victim's dismembered corpse in a set of distinctive luggage still bearing your own initials is arguably as dumb as you can get. Yet this really occurred, in a notorious 1919 incident known as the

"Suzuben Murder." A fancy trunk—emblazoned with the initials "A.Y."—helped police wrap up their, er, case in near-record time.

The Suzuben incident was not your everyday sleazy killing by a dim-witted culprit. Its main perpetrator was an elite bureaucrat out to fatten his wallet while people were rioting over the price of rice.

In the summer of 1918, hoarders and speculators sent rice prices through the roof. On July 23, housewives in the village of Uozu, Toyama Prefecture, raised a ruckus, setting off a chain reaction in major cities, culminating in full-fledged "Rice Riots" in Tokyo's Hibiya Park. To stabilize prices and ensure sufficient supply, the government initiated a rationing system and also procured *gaimai*, less-popular "foreign rice," mostly from China.

The Ministry of Agriculture assigned four trading companies to distribute the *gaimai*. Even though prices were controlled, the sheer quantity assured these companies enormous profits from brokerage fees. Sensing an opportunity, Akira Yamada, a thirty-year-old bureaucrat at the ministry responsible for procurement, made an arrangement with a sleazy rice broker named Benzo "Suzuben" Suzuki to divert some of the inventory, for a slight consideration.

The scene now shifts to the lower reaches of the Shinano River in rural Niigata Prefecture. On June 6, 1919, a milk delivery man pedaling along his route noticed a foul smell emanating from a trunk at the water's edge. He opencd the lid and dashed off frantically to the police to report he had found part of a human torso.

The Niigata police sent a cable to the Tokyo Metropolitan Police. For the past several days, the MPD had been badgered by the family of a man named, yes indeed, Benzo Suzuki, who had been missing since the evening of May 31. From a description of the corpse, Suzuki, or at least part of him, appeared to have been found.

Suzuki had told the last people he saw that he was planning to meet an Agriculture Ministry official named Akira Yamada (note the initials).

Investigators in Niigata, meanwhile, learned that on the morning of June 3, two men had arrived at Nagaoka Station on a sleeper from

Tokyo. They carried two distinctive leather trunks, so heavy the station porter could not lift them alone. The men, later identified as Sozo Watanabe (twenty-seven) and Shohei Yamada (thirty-eight), had then arranged to go boating on the Shinano River.

The owner of the vessel told police that Watanabe asked him to steer to a deep section of the river and, explaining the trunks contained contraband a friend had brought back from the war in China, shoved them overboard.

Watanabe had been an underclassman at the university Yamada attended. Realizing the police were closing in, Yamada asked Watanabe to confess to the rap, insisting that by claiming he had killed Suzuki during a struggle, he would receive a lighter sentence. Under persistent police grilling the story of the rice scam came out.

Yamada had proposed that he and Suzuki speculate in the market to the tune of 300,000 yen. Yamada asked Suzuki to put up the money on his behalf, after which Yamada would pay back his share in the venture out of the profits. Unfortunately the scheme collapsed, and an infuriated Suzuki demanded that Yamada cover his share of the losses, or 50,000 yen.

Yamada invited Suzuki to his home in Shinagawa on the evening of May 31, having already made the decision to murder him. After pouring drinks, Yamada pleaded for more time to get the money. As Suzuki began ranting for his money, Sozo Watanabe sneaked up behind him and struck him with a baseball bat. Yamada then strangled the unconscious Suzuki and cut his throat for good measure.

The two dismembered Suzuki's corpse and stuffed the parts into a pair of trunks, in their haste overlooking the fact that they bore Akira Yamada's initials. They sprinkled in moth pellets to mask the smell, and soon thereafter Watanabe, assisted by Shohei Yamada, a relative of Akira, headed for Nagaoka and the Shinano River.

Corruption in the bureaucracy leading to murder was without precedent, and the evidence in this case was overwhelming. Akira Yamada went to the Ichigaya Prison gallows on April 2, 1921.

THE LATE TAISHO PERIOD

NINETEEN TWENTY-THREE, the twelfth year of
Taisho, is best remembered as the year of the Great Kanto Earthquake.
When the quake struck just before noon on September 1, law enforcement suffered as much as the general population. Twenty-one of the
city's police stations and 254 *koban* were seriously damaged or completely destroyed. Among the dead were ninety-four police officers and
firemen, including the captain of the Honjo Aioi police station.

Tokyo's Kosuge Prison was devastated. The over 1,000 inmates were
temporarily released on the honor system, a custom going back to feudal times. Amazingly, all of them returned, apparently out of a sense of
obligation to the warden, Shirosuke Arima, who was known for his
stern but fair treatment. In Yokohama, where the devastation was even
greater, the local prison was not so fortunate. Its warden temporarily
freed 1,131 prisoners on their own recognizance. Of these, 140 failed to
return and the warden requested assistance from the navy shore patrol.
Later, naval ships were used to ferry several hundred convicts to temporary lodgings at Nagoya Prison.

The mob lynchings of thousands of Koreans and smaller numbers
of Chinese were anything but spontaneous. On September 3, Fumio
Goto, a security official in the Home Ministry, cabled outlying offices
that Koreans were committing acts of arson and ordered them rounded

Socialist writer Sakae Osugi (center) and his wife Noe Ito were among the leftists murdered by the military in the wake of the Great Kanto Earthquake.

up. The media, particularly the nationalist *Hokkai Times*, chimed in with inflammatory stories.

One of the first acts by newly appointed Prime Minister Gonnohyoe Yamamoto was a demand for the persecution to stop, but the damage had been done. The incident was to spur a young man named Daisuke Namba to fire a shot at then Crown Prince Regent Hirohito on December 27. He was found guilty of lese majeste and hanged a year later.

Rightists also took advantage of the confusion to kill scores of fellow Japanese, whom they viewed as "enemies" of the state. In the notorious Kameido Incident of September 4, Yoshitora Kawai, Keishichi Hirasawa and eight other labor activists were beheaded by cavalry troops based in Chiba.

Perhaps the best known victim of the carnage was a thirty-nine-year-old anarchist named Sakae Osugi. One of the country's most flamboyant rebels, Osugi had recently stirred controversy with an autobiography in which he railed against the oppressiveness of family and society. He had just returned from a sojourn in France.

On September 16, a captain of the *kempeitai* ("military police") named Masahiko Amakasu dispatched teams of soldiers to track down and apprehend Osugi. He was finally spotted around 5:30 P.M., waiting with his six-year-old nephew Munekazu as his wife, Noe Ito, twenty-nine, shopped for fruit near their house.

The three were driven to the military police compound at Kojimachi. Around 8:00 P.M. Osugi was taken into a conference room and seated. Amakasu later testified that he walked behind Osugi and locked his forearm across his throat in a judo stranglehold. It took about ten minutes for Osugi to die of asphyxiation. The process was repeated shortly afterward with Ito. Two enlisted men then strangled the boy using a hand towel. That night, their bodies were wrapped in burlap, bound with rope and tossed down an unused well.

On September 20, doctors performed autopsies on the victims. The report, only made public half a century later, noted that Osugi and his wife were also severely beaten before being strangled.

At his court martial in October, an unrepentant Amakasu delivered a rambling soliloquy on his motive for the slayings. "In just fifty or sixty years," he harangued, "our country has achieved the level of civilization that took five hundred or six hundred years in Western countries. If anarchists are allowed to oppose the ways of our sacred land, it will lead to the ruination of the Yamato race. [These people] are like parasites in the body of a lion. I cannot allow them to carry on."

The prosecutor at the trial was less than energetic in condemning Amakasu's crimes. After all, he conceded to the bench, these were "extraordinary times." Still, murder could not be disregarded; the prosecution requested a fifteen-year sentence. On December 8, the military court sentenced Amakasu to a ten-year term of imprisonment. Sgt. Keijiro Mori received a three-year sentence. Two MPs under his command were acquitted because they acted on orders.

Amakasu was quietly paroled after two and a half years. After spending eighteen months in France, he became director of a film production company in Manchuria and over the next decade engaged in a variety of intrigues. He committed suicide on August 20, 1945, to avoid capture by the Soviet Army. Amakasu achieved posthumous film stardom of sorts. Played by composer Ryuichi Sakamoto, he was prominently featured in the 1987 Bertolucci film *The Last Emperor*.

A Merry Chase through Chiba

Of all the sensational crimes that occurred in the Taisho period, one singular event stands out. In 1926, a feisty fugitive in northern Chiba captured the nation's rapt attention by eluding authorities for forty-two days.

The leading player in this drama was a stalwart wagoner named Kumajiro Iwabuchi, age thirty-five. The other dramatis personae included Kumajiro's wife, two mistresses, and an army of some seven thousand police, firemen and volunteers.

Although only about 155 cm tall, Iwabuchi was strong as an ox. While not particularly bright, he was cheerful and diligent, and was liked by those he encountered, who addressed him as "Kuma-san" ("Mr. Bear").

"Bear," unfortunately, had a fondness for strong liquor; he also had a surfeit of testosterone. He had fathered five children by his wife, Yone, and was on intimate terms with two other ladies. One, Kei Yoshizawa, decided she was tired of playing third fiddle and took up with another man. This infuriated Iwabuchi. In a drunken rage, he pummeled several people and found himself arrested and jailed for three months.

Shortly after his release on August 18, Iwabuchi went to Kei's home and bludgeoned her to death with a piece of firewood. After meting out similar treatment to her mother, he set off to hunt down Toramatsu Sugazawa, her would-be suitor. Sugazawa was not home, so Iwabuchi politely asked to borrow a match and used it to set fire to the Sugazawa home, which burned to the ground. Iwabuchi then fled into the sticks.

It is hard to conceive that one rustic running amok could generate such a response. Policemen, armed with revolvers and swords, were dispatched from the stations of Sawara, Tako, Omigawa, Narita and Yokaichiba. Their ranks were buttressed by volunteers and firemen. Other groups pitched in. Vigilante groups were formed, including "The Buddhist priest group to sermonize Iwabuchi."

The makeshift posses then scoured an area measuring 17.5 km from east to west and 15 km from north to south, but Iwabuchi, by now nicknamed "Onikuma" ("devil-bear"), was not to be found. Out of a sense of personal obligation and perhaps partly out of sympathy for the underdog, local farmers gave him food and provided hideouts, enabling him to evade the massive manhunt for several weeks.

The media, meanwhile, began directing barbs at the police. "For nearly half a month," satirized the *Tokyo Nichinichi Shimbun* of September 6, "Iwabuchi has managed to elude four thousand police and five thousand firemen. Once it's over, we can hardly wait for the movie spectacular, starring 'Lord Kuma the wagonmaster' and a cast of five thousand extras!"

Iwabuchi, who had vowed to kill Sugazawa, continued to appear sporadically, but the sight of him swinging a long scythe was enough to frighten off pursuers. On September 11, when a twenty-four-year-old patrolman named Kotaro Kono attempted to nab him, Iwabuchi slashed Kono with the scythe and he bled to death. Shocked by this violent resistance, police beefed up their search with another three hundred officers.

The media had better luck tracking him down. On the night of September 27, a man named Tada offered to lead two newspaper reporters, Sakamoto and Baba, to Onikuma's hideout.

As they approached, the "Devil-bear" shouted, "Who's there? I'll kill you!" With his disorderly hair and beard, he looked every bit the wild man he was. Tada calmed him down and introduced the two, who placated him saying, "*Zuibun gokuro sama.*" (You must be very tired.)

"Ah, Mr. Sakamoto," moaned Iwabuchi. "I'm so sorry. I've done some terrible things—killed people. Set fires. It's unforgivable."

"A lot of people see you as another Kunisada," said one obsequious reporter. This was a comparison to the legendary outlaw Kunisada Chuji, who evaded Tokugawa authorities throughout northern Kanto for over a decade in the 1840s.

Iwabuchi spread out some matting and, setting the deadly scythe beside him, swigged *shochu* (grain spirits) from a teacup.

Sakamoto inflamed Iwabuchi, saying, "Put an end to yourself like a man. We'll report it that way in the paper."

The fugitive informed them frankly that he had indeed decided to commit suicide. After several more cupfuls, he took the two reporters' hands in his and wept, "I've been so bad. Please write it down and tell everybody how sorry I am.

"But whatever you do," he begged them, his palms together in supplication, "Don't turn me in to the cops." The two promised, then rushed off around 2:00 A.M. to call in their stories by telephone.

By September 28, the police had conducted twenty-five sweeps, searching empty houses, storage sheds, caves and other likely hideouts. They had called on 1,917 households in the district, making door-to-door inquiries as many as thirty-four times, without success. Yet Iwa-

Firemen transport the corpse of "Devil Bear" Iwabuchi, who committed suicide after eluding thousands of searchers for 42 days.

buchi had boasted to the reporters that there were only two days on which he had nothing to eat.

The weather turned colder and the six weeks on the run, without a hot meal or a soft bed, began to take its toll on the fugitive. The next day three firemen, former acquaintances, found him lying before his family grave, having attempted suicide by slashing his own throat. Actually that attempt failed and he had finally ingested a lethal dose of strychnine. Instead of immediately informing the police, the three men carried him to the home of his older brother, Seijiro. He died without regaining consciousness.

The forty-two-day hunt for "Devil-bear" Iwabuchi involved the mobilization of 13,540 men and cost the state some 57,630 yen—the equivalent of several million U.S. dollars. And they never caught him.

Sneak Thief Dressed to Kill

Early in the morning of November 9, 1925, a school teacher living in Ebara in Tokyo's Shinagawa district was shot and killed by a burglar, who then stabbed to death a patrolman who tried to stop him from fleeing. Two nights later, the same thief held up a Buddhist priest in Totsuka. By November 14 he had killed a maid in Ibaraki City, an Osaka suburb, and on November 16 he robbed a temple in Osaka. Based on the description circulated by police, the same man was linked to three armed robberies that occurred in Yokohama in late October.

Later in November, Tokyo police officials received two letters from the culprit postmarked Kurashiki City in Okayama. It was by now obvious he was using robberies to fund his journey westward. One letter read, "I am the criminal who killed Torakichi Koda and Patrolman Iitaba. I am truly sorry you have been forced to work so diligently at your investigation . . . I advise you to post my description throughout the country. Exhort your subordinates, and don't fail to question even one traveler at the rail stations. I pray for your rigorous investigation."

It was rare enough for killers to write letters of apology for their acts, but the robber known as "Pisu-Ken" was an unusual fellow. He was able to elude the police dragnet thanks to a very convincing disguise. It seems Pisu-Ken could easily pass as a woman.

As one account described him, "He would remove his Chinese-style men's clothing and, from his *furoshiki* ("carrying cloth") take out a kimono. Over it, he wore a dark green coat made of Oshima brocade. His wig was coiffeured in an upswept style. When he covered his head and neck with a velvet shawl, his narrow face, delicate bone structure and slightly puckered lips enabled him to pass for a woman."

His real name was Seijiro Onishi and he was born in Hyogo Prefecture in 1887. His father operated theaters in Kobe and the family was at one time well off, but when he was about fourteen years old his father lost the business. Onishi stowed away on a freight train bound for Tokyo, where he was taken under the wing of the head of a group of pickpockets in Asakusa.

In 1904, at age eighteen Onishi was finally jailed, the first of a string of arrests for theft that kept him behind bars for most of his youth. It was at this time Onishi changed his name to Kenji Morigami, from which he became known as "Ken the Pistolero," or "Pisu-Ken."

Perhaps seeking even greater notoriety, he at one time lurked about the Tokyo residences of Prime Minister Takaaki Kato and Home Minister Reijiro Wakatsuki, hoping for an opportunity to assassinate them. Afterwards he traveled to mainland Asia but soon returned to Japan. In August 1908 he was arrested for a number of armed robberies in the Kansai area and sentenced to life imprisonment at hard labor. He was described as being less than a model prisoner, but an imperial amnesty cut time from his sentence and he was released in August 1923.

The ex-con was kept under close police observation, but he found honest work and arranged a marriage. Lulled into the impression that maturity had blunted his criminal urges, the police let down their guard.

That was a mistake. Onishi was about to demonstrate the meaning of "recidivism" in the true sense of the word.

In October 1925, he suddenly disappeared. He resurfaced in Yokohama, where he began a string of robberies, including the killing of the Tokyo patrolman on November 9.

With the nation starting to panic over where Pisu-ken might strike next, he slipped away by ferry from Shimonoseki, traveling to Pusan, Korea, and Dairen (Dalian), China. Masquerading as a Chinese, he made his way back to Japan in early December.

The owner of a restaurant in Kobe informed police that Pisu-Ken would be spending the night on the premises. In the early morning hours of December 12, 1925, a "do-or-die" squad of twelve detectives raided the establishment and pounced on him as he slept. Before he could get off a shot from the 8-round Browning automatic in his hand, the excitement apparently proved too much for him; he fainted.

Outside the police station, Onishi a.k.a. Pisu-Ken was obliged to pose for a commemorative photo with twenty-three detectives. He sits in the center of the front row, minus the wig, but dressed in his female garb. He is not smiling.

At the first session of his trial on September 7, 1926, at the Osaka District Court, the bench was forced to halt proceedings at 12:20 P.M. due to clamor in the courtroom. Onishi received the death sentence on September 25 and went to the gallows on December 6, at the age of forty.

SHOWA PERIOD
1926–89

HEISEI PERIOD
1989–

THE EARLY SHOWA PERIOD

SICKLY FROM CHILDHOOD and clearly not up to the demands of his position, Emperor Taisho passed away at age forty-eight. His fifteen-year reign came to an end on Christmas day 1926. He was succeeded by his son Hirohito. The first year of the new era, named Showa, was of only one week's duration; so was the final year, Showa 64, which ended on January 7, 1989.

As part of the observances during the period of imperial mourning, benevolence was accorded to wrongdoers. On February 7, 1927, amnesty was granted to 137,669 convicted criminals. Another 1,457 received "special amnesty"; sentences were reduced for 46,138 more.

These magnanimous acts did not deter authorities from constructing bigger and better penal facilities. On March 17, 1928, Osaka Prison, which had been under construction since 1918, was finally completed. The huge four-story brick building with elevators and a capacity of 3,155 became Japan's largest penal facility and remains so today.

The judicial system was also in for a remarkable change. After some two decades of study and debate, Japan adopted the system of trial by jury on October 1, 1928. Juries were empowered to decide questions of fact in cases punishable by death, imprisonment or penal servitude. Crimes deemed of the most serious nature were excepted. These included *fukeizai* (acts deemed discourteous to the imperial household), *taigyakuzai* ("treason"), and violations of the military regulations. Such cases were remanded to judges. If the maximum penalty in a case being tried was more than three years, the defendant was given the option of trial by judge.

As in England and the U.S., Japanese jurors numbered twelve. The criterion for jury selection included at least two years of continuous residence in the district and payment of at least 3 yen in national taxes. Jurors had to be over thirty years old and reasonably literate.

Defendants in jury trials could not appeal to a higher court; however, the judges, if they disagreed with the verdict, could order a retrial by a newly picked jury. Judge Masataro Miyake noted that of 135 cases of serious crimes ruled upon by juries, 66 returned verdicts of guilty. In the other cases, 52 of the accused were convicted on reduced charges. The remaining 17 were acquitted.

Hugh Byas, an Englishman who in the 1930s served concurrently as the Tokyo correspondent of the *New York Times* and *The Times* (of London), acknowledged that the introduction of the jury system indicated a desire by Japan to liberalize the processes of criminal law.

"We may . . . discount the criticism that jurors were too prone to acquit," Byas opines. "We have seen that procurators were unscrupulous in the methods they adopted to obtain a conviction and it is not far-fetched to suppose that the jurymen may have seen through some of the evidence placed before them.

"The fact that a system in which the question of guilt or innocence is separated from the question of punishment did not work well would not surprise anyone familiar with the Japanese character.

"Objectivity," Byas concludes, "is not a strong point with the Japanese."

Many criminals seemed uncomfortable about being judged by their peers and opted for the more conventional system. The experiment finally ended in 1943. (There has been talk recently of restoring it.)

On July 30, 1926, Matsukichi Tsumagi, a construction worker and ex-con from Yamanashi Prefecture, re-embarked on his criminal career. His modus operandi was known as *sekkyo goto*, which translates as "armed robbery with sermon."

After the Great Kanto Earthquake in 1923, residential areas sprang up in Tokyo's western suburbs. Because homes tended to be more dispersed, these new neighborhoods proved fairly easy to rob. Tsumagi's technique was to creep into people's bedrooms while they slept, quietly lower himself next to their pillows, and light up a cigarette. When the smell awakened the husband or wife, the first thing he or she would see was a stocky man in dark clothing sitting in the dark.

"For reasons that have become pressing, I need money," Tsumagi would say in a low voice. "I am really sorry to have to make my presence known while you are in the midst of sleep, but might you be kind enough to give me some? I hope you won't make any rash moves, sir. It would be bad if your wife got hurt."

What made Tsumagi memorable was his propensity to provide his victims with advice on crime prevention.

"Your house is easy to break into," he would say. "Look how easy it was for me to get in. Get yourself a dog. Not one with a pedigree—they're too friendly. You need a nasty mongrel. One that will bark at anybody."

"Well," he would say, after taking possession of whatever money was on the premises, "it will be sunup soon. I'd best be leaving. By the way, I'd appreciate if you waited a little while before calling the police. I took the liberty of cutting your phone line. But I think the nearest police box is at *2-chome*. Bye now."

The robberies were heavily reported in the media and one newspaper offered a reward of 1,000 yen, a figure equivalent to a journalist's annual salary.

Through this combination of the element of surprise and his rough charm, Tsumagi was nearly always successful in obtaining money. Police redoubled their efforts and finally nabbed him on February 23, 1929. He was charged with a total of ninety offenses, including two cases of bodily injury and one of attempted rape. He even managed to commit one of his robberies during that week-long first year of Showa.

On November 18, 1929, the Tokyo District Court sentenced Tsumagi to life at hard labor. He was released on parole in 1948 at age forty-eight.

No Jack the Ripper in Tamanoi

In the Japanese lexicon of crime, the term *barabara* ("scattered") refers to the dismemberment of a corpse. One case that helped make the term *barabara satsujin* ("mutilation murder") a household word in Japan is identified with the Tamanoi district in eastern Tokyo.

The case drew a good deal of attention due to its location, a seedy, low-class brothel district in Sumida Ward, on the large island between the Sumida and Arakawa rivers. The original Tamanoi gay quarters owed its existence to the Great Kanto Earthquake, which devastated Asakusa, forcing the brothels to relocate to the other side of the river.

On the morning of March 7, 1932, a painter living in the neighborhood spotted a large item enclosed in paper bobbing in a canal. Discovering to his horror that it was a human torso, he summoned police, who pulled out three separate parcels containing the upper and lower parts of a human torso and a head.

Perhaps because of the modus operandi established by another murderer who frequented a similar area in nineteenth century London, one would ordinarily have expected the victim to be female. Such, however, was not the case. The pathologist quickly determined that all three parts belonged to the same victim, a male estimated to be in his early thirties. The head bore numerous injuries, suggesting death was caused by multiple blows from a blunt object.

About one month passed with the police no nearer to establishing the victim's identity, and since the hands were still missing, no fingerprints were available.

An artist's sketch was circulated, but after another month it began to look like the case would go on the books as unsolved. Then around mid-September, police received a break. While on duty along the Sumida's bank about three years earlier, a policemen named Michio Ishiga had given directions to a vagrant he thought resembled the man in the sketch. Through this description, the victim was finally identified as Ryutaro Chiba, age thirty. Chiba was traced to the Hongo area, where he had shared a dwelling with a low-life named Ichitaro Hasegawa, thirty-three.

The police tracked down Hasegawa and took him in for questioning. He admitted knowing Chiba, but at first told detectives that he believed Chiba had returned to the countryside. Hasegawa seemed overly nervous, and under persistent grilling finally confessed to the murder.

In mid-April 1931, Hasegawa related, he first met Chiba in a park in Asakusa. Chiba had been sitting beside a girl he claimed was his daughter. He told Hasegawa he had lost his wife to a prolonged illness and he himself was sick as well. Out of sympathy to a man so down on his luck, Hasegawa gave him 50 *sen* (half a yen), a banana and some cigarettes.

The man told them he came from a wealthy family in Akita Prefecture, but had run away and taken sick. He could not return home. His tale was a total falsehood. Actually he was a vagabond and a drunk and told his hard-luck story to gain sympathy.

Hoping that Chiba's wealthy family would be eager to reward his acts of kindness, Hasegawa helped Chiba find work at a rail station. He also arranged a marriage between Chiba and his younger sister Tomi, thirty.

Chiba only lasted two months on the job, after which he sold his clothes and even his shoes to get money for drinking.

In November 1931, Chiba asked Hasegawa for a loan, telling him he would use the money to return to his family in Akita, sell off part of his landholdings, and obtain money to repay him.

The anticipated windfall never materialized, and an infuriated Hasegawa finally realized Chiba was a fraud. On the evening of February 11, 1932, at the Hasegawa residence in Hongo, Ichitaro smashed Chiba's forehead with a wrench, causing blood to flow.

Angrily Chiba rose to his feet, shouting, "You struck me."

Hearing his cue, Hasegawa's younger brother Chotaro, twenty-three, entered the room with a baseball bat and bludgeoned Chiba to death. After concealing the body beneath the kitchen floor, the two men went to a nearby public bath to wash off the bloodstains.

Three days later the brothers obtained a box to move Chiba's body. Finding it too heavy to carry, they dismembered it using a saw. Around February 23, they tossed the limbs into a canal in Oji. On March 6, they moved the remainder by taxi to Tamanoi and tossed the three large sections in the canal.

Based on the interrogations, the police were able to find Chiba's remaining parts. Upon learning of Chiba's deceptions, the judges at the Tokyo District Court were highly sympathetic, but murder simply could not be condoned. On December 17, 1932, Ichitaro Hasegawa was sentenced to twelve years imprisonment. Chotaro was sentenced to six years, and Tomi received three years probation.

The Man No Prison Could Hold

Prison escapes were fairly common occurrences during the Meiji period—a record 1,821 made successful getaways in 1881—and annual figures remained in the hundreds well into the first decade of the twentieth century. By the mid-1970s, however, the number in any given year never exceeded one digit. Perhaps it is a sign that criminals have become more submissive, or that Japanese prisons have become cozier.

In the annals of Japan's escape artists, no one comes close to matching Yoshie Shiratori, an indomitable character who could rate the title of the Japanese Houdini.

In 1933, Shiratori, then twenty-four, was arrested as an accomplice in a murder-robbery in Aomori City. He appealed his conviction but the court took no action and he languished in Aomori Prison for two years. Impatient for the wheels of justice to turn, he decided to free himself.

Obtaining a piece of wire, he jimmied the lock on his cell and, after having observed the timing of guard patrols closely, crept out just after midnight on June 18, 1936, exiting via the institution's rear gate. About five and a half hours later, all hell broke loose when he failed to respond to morning roll call.

Shiratori was captured two days later in a nearby cemetery, looking gaunt and very hungry. The guard was dismissed from his job and Shiratori was punished with an indefinite sentence, to be served in Tokyo's Kosuge Prison. In October 1941, the decision was made to transfer long-term inmates to rural prisons. Shiratori was sent to Akita, which borders on Aomori, and found his reputation as a jailbreaker had preceded him. Taking no chances, authorities put him in a tiny high-security cell with a small opaque window in the ceiling. After shivering through the winter, he began preparations for an escape.

First, Shiratori began developing his muscles by using his hands and feet to boost himself up the walls. He would work his way to the ceiling where, using a rusty nail, he began to chip away at the window frame in ten-minute sessions between the guards' rounds. Finally, after midnight on June 15, 1942, Shiratori took advantage of a summer storm to make his escape. He managed to replace his prison clothing and, following the route of the railroad line, made his way to Tokyo. On September 20, having walked for nearly three months, Shiratori appeared at the gate of Tokyo's Kosuge Prison and turned himself in, saying the only reason he had escaped was the unnecessarily harsh treatment in Akita.

This failed to win him any sympathy. After a winter-long sojourn in Kosuge, in April 1943 he was transported to Abashiri Prison in Hokkaido. Until finally closed in 1984, Abashiri was a grim and frozen place used to confine the country's worst offenders, and it was clear that the authorities intended to crush Shiratori's spirit once and for all. He saw it as another challenge.

Shiratori was forced to wear manacles even while in his cell. After he broke the first set and several subsequent pairs, his warders put him in leg irons and handcuffed his hands behind his back, locking them with a bolt. So tight were the cuffs, they cut through his flesh to the bone, and maggots squirmed from his open wounds. The sight was so pitiful even the guards began to feel pangs of guilt.

Plotting his next escape, Shiratori each morning at breakfast spat miso soup on the door frame. The salt soon caused the metal to corrode and weaken. On the night of August 26, 1944, taking advantage of the wartime blackout, he stripped to his loincloth and—dislocating both his shoulders—squeezed himself through the slot in the door used by the guards to insert the food tray.

Shiratori's escape made front-page headlines in the *Hokkaido Shimbun*. He hid out in the mountains and was not aware that the World War II had ended until May 1946. While en route to Sapporo, he fought and killed a teenager who had challenged him and was arrested shortly thereafter. Shiratori claimed justifiable homicide in self-defense, but was sentenced to death. Angered at what he perceived as yet another injustice, he once again made preparations to escape, this time from death row at Sapporo Prison. Using his metal dish as a shovel, he tunnelled beneath the concrete wall of his cell and made good on his fourth breakout on April 1, 1947. The next day's banner headlines read, "Shiratori in 4th Escape!"

Shiratori was recaptured but won a reprieve. He spent the next fifteen years without incident in Tokyo's Fuchu Prison, where he was treated with exceptional deference by the other inmates. In December 1962, he was given a provisional release. Refusing employment, which he felt would constrain his hard-won freedom, he worked as an itinerant laborer. He died in a hospital bed of heart failure in 1979 at age seventy-one.

O-Sada Serves a Grateful Nation

On February 26, 1936, a Wednesday, Tokyoites awakened to a heavy snowfall. Early that morning, junior army officers of the ultranationalist "Imperial Way" faction, angered over the success of liberals in the parliamentary elections held a week before, attempted a coup d'etat that came to be known as the *Ni-Ni-Roku Jiken,* or "2–26 Incident." From the command post at the Sanno Hotel, 1,400 infantrymen fanned out to occupy the nearby Prime Minister's Residence, Metropolitan Police headquarters and other buildings. Coup leaders denounced the civilian government and demanded a "Showa Restoration" that would override the constitutional monarchy.

Gunning down half a dozen civilian policemen who stood in their way, squads of soldiers shot to death Lord Keeper of the Privy Seal Makoto Saito, Finance Minister Korekiyo Takahashi and Inspector General of Military Education Jotaro Watanabe. Prime Minister Keisuke Okada avoided almost certain assassination by grudgingly allowing himself to be secreted in a closet, but soldiers mistakenly shot and killed his brother-in-law Denzo Matsuo.

The uprising was quelled four days later, upon the order of a furious Emperor Hirohito. Its instigators were court martialed and sentenced to execution by firing squad, or life imprisonment.

The arrival of spring failed to dispell Tokyoites' sense of angst. Blood had been shed, political discontent was in the air, and full-scale hostilities with China appeared imminent. People were desperate for a diversion.

The timing couldn't have been better for a sex-crazy harlot to lop off her lover's genitals with a kitchen knife.

The event, referred to tongue in cheek as the *Go-Ichi-Hachi Jiken,* or "May 18 Incident," set tongues wagging throughout the nation. It happened the night of May 17–18 at Masaki, a *machiai*—in present-day parlance a "love hotel"—in Oku, Arakawa Ward.

The perpetrator was Ms. Abe, first name Sada, age thirty-one . The deceased, Kichizo Ishida, forty-two, was the operator of Yoshida-ya, a

Japanese-style restaurant in Nakano. Ishida was an unrepentant playboy and his wife, Toku, ran the business. The couple had two teenage children.

Yoshida-ya specialized in eel dishes, and officers posted at nearby army garrisons made up a large share of its clientele. It made perfect sense to employ attractive waitresses who could keep the sake flowing.

Sada, a former geisha-cum-prostitute, had just moved back to Tokyo from Nagoya. Introduced to the restaurant via a job broker, she began work the same month as the coup attempt. Sexual harassment of female employees was commonplace, and Sada soon found herself the object of amorous signals from Ishida—such as nibbles on her earlobe. Unwilling or unable to resist these displays of affection, Sada gave in, and before long Ishida was sneaking away from the Yoshida-ya on "business trips" coordinated with Sada's own absences from work.

Sada, promiscuous as an adolescent and employed in the sex industry since she was eighteen, suddenly found herself in the throes of romantic passion. Her sexual demands proved insatiable, and initially the satyrlike Ishida was pleased to oblige. The couple pledged eternal love, consummating their vows with marathon sex bouts that hotel maids were shocked to see continuing even when they entered the room to serve the pair sake.

One physician speculated that perhaps Sada's insatiable sexual appetite was due to infection by *Trichomonas vaginalis*, a sexually transmitted protozoan parasite. It is possible, then, that what Sada perceived as prolonged ecstasy may have been no more than relieving an annoying itch.

Be that as it may, as their encounters became increasingly frenzied, the two began experimenting with what medical textbooks term the vagal maneuver, in which pressure applied to the carotid artery stimulates the vagus nerve. Sada would tighten the ornamental band from her *obi* around his neck, causing Kichizo's member to inflate impressively, further enhancing her sexual pleasure. As he teetered at the edge of consciousness, she moaned and spasmed in ecstasy.

Strangulation is a risky maneuver, and the couple had come close to going over the edge once before. Finally, Sada went too far.

About 8:00 A.M. on May 18, a Sunday, Sada told the proprietor of the Masaki hotel she was going out to buy some confections. She instructed that the gentleman was sleeping and not to be disturbed. When she failed to return by 2:30, the maid cautiously entered the small second-story room and, to her horror, discovered Ishida dead. On the sheet, written in fresh blood, were the characters *Sada, Kichi Futari-kiri* (Sada and Kichi, inseparable forever). The same words were gouged into his left thigh. "Sada" was written on his left arm. The source of the blood left nothing to speculation: his entire male apparatus was missing.

Police launched a city-wide dragnet for Abe, noting her alias used at the hotel (Kayoko Tanaka) and circulating a photo. Newspapers gave the story generous front-page coverage.

Abe later told police she planned to jump to her death from Mt. Ikoma in Nara Prefecture, and had a third class rail ticket to Osaka in her possession. Immediately following the crime, however, she did not behave as a person overcome by remorse. On May 19, she shopped and went to see a movie.

On May 20, Abe took a room at an Japanese inn at Shinagawa. After a bath, she sipped a beer and called for a masseuse. She drank two more beers while penning letters of farewell to her middle-aged patron in Nagoya and a close friend. She also wrote an emotional missive to her dead lover. Around 4 P.M., head of detectives Matsukichi Ando, forty-three, dropped by to check the inn's register. His eye stopped on Nao Owada. The name Nao was gender neutral, and, on a hunch, Ando asked to be shown to the room.

The maid entered just as Sada finished off her glass of beer.

"Madam, a man from the police is here," said the maid apologetically, stepping aside for the policeman.

"Excuse me, I am investigating an incident."

"Hey, relax," she told him. "Don't be so formal. You're looking for Sada Abe, right?"

Ando made no reply.

"Well that's me. I am Sada Abe."

"Don't tease me, dammit, I'm busy," Ando grunted, and turned on his heels to leave.

"No, *no*," she insisted. "I *am* Sada!"

And to erase any doubt from the officer's mind, she produced a piece of light brown *patronen papier* from her bodice and opened it to display an unmistakable piece of evidence linking her to the crime.

Tokyo's newspapers trumpeted her arrest with extra editions. One unflattering photo of her in custody, surrounded by hulking detectives, shows her hair slightly dishevelled and eyes out of focus.

The interrogation spanned eight sessions. Sada's attitude was unfailingly cooperative and polite. She testified she was the youngest of seven children. Her father operated a prosperous *tatami*-making business in Kanda. As was common for women of her status, she underwent formal schooling only to the sixth grade. At age fourteen, while at the home of a friend, she was forcibly introduced to sex by a university student. Afterward she began hanging out with bad company and when she reached eighteen, her father, deciding that she was incorrigible, sold her to a brothel in Yokohama—over the protestations of her mother and older sister.

She did not sound especially bitter over her fate.

Sada Abe being taken into custody at the Takanawa Police Station.

Of late, she had been earning a fairly good income as the mistress of a wealthy man and as a waitress.

As Ishida had complained of insomnia, she had purchased a quantity of Calmotine, an over-the-counter sedative that could be fatal when consumed with alcohol. That night Ishida took several tablets, and may have been in such a stupor that he was unable to resist her strangulation and save his own life.

Q: What made you feel like killing Kichizo?

Sada: I loved him so much, I wanted him all to myself. But since we were not husband and wife, as long as he lived he could be embraced by other women. I knew that if I killed him no other woman could ever touch him again, so I killed him. . . .

Q: Didn't you feel repulsed, walking around Tokyo with that thing you'd cut off him?

Sada: Why would I? It belonged to someone I loved. Everything of Ishida's had become mine. But I'm upset to hear people saying I ran off after stealing his money.

The media continued to embellish her story. On June 9, the Tokyo edition of the usually staid *Asahi Shimbun* quoted her as expressing the wish "to go to her death laughing, while mounting the steps of the gallows, clutching the 'keepsake' from Kichizo in her hand."

Abe was charged with second degree murder and mutilation of a corpse. At her first trial session on November 25 spectators began lining up outside the Tokyo District Court at 5 A.M. and dozens had to be turned away.

The prosecutor demanded ten years. On December 21, she was sentenced to six years, to include the seven months already served.

At her sentencing, she was asked if she wanted to make a statement for the record.

"The thing I regret most about this incident," she said, "is that I have come to be misunderstood as some kind of sexual pervert. If you investigate my life up to now, you will know whether or not I am a person with abnormal sexual desire. There had never been a man in my life like Ishida. There were men I liked, and with whom I slept without accepting money, but none made me feel the way I did toward him."

She became prisoner No. 11 at Tochigi women's penitentiary. Thanks to a special imperial amnesty in observance of the 2,600th anniversary of the ascension of Emperor Jimmu, she was discharged on May 17, 1941, exactly five years after the day of her crime. Supposing she had endured enough excitement, authorities helped her register under a new identity, Masayo Yoshida. She moved to Saitama Prefecture, and, amazingly, married at age thirty-six.

In 1947 her world fell apart once more when a reporter named Ichiro Kimura tracked her down and produced a lurid booklet entitled, "The Sex Confessions of Sada, the Amorous Woman of Showa." It was printed on low-grade paper, but people were hungry for diversions and it quickly sold one hundred thousand copies.

Whether intimidated by his wife's true identity, or merely aghast at the discovery that he was wed to the nation's most notorious female, the husband fled.

"Why is the public treating me so coldly," Abe demanded, "when I am making efforts to go straight?"

Abe launched a libel suit against Kimura. Afterwards her interview with author Ango Sakaguchi was published in a popular monthly magazine.

"How many times have you been in love?" Sakaguchi asked.

"Only once," she replied. "It was that person [Ishida]. It might seem strange to be in love at thirty-two, but I suppose there have been many people who died never having loved even once in their lives."

Sakaguchi later waxed romantic, saying that Sada's act involved the consumption of "total love" where the couple reached the ultimate stage. "This was not a crime," he asserted. "For her to cut off his member as a keepsake was the ultimate feminine act."

Abe settled in Tokyo's low-rent Shitaya district, living a modest and unassuming life for some twenty years. She received an award as "model employee" from the local restaurant association. The last "official" photo in which she appears was taken in August 1969.

In her declining years she is said to have entered a Buddhist nunnery. Her final fate is unknown.

The same can be said concerning the whereabouts of Ishida's penis. The caretaker at Tokyo University Hospital's specimen room was cooperative, but admitted to this writer that the inventory records were a shambles and was not able to confirm or deny its presence. The organ was last seen on public display at the Tobu Department Store in Asakusa shortly after World War II, in an exhibition sponsored by the Ministry of Health and Welfare, the Ministry of Education, the Tokyo Metropolitan Government and the Japan Teachers' Union. It appeared along with several other curiosities, including the reproductive apparatus of executed murdress O-Den Takahashi.

Reams of paper and several films, including Nagisa Oshima's erotic masterpiece *In the Realm of the Senses* (1976), have been devoted to retelling Sada's story. In 1998, Makazu Horinouchi published a definitive 438-page biography.

Her crime spawned the word "Sada-ism," and was to inspire at least fifty-three similar cases of assaults by women on male genitalia over the next six decades. Above all, perhaps, this story stood out for its supreme irony. The February 26 military coup d'etat—symbolic of male domination and violence—was very neatly offset in people's daily preoccupations three months later by the misadventures of a man completely carried away by carnal depravity. Which he paid for with his phallus *and* his life. Both were lost, neither recovered.

THE WAR YEARS

A "MASS MURDER," according to FBI criteria, begins at four. In 1938, Japan's most prolific killer surpassed that figure seven-fold.

On July 7, 1937, Chinese troops clashed with a Japanese army unit at the Lugouqiao (Marco Polo Bridge) on the outskirts of Beijing, initiating full-scale hostilities. The same month war broke out in China, a twenty-one-year old man named Mutsuo Toi from Kaio, a farming village close to Okayama's border with Tottori, paid 75 yen for a double-barreled shotgun and a supply of cartridges at the Katayama Gun Shop in Tsuyama. On October 27, about the time the local hunting season was to begin, Toi appeared at the Tsuyama Police Station requesting a second-class hunting permit. On the application form he noted, "Although my military conscription status is *hei* (the lowest of three levels of eligibility), when my condition improves, I intend to enter military service. I would hope [to use this gun] to improve my marksmanship beforehand so as to enable me to slay even one additional enemy soldier."

Whether or not this constituted Toi's true purpose in obtaining the shotgun remains uncertain, but the young man's patriotic spirit no doubt made a favorable impression; the permit was issued forthwith.

Ten months passed. At 2:40 A.M. on the morning of Saturday, May 21, 1938, police inspector Takeshi Imada was awakened at his small substation in Kamo-cho by a man from Kaio who said, "Something terrible has happened. My mother has been killed. Please come quickly."

After hearing the frantic man's account, Imada telephoned the police station at Tsuyama, twenty kilometers away, to summon help. Several hours passed before truckloads of police and firemen (who were often called in to assist in searches) headed up the narrow, winding road into the mountains.

No amount of preparation could have steeled them against the horrifying sight that awaited them. Toi had burst his way into twelve of the twenty-three homes in the hamlet and wiped out six entire households, shooting or stabbing to death a total of twenty-nine men, women and children and seriously wounding three others. The Tsuyama Incident was, aside from acts committed in wartime, Japan's largest single mass-slaying of modern times. It has few parallels in the world.

Toi, born in 1917, came from a prosperous family. His parents died of illness when he was only two and he was raised by his grandmother and a sister three years his senior. He was an exceptionally bright boy who excelled at his studies, but perhaps due to the sickness that plagued his family, the neighbors tended to shun him. In his late teens he developed a respiratory illness that proved to be tuberculosis. Under such conditions he was, not surprisingly, unable to form any romantic relationships with local females. When pronounced unfit for military duty in 1937, the villagers' scorn increased; the rejection by the women of the village may have been the final straw.

By the early spring of 1938, Toi was making repeated death threats against his neighbors, who were doubly nervous when they heard him firing his shotgun at targets. This prompted Inspector Imada to give him a stern citizenship lecture. Toi broke down in tears and agreed to sell his shotgun and surrender his sword, dagger and other weapons for safekeeping.

Imada, who survived the killings unscathed, later voiced his opinion that Toi had laid his plans so carefully that this capitulation may well have been part of the scenario that enfolded.

In April, Toi purchased another sword from a local collector, using the pretext of commemorating his brother-in-law's promotion to army sergeant. He then traveled to Osaka, where, under a pseudonym, he purchased a new shotgun and arranged to have it modified to accommodate nine shells with a single loading. He purchased a dagger from a local yakuza. Before leaving town, he spent the night with a high-class prostitute, who in a later deposition recalled that he had a great deal of money in his possession and that he had not made any unreasonable sexual demands. She added that Toi showed a pronounced fixation on Sada Abe, who had made national headlines in May 1936 for severing her dead lover's genitals, and who had actually serviced clients in the same Osaka brothel several years before.

After making additional preparations, Toi returned to his village around the middle of May. In the early evening hours of May 20, he climbed a utility pole and cut off electric power to the entire village. A brief rain fell that evening. Around 1 A.M. on May 21, Toi donned heavy clothing and wrapped his calves with leggings. He fastened two flashlights to his head with a leather strap, giving him the appearance of a vengeful wraith. He suspended a bicycle headlamp around his neck (a technique often adopted by locals while fishing at night). He thrust a Japanese sword through his waistband, stuffed his pockets with some one hundred shotgun shells and picked up his newly acquired Browning shotgun.

He entered the room where his seventy-five-year-old grandmother, Ine, slept and swung down an axe on her neck, decapitating her with one powerful blow. He then started toward his adjacent neighbors, the Kishidas.

Using shotgun and sword, Toi swept through the village, successively assaulting the households of Kishida, Nishikawa, another Kishida, four separate households headed by people with the surname Terai, and then Tanba, Ikezawa and Okamoto. His killing spree was estimated to have taken about ninety minutes; a few survived his assaults, but not many.

Finally, out of exhaustion or the sheer inability to shed any more blood, he ceased his rampage. He headed southwest into the hills, stopping around 3:00 A.M. to arouse a distant neighbor to request a pencil and paper.

Using the light from the two flashlights still bound to his head, Toi poured out his feelings. He wrote of his grandmother, who had raised him from childhood. He asked his older sister for her forgiveness.

"Over the four years of my illness," he wrote, "I cried from the cold and cruel treatment meted out to me by society. I cried for having few close relatives who could love me. People should be more sympathetic to TB sufferers. Being weak and unfortunate in this life, I hope I will be strong and happy in the next one."

In his final sentence, Toi wrote, "The dawn has almost arrived. It is time to die." He then removed the flashlights and other gear and arranged them neatly by his side. He pulled off his worker's boots. He unbuttoned his upper garment, set the rifle barrel at the center of his chest, and used his right big toe to work the trigger. The gun's recoil sent it flying about one meter away from his body.

A search party found him shortly before noon. The examining physician estimated the time of Toi's death at approximately 5:00 A.M.

At least four books have been written about the incident, the most detailed being Akira Tsukuba's fine account, *Tsuyama Sanjunin-goroshi*, published in 1981. Nozomu Nishimura and Seicho Matsumoto produced earlier works. It was gothic novelist Seishi Mizoguchi, however, who put Okayama on the map with his macabre story *Yatsuhaka-mura* ("The Village of the Eight Graves") in 1951. This was released as a Shochiku horror film, directed by Yoshitaro Nomura, in 1977. A 1996 remake, directed by Kon Ichikawa, was produced jointly by Fuji Television, Kadokawa Shoten and Toho studios.

Tsukuba, who interviewed witnesses and survivors for his book, notes that although the incident was widely reported by the newspapers, many unsolved questions remain regarding what drove Toi to kill. Many of those he sought out were understandably reticent to discuss it. Interestingly, the "official" local history of Kamo village refers to the incident in just two sentences: "During wartime, uncooperative people were disparaged with the term *hikokumin* [non-citizens], while those adults who passed their military physicals represented the flower of manhood. It was in these circumstances that the incident involving Mutsuo Toi occurred."

The largest mass-murder in Japan's modern history, Mutsuo Toi's 1938 slaying of 29 people was to inspire a ghoulish book and several films. [Newsclip: *Godo Shimbun* (now *San'yo Shimbun*), May 23, 1938]

Hear No Evil, Speak No Evil

FBI agent Robert Ressler is credited with coining the term "serial murder" in the 1970s while teaching cadets the science of criminal profiling. This program eventually developed into the FBI's now-famous Behavioral Sciences Unit. "Serial murderers" had previously been referred to in law enforcement circles as "stranger murderers."

Ressler thought that between their crimes, serial killers considered means of "improving" the drama of their actions, in a manner somewhat analogous to the old motion picture serials in which cliffhanger endings lured viewers to return to see the next installment.

Spurred by several recent cases, Japanese law enforcement has belatedly begun to adopt similar profiling methods, but in 1941, this science was not available to the Shizuoka Prefectural Police. And meanwhile, a serial killer who stalked by night was assaulting and murdering several people at a time.

At first, Kosaku Kimura, twenty-one, must have seemed a highly unlikely suspect. For one thing, he stood only 154cm tall and weighed just 44 kilograms—barely enough to overpower his female victims. He was also severely deaf, a disability he had suffered from from birth. While not entirely mute, he could only enunciate simple sounds.

Kimura was, despite his handicap, exceptionally bright. He also had an active imagination. He was especially enraptured by a series of samurai films called *Tange Sazen* featuring a nihilistic, one-eyed, one-armed anti-hero. Here was a handicapped figure Kimura could relate to.

At sixteen, Kimura had experienced an earlier run-in with the law in his home town of Nishigasaki, in western Shizuoka Prefecture, when he was arrested on charges of armed robbery, attempted rape and attempted murder of a geisha. His father prevailed on the mercy of the court and arranged for his son to enter Hamamatsu's municipal school for the deaf.

His record as a felon was covered up, and Kimura excelled at his studies, but the lure of Tange Sazen proved irresistible. In July 1941, Kimura purchased a fish knife and modified it to resemble a *tanto*, the short sword carried by samurai. On the morning of August 18, he crept into the window of an *okiya* (geisha dormitory) and used the knife to murder two twenty-year-old geisha by single thrusts to their hearts. He fled when a third, older woman overheard the ruckus and cried out.

Two days later, Kimura broke into the sleeping quarters of employees of the Kikusui restaurant, killing a sixty-year-old male employee, a sixteen-year-old maid and the forty-four-year-old female proprietor.

Kimura's next target, incredibly, was his own home. Short of funds for his tuition, Kimura's father had pressured him to withdraw from the school. On September 27, 1941, he assumed a disguise and killed his elder brother and sister-in-law, and assaulted other family members. He slipped back to his room without being recognized and feigned to have slept through the ruckus.

On the night of August 31, 1942, Kimura broke into a house in a rural village and killed a couple and injured their fifteen-year-old son, but fled before he could grab any money or rape the nineteen-year-old daughter, whom he had spotted on the street and followed home.

In November 1942, police arrested Kimura, not on material evidence, but on his prior arrest from 1938. Under questioning, he confessed to nine murders and six cases of serious injury.

During the police interrogation, instructors from Kimura's own school were used as interpreters using sign language.

Police:	What time did you leave your house?
Kimura:	About 2 or 3 A.M.
Police:	What was your intention?
Kimura:	I intended to kill people.

They also questioned him about his film idol.

Police:	Do you think you committed [the killings] as well as Tange Sazen [would have done]?
Kimura:	[In formal language] Yes, I do.
Police:	What is more satisfying for you, to rob or to kill?
Kimura:	If I kill and get some money as well, then nothing makes me happier.
Police:	But Tange Sazen didn't steal money, did he?
Kimura:	[As far as Tange is concerned] I only imitated the killing part.

The psychological evaluation noted that Kimura did not appear to show regret for his crimes. It nonetheless cited such extenuating factors as lack of parental love as a child and his severe handicap. His disability, his defenders asserted, had led to his suffering discrimination, so he should not be forced to take all the blame for his crimes.

These arguments were of little help in pleading his case, and after only four court sessions—Japan was at war and had little patience for legal maneuvering—Kimura was sentenced to death. On June 19, 1944, his appeal was overturned, setting the stage for his execution.

Kimura's father was found in the Tenryu River, one month after his son's arrest. He had committed suicide.

THE POSTWAR PERIOD

JAPAN'S DOMESTIC crime rate remained relatively low during the war years, not surprising considering millions of young males were serving in the military overseas. In the late stages of the war, the manpower pinch was not limited only to the military; three days prior to the October 21, 1943, order for mobilization of students, the Tokyo Metropolitan Police lowered its age requirements and began recruiting males aged sixteen to eighteen.

A directive that same month limited executions to seven prisons: Sapporo, Miyagi, Tokyo, Nagoya, Osaka, Hiroshima and Uragami (Nagasaki). The four men on death row in the Uragami prison were spared the gallows, in a manner of speaking. They were killed by "Fat Man," the second atomic bomb, which detonated almost directly above them on August 9, 1945.

As the Pacific War neared its conclusion, a bizarre twist was added to the orgy of death and destruction: a serial rapist-murderer began stalking women in Tokyo.

On August 17, 1946, a groundskeeper found the corpses of two women—one in a state of advanced decomposition—in a bamboo thicket behind the Zojoji temple, close to the location of what is now the Tokyo Tower. One was identified as Ryuko Midorikawa, seventeen, missing since August 6.

Midorikawa's family told police their daughter had gone to meet a "kindly" older man who had promised her a job. Their description led police to a forty-two-year-old laundryman and former Imperial Marine named Yoshio Kodaira. Kodaira was an ex-con, having served time for murder and assault. Under questioning, he confessed to raping and killing Midorikawa. With further urging, police were able to clear nine other murders starting from May 1945.

Of subaverage intelligence and afflicted with a stutter, young Kodaira had adopted well to military discipline. When his ship called at foreign ports, however, his mates initiated him to sex with foreign prostitutes, stimulating his appetite and giving him a taste for variety.

In May 1928, Kodaira's unit went into action in the so-called "Jinan Incident." When the Nationalist Chinese army made its march northward, Japan dispatched troops to protect its colony on China's Shandong Peninsula and the two sides clashed. During action in the city of Taigu, Kodaira took part in atrocities during which Japanese marine units broke into the homes of local Chinese, raped the female occupants, looted property and killed civilians.

"Four or five of my comrades and I entered a Chinese home, tied up the father, and locked him in the closet," he told police investigators. "We stole their jewelry and raped the women. We even bayoneted a pregnant women and pulled the fetus from her stomach. I also engaged in those depraved actions."

For his "meritorious" service, Kodaira was promoted to sergeant and awarded the Order of the Rising Sun, Eighth Class.

Kodaira, a dim and brutish boy with a family history of mental instability, had been exposed to sexual depravity in the military, and his atrocities against Chinese civilians were not only overlooked by his superiors, but rewarded. He returned home to a semifeudal society where men treated women as inferiors. After his discharge in 1929, he returned to Tochigi, took a factory job and married.

From 1932, he began serving a fifteen-year prison term for bludgeoning his father-in-law to death, but received an early parole in 1940.

Forensic investigators comb the scene where serial rapist-murderer Yoshio Kodaira killed his final victim in August 1946.

With so many men in uniform, the ex-con was able to cite his background as a decorated veteran and easily find work.

In early 1945, Kodaira found a job as a boiler operator at a naval facility in Tokyo's Shinagawa Ward. The facility maintained a dormitory for female workers and, with few other forms of recreation available, Kodaira fashioned himself a peephole and spent hours watching them bathing.

On May 25, Mitsuko Miyazaki, twenty-one, went to bid Kodaira farewell. He attempted to force himself on her, and when she struggled, he choked her into unconsciousness and raped her. He then strangled her and concealed her corpse in an air raid shelter.

By the war's end on August 15, Kodaira had added four more victims, and before 1945 was out, he had killed several more. Naive young women desperately searching for food or work were easy targets for Kodaira's sympathetic pose. He also admitted to having committed several dozen rapes.

His crimes continued through the summer of 1946, when Ryuko Midorikawa became his tenth and final murder victim.

Even while World War II was generating deaths by the tens and hundreds of thousands, much more primitive urges drove Kodaira to kill. In the end, he muttered a few words of remorse for his victims, but the court saw no grounds for mercy. He accepted his fate stoically, and it was not long in coming: he was hanged in Miyagi Prison on October 5, 1947.

An Enigmatic Crime

Just after the 3:00 P.M. closing time on January 26, 1948, a man entered the small branch of the Teikoku Bank in Shiinamachi, near Ikebukuro, and asked to speak to the manager. He presented a card identifying him as Dr. Jiro Yamaguchi of the Ministry of Health and Welfare and explained that there had been an outbreak of dysentery caused by water from the neighborhood well. As one of the persons stricken had been in the bank earlier that day, Yamaguchi had been assigned to treat all those who may have been exposed. The staff, caretaker and his family were summoned.

Opening up a case containing labeled bottles, he asked them to produce their teacups. He warned them to swallow the "medication" straight down, since it could damage the enamel of their teeth. He demonstrated by taking a few drops from the bottle in an eyedropper and tilting back his head, drinking it himself. Sixteen people obediently complied, then waited uncomfortably for him to administer a second, separate dose. Moments later they were writhing in agony. The man fled with 180,000 yen in cash and a check, but left behind a large amount of cash and twelve dead bodies.

The crime itself was unusual enough; bank robberies were almost unheard of in Japan. The technique used by the murderer was even more bizarre.

Based on descriptions from the four survivors, police had an artist draw a composite sketch—the first ever used in Japan. A profile of the

In Japan's most enigmatic crime, a robber posing as a public health official murdered 12 people at the Teikoku Bank.

criminal was also produced. In a memorandum to the U.S. occupation authorities dated June 26, 1948, this police document stated:

"The criminal is likely to be a person with knowledge of public health who was trained as a doctor, dentist, pharmacist, or person engaged in production or sales of chemicals; who had contacts with occupation forces; who was a repatriated Japanese or returned former serviceman, probably a medical corpsman; or someone familiar with training in epidemic prevention in areas hit by floods, and so on."

The previous October 14, a bank in another part of the city had been visited by a doctor for essentially the same purpose, but with two important exceptions: he used the name Dr. Shigeru Matsui on his card, and no one died. The real Matsui was easily traced, and had an airtight alibi for the time of the crime. Police then attempted to track down every person with whom the doctor had exchanged business cards. The trail eventually led them to a tempera artist in Otaru,

Hokkaido, named Sadamichi Hirasawa, fifty-seven, who had been in Tokyo on the day of the crime, and who had no firm alibi. Moreover, Hirasawa had come into a large amount of money whose source he could not explain. After two months of daily grillings, Hirasawa confessed. He was tried, convicted and sentenced to death.

Even though Hirasawa's behavior seemed suspicious, questions immediately arose as to where he obtained the poison kit (it was never found). Others wondered how an artist with no medical background could give such a professional and convincing performance.

Hirasawa's defenders offered another reason for Hirasawa's sketchy memory and eccentric behavior: Korsakoff's psychosis, a not uncommon disorder also referred to as the amnesic-confabulatory syndrome. In May 1925, while in his early thirties, Hirasawa had been bitten by a rabid dog and forced to undergo inoculations to prevent rabies. He spent most of the next three months in a delirium and never recovered fully.

In its acute phases, Korsakoff's psychosis is characterized by impairment of recent memory and confabulation, i.e., the fabrication of ready answers or the recital of fictitious experiences. A person exhibiting such symptoms seldom gives the same story twice.

The fact that no Minister of Justice ever signed the order to proceed with Hirasawa's execution is seen as evidence that doubts persisted as to his guilt.

While on death row at Sendai Prison, Hirasawa was permitted to resume his profession. He produced an average of 40 paintings per year—some 1,200 in all. He not only outlived Yoshio Yamada, the head of his first defense team, but his next two lawyers as well.

Sadamichi Hirasawa eventually became the world's longest-serving prisoner on death row. After nearly forty years in prison, he passed away in May 1986, still professing his innocence.

In the spring of 1951, Seicho Matsumoto, a forty-two-year old writer from Kyushu, published a short story in an extra issue of *Shukan Asahi* magazine. He was to become Japan's most controversial novelist, producing a huge body of works over the next four decades.

Matsumoto's formula, described as "social realism," examined the dark underside of Japanese society. One of his established techniques was to reconstruct incidents according to his own hypotheses, based on research, inside sources, shrewd guesswork—and sometimes wild speculation.

For one year from January 1960, Matsumoto serialized "Nihon no Kuroi Kiri" ("Japan's Black Mist") in the prestigious monthly magazine *Bungei Shunju*, fictionalizing the Teikoku Bank Incident and other notorious incidents from the occupation era. Matsumoto surmised a connection between the killer and Unit 731, a chemical and biological warfare detachment based in Pingfan, near Harbin, Manchuria, where it had originally been given the purposely vague name of "Water Supply and Prophylaxis Administration of the Kwantung Army."

Members of the unit were allegedly excepted from prosecution for war crimes in exchange for details of their research, and perhaps for this reason information on their activities is inconclusive. One hypothesis is that the unit developed use of poisons as an assassination technique.

A decade and a half after Hirasawa's death, interest remains high over the question of his guilt or innocence. Perhaps the true story of what happened at the Teikoku Bank that day, and why, may yet come to light.

RIGHTISTS AND LEFTISTS

IN JULY 1950, one month after the outbreak of the Korean War, allied occupation authorities issued a directive for a "Red Purge" of leftists from the ranks of Japan's civil servants and the media. The decade that followed was marked by vigorous and vehement political confrontations between the left and the right—non-shooting warfare that occasionally led to fatalities.

The struggle escalated on the night of January 21, 1952, when Sapporo police inspector Kazuo Shiratori, thirty-six, was shot from behind and killed by assailants on bicycles. Kuniji Kobayashi, chairman of the Japan Communist Party's Sapporo district branch, was later arrested for plotting the murder. Although he proclaimed innocence, Kobayashi was sentenced to twenty years in prison.

Ten other suspects sought for Shiratori's murder fled to mainland China. One of them, Michiya Tsuruta, was still residing in Beijing as late as 1997.

In the 1952 May Day Incident, leftists converged on the Imperial Palace square and a riot ensued in which police shot two demonstrators dead. Charges were filed against another 1,230. The rioters attacked Kazuo Koyama, thirty-one, a patrolman assigned to photograph the crowd. He lingered for four years before dying.

Tekiya (guilds of rough-and-tumble street peddlers) gained control

A young right-wing assassin cuts down Socialist leader Inejiro Asanuma as he speaks before a party gathering.

of the black markets in major Japanese cities within days of the war's end, and by the 1950s their principals had accumulated considerable wealth and power. Occupation authorities failed to suppress the underworld, but this ultimately worked to their advantage. Gangs such as the Kobe-based Yamaguchi-gumi dominated the docks, and during the Korean War proved themselves indispensable in keeping leftist unions from interfering with military shipments.

Hordes of leftists continued to demonstrate against the Liberal Democratic Party-led government, but it was the right wing that displayed true fanaticism. On October 12, 1960, Inejiro Asanuma, secretary-general of the Japan Socialist Party, was cut down on the rostrum of the Hibiya Public Hall by a sword-wielding teenager. Four months later, while *Chuo Koron* magazine was serializing *Furyu Mutan*, a controversial novel by Shichiro Fukazawa viewed by rightists as derogatory to the emperor system, another teenage rightist attacked the home of its publisher, seriously injuring his wife and killing the couple's housekeeper.

Around 1970, the National Police Agency estimated there were approximately four hundred rightist organizations with a membership of about 125,000.

Author Yukio Mishima harangues Self-Defense Forces troops at Ichigaya, Tokyo, minutes before his suicide by seppuku.

Yukio Mishima, forty-five, was a gifted but eccentric writer with reactionary political views. He made worldwide headlines with a spectacular suicide. On November 25, 1970, he and several members of the private army he had organized two years earlier, the *Tate no Kai* (Shield Society), seized control of the office of the commanding general, Eastern Headquarters of the Ground Self-Defense Forces in Ichigaya, near downtown Tokyo.

The commander was Lieutenant General Kanetoshi Mashida, who had been acquainted with Mishima and granted him an appointment at 11 A.M. Before Mishima's contingent was ushered into the general's office, an aide questioned them about their swords, but Mishima assured them they were for "ceremonial use."

On entering the room, Mishima told the general, "Here, look at this fine Japanese sword," and unsheathed it. While the general was admiring the sword, the writer's four companions surrounded him and immobilized him in his chair. Mishima then demanded that the troops be summoned. When they gathered, he delivered an emotional ten-minute speech attacking what he called the "spinelessness" of Japan's antiwar Constitution, and criticized the weakness of the Self-Defense Forces.

The servicemen were not the least persuaded by Mishima's charisma; they taunted him with a hail of epithets and angry heckling and a few even tried to tear down the banners Mishima's companions had unfurled from the balcony.

Mishima's harangue ran out of steam. Finally, he said, "I am going to shout 'Banzai' for the emperor," and went back inside.

As General Mashida watched in horror, Mishima plunged a dagger into his abdomen and a student, Masakatsu Morita, delivered the coup de grace. Morita then used the same procedure to follow his mentor. The three surviving students placed the two men's severed heads neatly on the bloodstained carpet and walked out of the room with dazed expressions, a still-bound Mashida in tow.

A half decade later, on March 23, 1976, a young actor named Mitsuyasu Maeno, also nostalgic for the traditional means of death, went out in an even more spectacular way. Inspired by the selfless heroics of the *tokkotai* (Kamikaze corps), he crash dived a light plane into the home of right-wing fixer Yoshio Kodama. Maeno had deeply admired Kodama, but was stung by the evidence of wrongdoing in the Lockheed bribery scandal and decided to crash his plane into the roof of Kodama's home in the Tokyo suburb of Setagaya. Maeno was the sole casualty.

The Left Ascends

From the 1960s, the leftist student movement began to supplant the right in terms of political violence. Students drew much of their inspiration from Mao Tse-tung's exhortations to take up armed struggle against the state.

The ultra-radical Sekigun-ha ("Red Army Faction"), founded in 1969, did not wait long before getting attention. On March 31, 1970, a Japan Air Lines' (JAL) Boeing 727 called "Yodo" with 131 passengers and a crew of 7 was hijacked on its domestic flight from Tokyo to Fukuoka by a team of nine Red Army Faction members. Attempts to trick them failed and they were ultimately flown on to Communist North Korea.

The Red Army Faction had combined with branches of a group calling itself "Keihin Ampo"; it was largely from the Yodo incident that the name "United Red Army" first became familiar to the public.

In 1971 leftists staged fifty-one attacks on police boxes, court buildings and universities. On June 17, Red Army radicals opposed to the terms of the agreement on the reversion of Okinawa to Japanese control staged a major riot in Tokyo's Meiji Park, during which the riot police were attacked with pipe bombs, injuring a total of thirty-seven policemen. On August 22, a twenty-one-year-old Self-Defense Force soldier guarding an armory in Asaka, Saitama Prefecture, was stabbed to death by members of an obscure radical faction who attempted to break in and obtain weapons. On September 16, three riot policemen from Kanagawa Prefecture were killed and numerous others injured by a fusillade of Molotov cocktails and other brickbats during violent demonstrations at Sanrizuka, Chiba Prefecture, by leftists opposing the construction of a new international airport at Narita.

On Christmas Eve 1971, the notorious "Christmas Tree Bombing" incident occurred adjacent to a police box across the street from the Isetan Department Store in Shinjuku. The explosion injured twelve, including policemen and passersby.

Following a massive police crackdown, a core group of radicals fled to a mountain redoubt in Gunma Prefecture, where United Red Army "chairman" Tsuneo Mori and "vice-chairman" Hiroko Nagata oversaw a vicious purge of the ranks, ordering the deaths of fourteen members. When police swooped in to arrest them, five armed members, led by Kyoto University student Kunio Bando, twenty-five, managed to slip away and barricade themselves in a pension in nearby Karuizawa, holding Yasuko Muta, the caretaker's wife, as a hostage.

Knowing a police assault was imminent, the radicals set up formidable barricades throughout the building. The siege of the Asamasanso lasted ten days. Finally on February 28, what was to be a day-long assault, broadcast live on nationwide television, began. Using homemade bombs and shotguns, the radicals viciously resisted every meter of the police advance with a tenacity that would have done justice to the defenders at the Alamo or Bastogne. Two policemen died from gunshot wounds and over a dozen were seriously injured. The radicals were captured unharmed, although they received a pummeling at the hands of angry cops before being hauled off to jail.

Soon after the smoke and tear gas began clearing from the Asamasan-so, horrifying revelations began to surface of another atrocity: the Red Army "lynchings" that took place under the command of the army's "chairman" and "vice chairman," Mori and Nagata. During summary trials, fourteen rank-and-file members of the group had been arbitrarily found guilty of offenses, some extremely trivial, and executed.

Tsuneo Mori committed suicide in his prison cell on New Year's day, 1973. Hiroko Nagata's appeal against the death sentence was turned down by the Supreme Court in 1993. In her two decades on death row, she has written several books about her experience. Because of her poor physical condition, which went untreated while in prison, she has attracted the attention of a support group that is campaigning for amnesty. (It is unlikely she will be executed; no woman has been hanged in Japan since 1971.)

Leftwing violence had yet to run its course. On August 30, 1974, the "East Asia Anti-Japanese Front," another leftist group with possible links to the Red Army, detonated a bomb outside the headquarters of Mitsubishi Heavy Industries in Marunouchi in central Tokyo. It occurred during the lunch hour, killing 8 people and seriously injuring 240. Over the next several months, other bombs went off in front of major firms, including Mitsui & Co. and the Taisei group.

The United Red Army made a bloody debut on the international scene when three of its "soldiers" shot up the terminal at Tel Aviv's Lod Airport on May 30, 1972, killing twenty-six people and wounding over one hundred. Their other incidents of note included the hijacking of a JAL plane from Dubai to Libya (July 1973); the seizure of the U.S. embassy in Kuala Lumpur and humiliating the Japanese government by gaining release of five imprisoned comrades (August 1974); the seizure of the French embassy in the Hague, Netherlands, to demand release of a comrade jailed in France (September 1974); the hijacking of a JAL jetliner to Dhaka, Bangladesh, to secure release of other radicals (September 1977); and attacks in Jakarta (May 1986), Rome (June 1987) and Naples, Italy (April 1988).

Few countries, even "rogue states," found much use for a dwindling number of aging Japanese radicals. As havens in eastern Europe, the Middle East and North Korea became increasingly less accommodating, the Red Army members dispersed and fled to South America and Southeast Asia. In April 1988, Yu Kikumura was apprehended with a car full of explosives in New Jersey, USA. Over the next decade, the apprehensions continued with Hiroshi Sensui (Manila, June 1988); Yukiko Ekita (Romania, March 1995); Kazue Yoshimura (Peru, May 1996); Tsutomu Shirosaki (Nepal, September 1996); Haruo Wako and five others (Lebanon, February 1997); Yoshimi Tanaka (Thailand, June 1997); and Jun Nishikawa (Bolivia, November 1997).

Fusako Shigenobu, a diehard revolutionary who is credited with founding the Red Army, had been on Interpol's wanted list since August 1975 and remained at large. On November 8, 2000, police, acting on a tip, announced she had been apprehended at an Osaka hotel while dressed as a man. Traveling on several false passports she had apparently been on the move for several years. She made several trips to Japan to meet supporters.

On April 14, 2001, the fifty-five-year-old Shigenobu, who is likely to be prosecuted on a number of charges, announced to a group of supporters in Tokyo that the Red Army was officially disbanded.

URBAN CRIMES AND CELEBRITY CRIMINALS

IN JULY 1960, Hayato Ikeda succeeded the unpopular Nobusuke Kishi as prime minister. In December he announced a ten-year plan aimed at doubling the national income. Thanks to successive 10 percent annual rises in GNP growth his efforts succeeded, well ahead of schedule, but the growing affluence also spurred thieves to make greater efforts to grab a share of this wealth. On December 10, 1968, a young robber tricked four Nippon Trust Bank employees into vacating their car and then drove off with the equivalent of over U.S. $800,000 in the trunk.

The details of the crime have been meticulously recorded. Just after 9:00 A.M. on that rainy December day, a black Nissan Cedric, carrying four employees of the Nippon Trust Bank's Kokubunji branch, headed for the Toshiba factory in Fuchu City. In its trunk was 294,307,500 yen in three large trunks—the winter bonuses for the Toshiba workers.

As the car passed a lonely stretch of wall beside Fuchu Prison, the driver was frantically waved to a halt by a young man disguised as a motorcycle policeman. In an excited voice, the "cop" told the bank employees that their manager's home had been bombed, and that another bomb might have been planted in their car.

The bank workers were aware of a bomb threat and immediately cooperated. The policeman slid under the car to inspect the undercar-

The police montage photo of the 300 million yen Toshiba robber. Mysteriously, the face shown here was of a man who had died in an accident one year *before* the robbery!

riage, and suddenly smoke began pouring out from beneath the car.

"It's a bomb!" he shouted. "Run for it!"

As the four men dashed for safety, the "cop" started the engine and drove off with the money. Police soon set up roadblocks throughout western Tokyo, but by then the culprit had made his getaway.

An exhaustive investigation determined the robber's movements subsequent to the crime, which indicated meticulous planning from as early as half a year before. The numerous clues, including the robber's fingerprints, all led to dead ends. The massive and prolonged manhunt continued until the statute of limitations expired in 1975 and cost some 1 billion yen— over three times the amount of money stolen. Neither the man nor the money were ever seen again.

Among the possible suspects was the teenage son of a motorcycle policeman with a record of delinquency, who mysteriously died from suicide by poisoning four days after the robbery. The young man's corpse was viewed by the four bank staff, who noted a "resemblance." This, however, raised more questions than it answered. How could a teenager acting alone have obtained the details of the bank transport, let alone devise a nearly perfect crime? And, equally important, what happened to the money? Theories abound, but in the more than three decades since then no answers have been forthcoming.

Glico-Morinaga

Starting from the spring of 1984, police in the Kansai region were challenged by a canny gang of criminals who issued repeated mocking challenges and taunted them unmercifully over a period of about eighteen months. What was to become known as the Glico-Morinaga Incident began with the kidnapping of Katsuhisa Ezaki, president of the Ezaki-Glico company, out of his own bathtub on the night of March 18, 1984. After Eguchi managed to escape, the criminals turned from ransom demands to corporate extortion, announcing that Glico candy products would be laced with poison, ominously warning, "If you eat Glico candy, you'll be sorry." They were probably inspired by the still-unsolved incident in the U.S. in which seven people died of cyanide poisoning in the autumn of 1982 after having taken Tylenol.

In addition to Glico, the same gang made extortion attempts against at least five other major confectionery and foodstuffs manufacturers: House, Morinaga, Fujiya, Marudai and Surugaya. The criminals sent a constant stream of typewritten letters to the local media, phrased in acerbic Kansai dialect and signed "The Phantom with 21 Faces," an allusion to a fictitious criminal genius created in the 1930s by popular mystery novelist Edogawa Rampo.

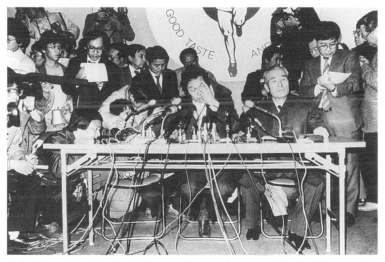

Ezaki-Glico president Katsuhisa Ezaki meets the press after escaping from his kidnappers. The statute of limitations expired with no arrests.

Several times police were close to an arrest, but each time the culprit (or culprits) managed to escape. One was photographed by a security camera while placing a box of poison-laced Glico candy on a convenience store shelf. Another suspect, nicknamed the "Fox-eyed Man" for the distinctive shape of his eyes, was tailed by a detective while on the way to pick up extortion money but managed to slip away.

After having instigated at least seventeen attempts at extortion, kidnapping, violation of postal regulations and other crimes, the gang announced a halt to their activities in August 1985. While "21 Faces" publicly humiliated the police, it has yet to be determined if he realized any material gains. No company has admitted to paying the extortionists, but this does not rule out gains through some indirect means, such as stock manipulation. The gang members' identities, and their true motives, remain an enigma to this day. The statute of limitations for the Ezaki kidnapping expired in March 1994 and the final charge, of attempted murder by use of poison, expired in 2000.

A Man with a Grudge

In February 1968, a Japan-born Korean roughneck with a long criminal record carried a hunting rifle into a bar in Shimizu, Shizuoka Prefecture, and shot dead two Japanese gangsters. Kim Hee Roh then fled by car to a Japanese-style inn at Sumata hot springs and used his hunting rifle and several sticks of dynamite to hold thirteen Japanese hostages.

Kim then demanded that the police in Shimizu make a public apology for their "humiliating" treatment of Koreans. NHK (Japan Broadcasting Corporation) viewers were astounded to see the head of the Shimizu police, red-faced and perspiring heavily, appear in a seventy-five-second TV spot, in which he apologized and pleaded for Kim to give himself up. The standoff lasted five days, during which time Kim gained a national audience. Reporters flocked to the isolated rural spa to interview him, and he obliged, holding his scope-mounted hunting rifle and flaunting the dynamite for the cameras.

In the days that followed, Kim displayed a talent for communication that belied his history as a grade-school dropout and ex-convict.

"Do you know what sort of prejudice we Koreans have to put up with?" Kim harangued the reporters. "Soga, the man I shot, had already put the squeeze on me for over 400,000 yen. When you kill people like him, you're doing society a big favor.

"As a kid, I was so poor I had to drink soy sauce diluted in water to stop the hunger pangs. When I was twelve years old, I got caught shoplifting. The Japanese cop called me *Chosen yaro* [Korean bastard] and threw me judo-

Kim Hee Roh took 13 people captive in a hot springs hotel and spent five days haranguing the media over discrimination he had suffered as a Korean.

style and put a choke hold on me. Even in jail, we Koreans got treated worse than Japanese."

When a newspaper reporter asked if he intended to surrender, Kim replied, "I've been hearing lots of calls to give up over the radio and television, I think my death is just a matter of time. I think I will be obliged to stage my own execution as punishment for all the disturbances I've caused.

"But I don't intend to die until the mass media make people aware of this situation [discrimination against Koreans]," he asserted.

During another of his "press conferences," Kim told reporters assembled in front of the inn, "The TV makes it look like I'm a nuisance. But that's just what a few Japanese are saying. Actually I'm risking my life to fight against Japanese persecution. This is a problem that every Japanese has to take responsibility for. If I die, it's going to create an international incident."

Kim's performance was cut short when police mingling with news reporters pounced and arrested him. He served thirty years in prison. His "mini coup d'etat" for the dignity of Japan's maltreated Korean minority made him a national hero in South Korea. Upon release from prison in 1999, the seventy-three-year-old Kim immediately headed for Pusan, and Japanese breathed a sigh of relief to be rid of him. Kim was given an emotional welcome "home"; soon afterwards, however, he was back in jail for having run amok, allegedly while on drugs.

Crime Goes Abroad

According to Japan's Criminal Code, homicide is punishable by the death penalty or imprisonment at forced labor for life or for not less than three years. Commission of a crime outside Japan does not exempt a killer from prosecution. Article 3 of the same document stipulates that the law applies to Japanese who commit murder *outside* Japan as well. As demonstrated by two sensational cases that occurred in the 1980s, however, this stipulation has some glaring flaws.

On January 18, 1984, *Weekly Bunshun* magazine began carrying a series of articles entitled "*Giwaku no Judan*" or "Bullets of Suspicion." The articles alleged that while visiting Los Angeles in November 1981, Tokyo businessman Kazuyoshi Miura had arranged for his heavily insured wife, Kazumi, to be murdered.

For the next year and a half, Miura's entire life story was paraded before the media. Finally on September 11, 1985, he was arrested on suspicion of assault with attempt to kill.

The crime for which Miura was later convicted occurred on August 13, 1981, in Los Angeles. Motivated by the promise of money and eventual marriage, Miura's twenty-five-year-old girlfriend, Michiko Yazawa, confessed to entering the Miuras' room at the New Otani Hotel and striking Miura's third wife Kazumi on the head with a length of metal pipe in a botched murder attempt.

Yazawa's confession led to Miura's arrest and sentencing, on August 7, 1987, to a six-year prison term.

This, however, was merely seen as a temporary measure to keep Miura behind bars until he could be charged for the alleged killing of his twenty-nine-year-old wife for 150 million yen in life insurance. On November 17, 1981, while on a subsequent visit to Los Angeles, Miura was suspected of engineering his wife's fatal shooting in what was made to appear a robbery attempt. Kazumi died on November 30, 1982, never having regained consciousness.

Japanese-American police officer Jimmy Sakota, named to head the Asian Criminal Special Unit attached to the Los Angeles district attorney's office, reopened the 1981 shooting incident and conducted an aggressive investigation. Based on largely circumstantial evidence, Miura was convicted on March 31, 1994, of murdering his wife. He appealed and five years later the Tokyo High Court overturned the ruling on grounds of insufficient evidence.

Miura was briefly freed but ordered back to prison to serve out the sentence for the first attempt on his wife's life, not for the murder itself. He was finally released from Miyagi Prison on January 17, 2001. The story is by no means over, as he still faces civil action from the insurance companies, which are demanding restitution of his claims.

Kazuyoshi Miura continues to portray himself as a victim of the media, and the media, to some degree at least, appears willing to humor him. He operates a home page (www.h3.dion.ne.jp/~yoshie-m/) set up by his wife.

Le Cannibale japonais

Six months before Kazumi Miura was shot in Los Angeles, another shocking murder involving a Japanese took place in France. On June 11, 1981, a twenty-five-year-old Dutch student named Renee Hartevelt arrived at the Paris studio of Issei Sagawa, thirty-two, a French literature graduate student at the Sorbonne. She had been hired by Sagawa to record German poetry.

"French girls tended to be circumspect, but Rene, being Dutch, was quite easygoing and we got along well," he was to write cryptically in his autobiographical novel, *In the Mist*. On a tape, which served as evidence, her voice abruptly halts with the sound of a muffled shot, made by Sagawa firing a bullet into her brain from a silenced .22 caliber rifle.

Sagawa, by his own admission, then disrobed her corpse and—very briefly—had sex. He dragged her corpse into the bathtub and took two rolls of film while he dismembered the body. After undressing her, he sliced off pieces of her flesh, which he consumed raw, describing its taste as "not too different from *toro* [the high-quality fatty meat of the tuna]. It was only after swallowing that I felt a rich aftertaste . . ." He also described how he sautéed other cuts from her body, adding salt, pepper and seasonings before eating. After carving up the corpse, he went to bed. Sagawa recalled he slept well that night.

Sagawa's awkward attempt to dispose of her body in two suitcases led police straight back to his apartment and he was arrested on June 17. His family retained the services of one of France's top criminal lawyers, who in 1984 succeeded in arranging for Sagawa to be deported back to Japan after spending twenty-one months in jail and fourteen more in a mental hospital.

He returned to Japan in May 1984 to be treated at a hospital. In September 1985, Sagawa's family withdrew him from the mental institution. Neither his doctors nor the Japanese police could take any action as he had entered the institution voluntarily and was free to leave.

"His release from the hospital came as a shock," Susumu Oda, a noted criminal psychiatrist, is quoted as saying in the weekly magazine *Shukan Shincho*. "Sagawa has a combination of sexual disorder and personality disorder. This means he is not psychotic, but is diagnosed as suffering from psychopathy. Although people in his state can be dangerous to others, they are excluded from the list [of patients] who require hospitalization.

"In such a case he should have been charged under criminal law, but the French did not do it. So he is not receiving any care. It's a weird situation."

The explanation as to why Sagawa was never prosecuted in Japan is a bit vague; one source reports the French police considered the case closed and were unwilling to send their files to Tokyo. If so, then Japan has been unfairly criticized for not pursuing the case.

That still leaves the Japanese media open to criticism for its tasteless coverage. In 1983, playwright Juro Kara received the prestigious Akutagawa literary prize for his *Letters from Sagawa*, which author Ian Buruma savaged as a "kick in the teeth of the murdered girl and her loved ones."

Sagawa insists he initially tried to slip into anonymity, but his reputation preceded him. His applications to tutor French were refused. He tried washing dishes, but with his poor physical condition, he usually wore out after one day on the job. Then in 1989 child serial murderer Tsutomu Miyazaki was arrested and the media turned to Sagawa—an acknowledged authority on criminal pathology—for astute comments. Sagawa's antics were eventually to earn him the sobriquet of "Japan's only celebrity cannibal."

"I was overwhelmed with work," he recalls. "Through a friend's introduction, I ran installments of my novel in a literary magazine. And I wrote the subtitles for a film about some guy who exhumed corpses, peeled off their skin and used it to make handbags. I really felt gratified when I saw my name in the screen credits."

Sagawa was later tabbed for a role in a porno film by director Toru Nishimura. Banking on his screen success, he was afterwards seen in public escorting starlets to theaters and making overseas publicity trips.

"But my father, who dislikes the mass media, went around to publishers asking that they refrain from giving me work," Sagawa said in an interview.

The cannibalism incident was to play havoc on Sagawa's family. His father stepped down from his position as president of a machinery company and later suffered a thrombosis that caused him to lose his ability to talk. His mother became neurotic. His younger brother developed a respiratory problem.

After watching a screening of *The Silence of the Lambs* in 1992, Sagawa was quoted in the *Asian Wall Street Journal* as finding Hannibal Lecter "unrealistic and comical."

"He was portrayed as a monster and ate everything," said Sagawa. "Normally a cannibal is delicate and selects his victims carefully."

In February 2001, he was still clamoring for media attention, this time through the publication of *Manga Sagawa-san*, a book of crude self-illustrated cartoons that relates his crime in graphic detail.

"I am more or less broke and dependent on occasional handouts from a caucasian female friend," Sagawa told *Shukan Shincho*. "I get a small amount from writing and some assistance from my family. I'd be glad to do more comics if anyone asks me."

FACELESS KILLERS, UNKNOWN MOTIVES

IN JAPANESE A RANDOM assailant is called a *torima*, literally a "passing demon." A history of the Showa period records forty major incidents from 1928 to 1988, but seven occurred in the final full year of Showa (1988).

In January 1959, residents of Tokyo's Arakawa Ward were terrorized by a *torima* who sporadically slashed young women as he pedaled past on a bicycle. One of his twenty-one victims, a junior high school student, died. Eyewitnesses described him as around fifteen or sixteen years of age, but no arrest was ever made. Gunji Kawamata, a twenty-nine-year old Tokyo sushi chef who grabbed a fish knife and went on a drug-induced rampage in June 1981, killed a housewife and two children, wounded two others, then took a female hostage and held off police for seven hours before giving himself up. His life sentence was confirmed in January 1983.

Torima incidents belong to the larger category known as *moso hanzai* or "delusionary crimes," assaults and other vicious crimes committed not for the usual motives of monetary gain, hatred or revenge, but to satisfy some demented urge, or even for pleasure. They also include forms of erotomania such as stalking and sex-related acts such as voyeurism and theft of women's underwear from clotheslines.

When one motive for killing feeds on another, the result can be especially shocking. Kiyoshi Okubo, born in Gunma Prefecture in 1935, grew up a petulant, spoiled mama's boy who liked to molest little girls, and eventually wound up serving three prison sentences for rape. After he was released on parole from his third sentence, on March 2, 1971, he pledged to go straight, but only a short time after leaving prison, he went on a seventy-three-day spree of rape and murder in Gunma Prefecture.

Of slightly foreign appearance, thanks to a Russian maternal grand-mother, Okubo would don a beret and a cossack blouse. Driving a sporty new cream-colored Mazda Rotary Coupe, he cruised the cities and towns of Gunma hunting for women. His usual ruse was to pose as an artist, propositioning young women to "model" for him. His shiny new car and thin veneer of sophistication were enough to convince them. He approached well over one hundred and persuaded dozens to join him for a drive. He may have raped as many as fifty. He confessed to murdering eight.

Impatient with the pace of the police investigation during the killing spree, the brother of one of the women who had disappeared organized a citizens' posse, and teams of men cruised Gunma roads in search of the man matching Okubo's description. After a four-day manhunt, on May 14, 1971, they found him and turned him over to the police.

Okubo was initially arrested on the charge of abduction with intent to perform an immoral act. Getting him to confess was like extracting teeth. He teased and taunted police interrogators for over two months, only showing where he had buried his final two victims on July 30.

Okubo's rationale for his spree of rape and murder was a hatred for the police.

"I became the brute that I am because of the police," he told a re-porter who interviewed him in jail. "They treated me in a way that com-pletely destroyed my humanity. It made me rebel against authority."

Okubo did not appeal his death sentence and insisted he was fully prepared to die. He went to the Kosuge Prison gallows on January 23,

1976. According to Kimiko Otsuka's work on executions, when the warden informed Okubo the sentence was to be carried out, he completely lost his nerve, collapsing to the floor of his cell unable to walk. Two guards had to hold him upright until the noose could be placed around his neck. His last sound was a gasp of self-pity just before the trap was sprung.

Strange Voices

In August 1988, a four-year-old girl disappeared from a community close to the boundary between Saitama Prefecture and Tokyo. About five months later, the ashes of the dead girl, placed in a cardboard box, were left in front of her home. In October the same year, a seven-year-old girl was last seen walking along a street in Saitama before disappearing. Parents of small children increased their vigilence, but two more girls, aged four and five, disappeared in December 1988 and June 1989.

On July 23, 1989, a young man was caught in the act of molesting a

Infatuated with his collection of thousands of sadistic videos, child-killer Tsutomu Miyazaki (center, wearing eyeglasses) killed four girls before he was captured.

child in Hachioji City, but was thwarted by the girl's father, who grabbed him and called the police. The suspect, Tsutomu Miyazaki, was a reclusive twenty-seven-year-old printing shop worker with a physical deformity. Investigators who went to his home found a room almost filled to overflowing with over five thousand sick videos, one of which showed one of the missing child victims.

Miyazaki confessed to raping, and in two cases cannibalizing, his victim's corpses, which he abandoned in wooded areas of Saitama and Tokyo. He explained his attraction to children by saying adult women made him feel "uncomfortable." He blamed his crimes on "rat people" who spoke inside his head, ordering him to kill. He appeared unmoved by his victims and indifferent to his own fate.

Psychiatrists' opinions differ as to whether Miyazaki suffers from multiple personality disorder or schizophrenia. In April 1997, the court judged Miyazaki was responsible for his actions and handed down the death sentence. Miyazaki's articles from prison appear regularly in *Tsukuru*, a monthly magazine. He does not have a computer in his cell, but operates an Internet home page through an intermediary and replies to questions in his own handwriting (www.tctv.ne.jp/members/nisijima/keimusyo/miyazaki-qa.html).

On June 28, 2001, the Tokyo High Court confirmed Miyasaki's death sentence.

Sakakibara Seito

In the early morning hours of May 27, 1997, person or persons unknown placed the severed head of an eleven-year-old retarded boy outside the gate of a junior high school in Suma Ward, Kobe. The killer, who identified himself with cryptic characters that were assumed to be read "Sakakibara Seito" (literally, Apostle Sake Devil Rose), left two messages crammed in the victim's mouth. One read, "Well, this is the beginning of the game. Stupid police, stop me if you can. It's great fun for me to kill people."

Jun Hase had been missing for several days when his head appeared at the school. His body was later found on a hill seven hundred meters from his home. A dark sedan was seen driving away from the school gate at approximately the time the head was believed to have been delivered. This initially set investigators hunting for a man in his thirties or forties.

The killer's dramatic method of delivering his grisly work struck tangible fear into the hearts of residents. Police patrols began escorting local children to and from their schools.

As the investigation proceeded, the tabloids, as is their usual practice, invited psychiatrists, mystery authors and other pundits to speculate over the killer's cryptic name and his message, which made references to Nazi ideology and showed chilling parallels with Zodiac, a prolific serial killer who haunted northern California from the late 1960s and who was never caught. Rumors flew that the twisted criminal might seek out his next victim further afield, perhaps even as far away as Tokyo.

The notes drew some interesting comments. One analyst, who pointed out the grammar was "flawless," speculated the writer was probably a teacher of the Japanese language. It was later surmised that the writer had first typed his messages out on a Japanese word processor (which would have facilitated correct grammar) and then copied it on paper by hand. Another was convinced the writer had "almost certainly" studied in mainland China, going so far as to name the area of the country where he studied.

On the evening of June 28, police announced an arrest: a fourteen-year-old junior high school student who had known Hase. He had preceded Hase's murder by bludgeoning to death a ten-year-old girl in mid-March. Just fifteen minutes later and only one hundred meters away, another girl was stabbed, though not fatally. She told police she thought her assailant was of junior high school age. For whatever reason, the investigation was not effectively pursued.

No one had a plausible explanation as to how anyone so young could kill so cold-bloodedly. Some reports speculated that the boy had snapped after the January 1995 earthquake that had devastated his home city. He apparently enjoyed torturing and killing stray cats, and at some point moved on to human victims. He was traced by handwriting samples and supicions voiced by those who knew him at school, but police took weeks to act, reluctant to move in spite of mounting evidence that pointed to the youthful perpetrator.

Although a weekly magazine ran a class picture in which the killer appeared, the Family Court protected his identity, and the results of his psychiatric evaluation were not made public. When he was eighteen, a weekly magazine reported that he told an instructor at his reform school that his ambition was to become a writer.

The incident in Kobe was just the first of a number of serious crimes by juveniles to be committed over the next several years, and some even believe Sakakibara was the catalyst. Amidst public pressure that the laws were overly lenient, and to seek justice for victims, the Diet on November 29, 2000, ratified a new law lowering the age of criminal responsibility from sixteen to fourteen.

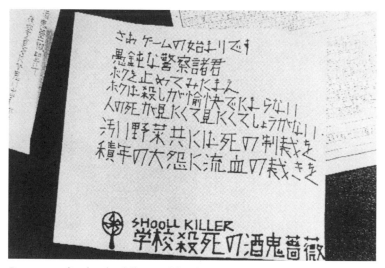

Even more startling than this chilling note left in the victim's decapitated head was the fact that its author was only fourteen years old. The symbol is reminiscent of notes sent by California's notorious "Zodiac" serial killer.

A Decade in Captivity

In January 2000, another bizarre incident came to light. Responding to a call from a mother terrified by her son's violent behavior, public health workers in Kashiwazaki City, Niigata Prefecture, went to a house and discovered a pale, emaciated young woman, wrapped in a blanket that had been sewn up into a bag. Her name was Fusako Sano and she had been missing since November 13, 1990.

Nobuyuki Sato, thirty-seven, a chronically unemployed man with a prior arrest record, had abducted Sano, then age nine, at knife point, forced her into the trunk of his car, and driven her to his house. Threating her with a knife and a stun gun until she was totally compliant, he held her prisoner in his room for nine years and two months. Sato's mother, terrified of his habitually violent behavior, claimed she had never seen the girl before. Her son had banned her from his room for the past ten years, she said, and in any case she was out of the house most of the day selling insurance.

Sano, so weak she could barely walk, was reunited with her own mother at the local police station. The Kyodo News agency reported she had atrophied leg muscles and reduced bone weight, and was suffering from posttraumatic stress disorder as a result of her ordeal.

The Niigata police was publicly humiliated when it was subsequently learned that in 1989 Sato had been arrested in an attempt to kidnap another girl, yet had not been approached as part of the routine investigation into Sano's disappearance, even though he was still on probation at the time. It was later revealed that after Niigata Prefectural Police superintendent Koji Kobayashi was informed of the situation, he and other high-ranking officers continued to entertain a visiting inspector from the National Police Agency at a hot springs hotel, drinking and playing mahjongg until late into the night. As if this weren't enough, it was learned that Kobayashi was accused of approving a falsified police report that attempted to take credit for "liberating Sano," when in fact police at the local station had refused to respond to the health worker's call for assistance. Kobayashi resigned in disgrace.

THE AUM DEBACLE

THE JAPANESE WORD *jakyo*, meaning a "perverse or dia-
bolical religion," is written with the characters for "annoying" and
"teaching." A 1995 paperback entitled *Itan no Kyodan* introduces some
two dozen of the more extreme sects that have come and gone over the
centuries. Most were transitory, but a few are still in business.

In the spring of 1989, the AUM *Shinrikyo*, known in English as
"AUM Supreme Truth" (see note on page 238), applied to the Tokyo
Metropolitan Government for registration as a religious body with tax-
exempt status. The bureaucrats at city hall had reservations. Its founder,
Chizuo Matsumoto a.k.a. Shoko Asahara, a partially blind masseur,
had a record of several arrests, including assault and fraud, and parents
had already begun to file complaints that AUM was "stealing away"
their children.

When the officials dragged their heels, AUM began bullying tactics,
demonstrating outside city hall and filing a lawsuit against the government. By August the officials caved in and the cult was officially incor-
porated as a religious body. This not only gave its commercial activities
tax-exempt status, it also accorded it the right to own property as an
organization, and protection from any state or other external interfer-
ence. The latter effectively shut out the police until it was almost too late.

AUM's success in getting its way established a quintessential pattern: first bullying and harassment, and when threatened, assuming the role of persecuted victim. Shoko Egawa, a gutsy female investigative reporter who tracked the cult's activities from its onset, noted that within eighteen months after its incorporation, the cult was involved in no fewer than sixty civil and criminal lawsuits. Six years later, Asahara was once again in police custody, this time on multiple charges that included instigation of mass murder.

Asahara, son of an impoverished weaver of tatami mats in Kumamoto Prefecture, had received training at special schools for the visually impaired. He was clever, manipulative and physically strong, and soon learned that he could usually get his way by bullying. After failing to gain entry to university, he considered his prospects and realized that emulating a new religion would be the surest way to generate large amounts of money and obtain the adoration he desired from female followers. He picked some of the brightest adherents of Agon-shu, a firewalking sect, and gave them a stake in the spoils. Skillfully generating propaganda, they enthusiastically proselytized and attracted growing numbers of naive young believers who were easily convinced, among other things, that Asahara had the power to levitate or walk through solid walls.

Meanwhile, a young human rights lawyer named Tsutsumi Sakamoto had been battling the cult on behalf of family members. Less than three months after the Tokyo government gave AUM its official recognition, the cult had blood on its hands. On November 3, 1989, a team of AUM adherents, including a karate expert and a physician, crept into Sakamoto's apartment and murdered him, his wife and the couple's infant son. After mangling their victims' teeth to prevent identification, the three bodies were buried in separate areas of the Japan Alps.

It was subsequently learned that a program director at Tokyo Broadcasting System (TBS) television had allowed key members of AUM's leadership to preview segments of an interview with Sakamoto prior to its airing. Sakamoto's denunciations of the cult were relayed to guru Asahara, who, in a fit of pique, ordered his followers to murder him. November 3 being a national holiday, Sakamoto did not go to his office, so AUM's hit team was forced to break into his apartment, and slew his family as well. TBS also kept quiet and informed neither Sakamoto (who might have taken steps to protect himself) nor the police, even after Sakamoto and his family disappeared.

The Sakamoto slayings were not AUM's initiation into murder. Shuji Taguchi, an adherent who requested permission to quit the cult, had been strangled to death on Asahara's orders a year before. Aside from nerve gassings and more sensational murders, it may never be ascertained how many people were killed. AUM operated its own clinic, and suspicions have been raised that several older members may have been killed after signing over their assets.

Taking a cue from Soka Gakkai, a lay Buddhist sect with membership numbering in the millions that founded the Komeito (Clean Government) Party in the 1960s, Asahara and several of his followers ran for seats in the national Diet. None were successful, but membership continued to grow, and AUM plowed its revenues into yoga schools and ramshackle retreats, at Namino, a mountain village in Asahara's home prefecture of Kumamoto, and at Kamikuishiki, in the foothills of Mt. Fuji. Wherever they settled, they promptly became a public nuisance. Protest signs sprouted, city offices refused to register cult members as residents, and local schools would not allow members' children to register.

In the years from 1989 to 1995, AUM's story came to resemble the plot of a Sax Rohmer novel. Asahara's minions were analogous to Kali-worshipping Thugs, who, at the orders of their sinister guru, killed out of religious fervor. The exotic weaponry was fully the equal of a Dr. Yen Sin or Fu Manchu. In addition to efforts to establish a cottage industry to produce conventional firearms, AUM's laboratories, working through dummy companies, procured tons of raw materials needed to synthesize the toxic nerve gas sarin and an even more lethal variety called VX. They also began research into biological agents, including anthrax and botulism, and a plasma-ray gun. A surplus helicopter was purchased from the Russians and shipped to Kamikuishiki. Fortunately, it was never put to use for any nefarious purpose.

Bizarre events followed in succession. In 1993, noxious smells began emanating from an AUM facility in central Tokyo. Only much later was it learned that cult scientists were attempting to cultivate anthrax.

AUM struck next in the peaceful rural city of Matsumoto in Nagano Prefecture. On the night of 27 June, 1994, seven people died and several hundred were sickened to various degrees by a mysterious cloud of gas. The mystery deepened several days later when tests determined the gas to be sarin, a toxic nerve agent developed by German scientists in the 1930s. The same person who first reported the gas attack to police was initially regarded as a suspect. The bewildered investigators were clearly out of their league.

Events began to build to a head from the start of 1995. On New Year's Day, 1995, the *Yomiuri Shimbun* reported that police had detected sarin residue in the soil near Aum's compound in Yamanashi Prefecture. On January 13, *Shukan Shincho* magazine hit the stands carrying a story entitled, "The Judges in a Lawsuit against AUM Were Sarin Victims." AUM, *Shukan Shincho* revealed, had been involved in a dispute over the sale of a plot of land in Matsumoto. The plaintiff sought to nullify the sale on grounds that AUM had purchased the land fraudulently through a dummy company.

The case was being heard by three judges, who lived in a three-story building adjacent to the Meiji Life Insurance dormitory, where a large number of casualties occurred. Judge Kiyoshi Aonuma, who had been assigned to write the court's opinion, was still ailing, causing a delay in the final ruling.

On January 17, a major earthquake devastated the city of Kobe. The same morning, the February 1995 issue of *Marco Polo* magazine appeared on newsstands. It contained a story about the Matsumoto sarin incident by Kyle B. Olsen, an American expert on chemical warfare, who grimly predicted, "Next time the criminals will select a larger stage, and one that will result in a greater tragedy."

Another AUM-related incident made the news, when on February 28, Kiyoshi Kariya, a sixty-eight-year old notary public, was snatched off the street near his home in broad daylight. Kariya had clashed with members of the sect while trying to prevent his younger sister from making further donations—she had already been pressured to contribute over 60 million yen. He had relayed his fears of an abduction by AUM to several others. A security camera mounted at the entrance to the Chuo Expressway enabled police to trace the van used to abduct Kariya to a rental company, and through it, to AUM.

This abduction led to AUM's undoing. The Tokyo Metropolitan Police Department (MPD) is not only less tolerant of criminal misconduct than the prefectural organizations; it also maintains a powerful public security section and can muster enormous investigative resources. Through its inside sources, AUM got word of an impending police raid and decided on a preemptive strike. On Monday, March 20, 1995, Japanese authorities got a nasty lesson in the consequences of investigative inertia. During the peak of the rush hour, members of the cult released sarin on three subway lines that converged on Kasumigaseki, where the headquarters of both the National Police Agency and the MPD are located. Twelve were to die and over five thousand were injured—a miraculously small number, considering Asahara and his minions had aimed for *poa* (altruistic murder) on a massive scale. Hastily prepared low-grade sarin and the fact that the following day was a holiday, leading many workers to extend their weekend, kept the casualties much lower than they could have been.

On the morning of March 30, an incident occurred that shocked the Japanese public as much if not more than the subway gassing. As National Police Agency Superintendent Takaji Kunimatsu walked from his apartment to a waiting limousine, he was shot and seriously wounded by a gunman with a Colt revolver. Although AUM was suspected, his assailant, who fled by bicycle, was never apprehended.

AUM vociferously denied the charges against it, and the media appeared to waver until Antonio Pagnotta, an Italian photographer,

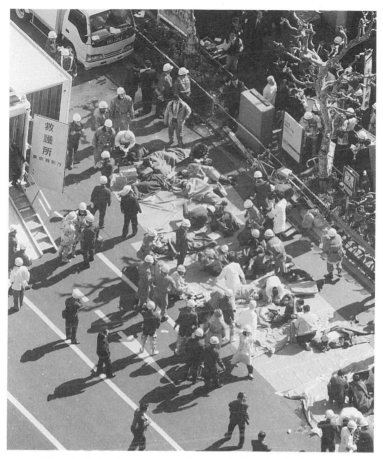

Victims of the sarin attack on March 20, 1995, being treated in front of Tsukiji Station.

electrified an April 3 press conference at the Foreign Correspondents' Club of Japan by telling cult spokesman Fumihiro Joyu, "You are lying." To prove his point, Pagnotta waved photos he had taken by circumventing police lines and thrusting his camera through a ventilation fan at AUM's No. 7 Satyam, an eerie complex near Mt. Fuji with sinister piping apparatus snaking from its exterior. The photos, which were later confirmed to show the equipment with which AUM had produced sarin, contradicted AUM's repeated insistence that the plant, which in any case it claimed was for producing insecticide, no longer existed.

Soon the tabloids and weekly magazines were reporting on AUM's bizarre initiation rituals with mind-altering drugs; intimidation and abductions of believers' family members; stimulant drug transactions with crime syndicates; "lynchings" of insubordinate members; operation of prostitution clubs; attempts to infiltrate and subvert the military and the police; break-ins at high-tech military research laboratories; plans to assassinate politicians, government officials and media personalities; and so on.

All these paled before the growing body of evidence that Asahara, influenced by the prophesies of French seer Nostradamus and through his own apocalyptic vision of Armageddon, was prepared to kill large numbers of people.

Six years after the release of sarin on the Tokyo subways, the lengthy process of trials and appeals for Chizuo Matsumoto and several dozen of his minions is ongoing. Despite legal harassment, the cult, since renamed Aleph, still exists. Its founder is unlikely to ever be released from prison, but the line of succession is clear. Like any traditional Japanese business, control will almost certainly be passed along to the proprietor's oldest son.

NOTES TO TEXT

NOTE TO PAGE 14

Three separate laws were in force during most of the Tokugawa period. The first, enacted in 1614, was prescribed for the *Kuge* ("Court Nobles"). A statute called the *Buke Shohatto* ("Laws for the Military Houses") was imposed upon the *daimyo* in 1615 and subsequently underwent several revisions.

For commoners, laws were announced in the form of *kosatsu* (tablets posted in public places in Edo and elsewhere). The details of the law were deliberately withheld from the public. Under Shogun Yoshimune, legal procedure and penal laws were finally compiled into the *Osadamegaki Hyakkajo* ("Edict in 100 Articles") in 1742. The *Edict* was further revised and amended in 1790.

John Carey Hall, who published a translation of the *Osadamegaki Hyakkajo* in 1913, noted that the bulk of the edicts was "old custom, modified by recent judicial decisions." He also pointed out that the *Edict* was never printed in Tokugawa times, and that "great variations [existed in] the manuscript copies of it which were in use in the tribunals." The *Edict*, Hall adds, was only directly operative in the eight Kanto provinces, the cities of Kyoto, Osaka and Sumpu, and minor distant strongholds and ports. Nonetheless, Article 21 in the 1635 amendment to the *Buke Shohatto* stipulates that "In all matters the example set by the laws of Edo is to be followed in all the provinces and places," thus ensuring its adoption throughout the country, at least to some degree.

NOTE TO PAGE 230

AUM, pronounced "ohm," is a composite of three different letters of the Sanskrit alphabet, whose English equivalents are "a," "u," and "m." These represent a trinity of three supreme Hindu Gods: Brahma, the creator; Vishnu, the preserver; and Shiva, the destroyer. In Hinduism the sign also represents the whole universe. When spoken in unison, the three letters are believed to generate a sense of well being, and Hindus preceded any chants by uttering the syllable.

BIBLIOGRAPHY

In Japanese:

Abe, Akira. *Edo no Autorou*. Tokyo: Kodansha, 1999.

Aizu, Shingo, and Nagayama, Yasuo. *Kindai Nihon no Satsujin Fairu*. Tokyo: Koei, 1996.

Aoki, Osamu. *Nihon no Koan Keisatsu no Shinjutsu*. Tokyo: Kodansha, 2000.

Aoki, Tamotsu et al. *Hanzai to Fuzoku*. Tokyo: Iwanami Shoten, 2000.

Asahi Shimbun Hyaku Nen no Kiji ni Miru Gaikokujin on Ashiato. Tokyo: Asahi Shimbunsha, 1979.

Asakura, Kyoji. *Dokufu-den*. Tokyo: Heibonsha, 1999.

— —. *Yakuza (For Beginners Series)*. Tokyo: Gendai Shokan, 1990.

Atlas Tokyo: Edo/Tokyo through Maps. Tokyo: Heibonsha, 1986.

Ayabe, Tomoko. "Kami ni Natta Dokufu—Kijin no Omatsu," pp. 64–70. *Denki Series No. 17 (Bessatsu Rekishi Tokuhon)*. Tokyo: Shin Jinbutsu Oraisha, 1980.

Bakumatsu Jinbutsu Jiken Sanpo. Tokyo: Jinbunsha, 1995.

Beato, Felix, and Yokohama Kaiko Shiryokan. *Bakumatsu Nihon no Fukei to Hitobito*. Tokyo: Akashi Shoten, 1987.

CIDO Productions, etc. *Ryoki Satsujin no Katarogu 50*. Tokyo: Japan Mix Inc., 1995.

Edo Machibugyo (Gakken Rekishi Gunzo Library). Tokyo: Gakushu Kenkyusha, 1995.

Edo Sambyaku Han Hankacho (Bessatsu Rekishi Tokuhon). Tokyo: Shin Jinbutsu Oraisha, 1996.

Edo Shohan Kaiki Fushigi Jikencho (Bessatsu Rekishi Tokuhon). Tokyo: Shin Jinbutsu Oraisha, 1995.

Edo Tokyo Rekiseki Mappu (Bessatsu Rekishi Tokuhon). Tokyo: Shin Jinbutsu Oraisha, 1995.

Endo, Makoto. *Teigin Jiken Saiban no Nazo*. Tokyo: Gendai Shokan, 1990.

Fujisawa, Morihiko, and Ito, Seiu. *Nihon Keibatsu Fuzoku-shi*. Tokyo: Fujimori Shoten, 1982.

Fujita, Satoru. *Toyama Kinshiro no Jidai*. Tokyo: Koso Shobo. 1992.

Goda, Ichido. *Nihon Ryoki, Zankoku Jikenbo*. Tokyo: Fusosha, 2000.

Hanzai no Showa-shi, Vols. 1–3. Tokyo: Sakuhin-sha, 1984.

Hara, Taneaki, and Osatake, Takeshi. *Edo Jidai Hanzai Keibatsu Jireishu*. Tokyo: Kashiwa Shobo, 1982.

Hayashi, Kazu. *Missetsu Edo Ichidai Onna*. Tokyo: Nihon Koron-sha, 1936.

Hayashi, Reiko. *Edo Mise Hankacho*. Tokyo: Yoshikawa Kobunkan, 1982.

Higuchi, Hideo. *Edo no Hankacho*. Tokyo: Shin Jinbutsu Oraisha, 1995.

Hinotani, Teruhiko. *Edo Jidai no Jikencho*. Tokyo: PHP, 1985.

———. *Kyoto Meibugyo no Rekishi Tokuhon*. Tokyo: Seishun Shuppan-sha, 1998.

Hiramatsu, Yoshiro. *Edo no Tsumi to Batsu*. Tokyo: Heibonsha, 1988.

Honda, Yutaka. *Edo no Hinin*. Tokyo: San'ichi Shobo, 1992.

Hon no Mori Henshubu, ed. *Abe Sada: Jiken Chosho Zenbun*. Tokyo: Kosumikku International, 1997.

Horinouchi, Masakazu. *Abe Sada Seiden*. Tokyo: Joho Senta Shuppankyoku, 1998.

Ienaga, Saburo, ed. *Nihon no Rekishi*. Vol. 5 (revised edition). Tokyo: Horupu Shuppan, 1987.

Iizuka, Yuichiro. *Engeki to Hanzai*. Tokyo: Bukyosha, 1930.

Ikenami, Shotaro. *Edo Kiriezu Sampo*. Tokyo: Shinchosha, 1989.

Imado, Eiichi, ed. *Torimono no Sekai*. Vols. 1–3. Tokyo: Nihon Hoso Shuppan Kyokai, 1986.

Imai, Kingo. *Hanshichi wa Jitsuzai shita*. Tokyo: Kawade Shobo Shinsha, 1989.

Ino, Kenji. *Yakuza to Nihonjin*. Tokyo: Gendai Shokan, 1993.

Inoue, Kazuo. *Nihon Zangyaku-shi*. Tokyo: Sogo Tosho, 1972.

Ishii, Ryosuke. *Edo no Keibatsu*. Tokyo: Chuo Koronshinsha, 1964.

———. *Hitogoroshi/Mittsu*. Tokyo: Akashi Shoten, 1990.

Ishikawa Jun'ichi, ed. *Tokyo Kemono Michi*. Tokyo: Heibonsha, 1990.

Itoya, Hisao. *Kotoku Shusui*. Tokyo: Shimizu Shoin, 1973.

Iyoda, Yasuhiro et al. *Terebi-shi Handobukku*. Tokyo: Jiyu Kokuminsha, 1998.

Kaku, Kozo. *Dai-keishi Kawaji Toshiyoshi*. Tokyo: Shuppan Geijutsusha, 1999.

Kamata, Tadayoshi. *Meikyu-iri Jiken to Sengo Hanzai*. Tokyo: Okokusha, 1989.

Kanzaki, Kiyoshi. *Taigyaku Jiken: Kotoku Shusui to Meiji Tenno*. Vols. 1–4. Tokyo: Ayumi Shuppan, 1976–77.

Kata, Koji. *Showa Jiken Shi*. Tokyo: Isseisha, 1985.

———. *Edo no Jikenbo*, Tokyo: Rippu Shobo, 1979.

———. *Nihon no Yakuza (Shimpan)*. Tokyo: Daiwa Shobo, 1993.

———. *Showa Daitoden*. Tokyo: Gendaishi Shuppankai, 1975.

———. *Showa Hanzai Shi*. Tokyo: Gendaishi Shuppankai, 1974.

———. *Tokyo Jiken-shi*. Tokyo: Isseisha, 1980.

Kawada, Hiroshi. *Meiji Yonjusannen no Tentetsu*. Tokyo: Shakai Shisosha, 1993.

Kawai, Atsushi. *Hayawakari Edojidai*. Tokyo: Nihon Jitsugyo Shuppansha, 1999.

Kinoshita, Naoyuki, and Yoshimi, Toshiya, ed. *Nyusu no Tanjo: Kawaraban to shinbun nishiki-e no joho sekai*. Tokyo. University of Tokyo Press, 1999.

Kitajima, Masamoto. *Mizuno Tadakuni*. Tokyo: Yoshikawa Kobunkan, 1969.

Koishikawa, Zenji. *Hanzai no Minzokugaku*. Tokyo: Hihyosha, 1993.

———. *Hanzai no Minzokugaku 2*. Tokyo: Hihyosha, 1996.

Koizumi, Terusaburo. *Taisho Hanzai-shi Shotan*. Tokyo: Daigaku Shobo, 1955.

———. *Meiji Hanzai-shi Seidan*. Tokyo: Daigaku Shobu, 1956.

———. *Meiji/Taisho/Showa Hanzaishi Seidan*. Tokyo: Hihyosha, 1997.

Kojima, Noriya. *Meiji Iko Daijiken no Shinso to Hanrei*. Tokyo: Kobunsha, 1935.

Konta, Yozo. *Edo no Kinsho*. Tokyo: Yoshikawa Kobunkan, 1981.

Koyama, Matsukichi. *Meihangan Monogatari*. Tokyo: Jinbutsu Oraisha, 1968.

Kurahashi, Masanao. *Nihon no Ahen Senryaku: Kakureta Kokka Hanzai*. Tokyo: Kyoei Shobo, 1996.

Kurashige, Teisuke. *Wagakuni no Kakegoto-shi*. Tokyo: Nihon Jitensha Shinkokai, 1977.

Kusayanagi, Daizo, ed. *Nijisseiki Foto Dokyumento*. Vol. 2. Tokyo: Gyosei, 1992.

Kyakuno, Sumihiro. *Meiji Keisatsu no Hiroku*. Matsuyama: Ehime Shimbun Sabisu Senta, 1976.

Maesaka, Toshiyuki. *Nippon Kijin-den*. Tokyo: Shakai Shisosha, 1996.

Mainichi Shimbun. *Sengo no Judai Jiken Hayamihyo*. Tokyo: Mainichi Shimbunsha, 1987.

Masukawa, Koichi. *Tobaku no Nihon-shi*. Tokyo: Heibonsha, 1989.

Matsumoto, Seicho, ed. *Meiji Hyakunen 100 Daijiken*. Vol. 2. Tokyo: San'ichi Shobo, 1968.

———. *Nihon no Kuroi Kiri*. Vols. 1–2. Tokyo: Bungei Shunju, 1974.

Matsumura, Yoshihiko. *Akujotachi no Showa-shi*. Tokyo: Raibu Shuppan, 1992.

Miyatake, Gaikotsu, ed. *Baishunfu Imei-shu*. Tokyo: Hankyodo, 1921.

Miyazaki, Manabu. *Kami ni Inorazu: Osugi Sakae wa Naze Korosaretanoka*. Tokyo: Asuka Shinsha, 2000.

Morikawa, Tetsuro. *Nihon Meikyuiri Jiken*. Tokyo: San'ichi Shobo, 1978.

———. *Zankoku Nihon Keibatsu-shi*. Tokyo: Tokuma Shoten, 1981.

———. *Edo Ansatsu-shi*. Tokyo: San'ichi Shobo, 1981.

———. *Bakumatsu Ansatsu-shi*. Tokyo: San'ichi Shobo, 1967.

———. *Showa Ansatsu-shi*. Tokyo: Mainichi Shinbunsha, 1994.

Morinaga, Taneo. *Runin to Hinin*. Tokyo: Iwanami Shoten, 1993.

Murano, Kaoru, ed. *Nihon no Shikei*. Tokyo: Tsuge Shobo, 1990.

Murofushi, Tetsuro. *Nippon no Terorisuto: Ansatsu to kuu deta no Rekishi*. Tokyo: Kobundo, 1964.

Nagamatsu, Senzo. *Meiji Taisho Jitsuwa Zenshu.* No. 8. *Sagi Oryo Jitsuwa*. Tokyo: Heibonsha, 1930.

Nakajima, Shigeo. *Jiken de Miru Meiji Hyakuwa*. Tokyo: Rippu Shobo, 1992.

———. *Meiji Hankacho*. Tokyo: Heibonsha, 2000.

Nakamura, Fumio. *Taigyaku Jiken to Chishikijin*. Tokyo: San'ichi Shobo, 1981.

Nakao, Kenji. *Danzaemon: Oedo mohitotsu no shakai*. Osaka: Kaihoshuppan-sha, 1994.

———. *Edo no Danzaemon*. Tokyo: San'ichi Shobo, 1996.

Nakazawa, Ichiro. *Chichibu Jiken*. Tokyo: Shin Shuppansha, 1991.

Nawa, Yumio. *Jitte, Torinawa Jiten*. Tokyo: Yuzankaku Shuppan, 1996.

———. *Gomon Keibatsu-shi*. Tokyo: Yuzankaku Shuppan, 1987.

———. *Machigai Darake no Jidaigeki*. Tokyo: Kawade Shobo, 1989.

Nichigai Associates, ed. *Nijisseiki Goyomi*. Tokyo: Nichigai Associates, Inc., 1998.

Nihon Fuzokushi Gakkai, ed. *Meiji no Tokyo Hyakuwa*. Tokyo: Tsukubane-sha, 1996.

Nihon no Keisatsu. Tokyo: Nikko Seihan, 1968.

Nomura, Yoshifumi. *Otsu Jiken*. Fukuoka: Ashi Shobo, 1992.

Obinata, Sumio. *Nihon Kindai Kokka no Seiritsu to Keisatsu*. Tokyo: Azekura Shobo, 1992.

Ohama, Tetsuya, and Yoshiwara, Ken'ichiro, eds. *Edo-Tokyo Nenpyo*. Tokyo: Shogakkan, 1993.

Oka, Tadao. *Meiji Jidai Keisatsukan no Seikatsu*. Tokyo: Yuzankaku Shuppan, 1974.

Okamoto, Takashi. *Kaibo Kotohajime: Yamawaki Toyo no hito to Shiso*. Tokyo: Doseisha, 1988.

Okitsu, Kaname. *Meiji Shimbun Kotohajime*. Tokyo: Taishukan Shoten, 1997.

Oku, Takenori. *Sukyandaru no Meiji: Kokumin wo Tsukuru tame no Ressun*. Tokyo: Chikuma Shobo, 1997.

Okubo, Haruo, *Oedo Keijiroku*. Tokyo: Roppo Shuppansha, 1985.

———. *Edo no Hanzai to Keibatsu*. Tokyo: Kobundo Shuppansha, 1988.

Onihei Hankacho no Subete (Bessatsu Rekishi Tokuhon). Tokyo: Shin Jinbutsu Oraisha, 1994.

Ooka Echizen Itsuwashu (Bessatsu Rekishi Tokuhon). Tokyo: Shin Jinbutsu Oraisha, 1994.

Otsuka, Kimiko. *Shikeishu Saigo no Shunkan*. Tokyo: Kadokawa Shoten, 1996.

Otsuka, Shin'ichi. *Hanzai to Fuzoku*. Tokyo: Iwanami Shoten, 2000.

Sakaguchi, Hiroshi. *Asamasan-so 1972*. Tokyo: Sairyusha, 1993.

Sakamoto, Taketo. *Kotoku Shusui: Meiji Shakaishugi no Ittosei*. Tokyo: Shimizu Shoin, 1984.

Sanayama, Seika. *Nezumi Kozo Jirokichi, Tochuken Kumoemon*. Tokyo: Kaizosha, 1927.

Sasama, Yoshihiko. *Edo Machi Bugyosho Jiten*. Tokyo: Kashiwa Shobo, 1991.

Sato, Kiyohiko. *Kidan Tsuiseki: Bakumatsu, Meiji no Hatenko na Hanzaishatachi*. Tokyo: Daiwa Shobo, 1991.

———. *Datsugokushatachi: Kanri Shakai e no Chosen*. Tokyo: Seikyusha, 1995.

Sato, Tomoyuki. *Shikei no Nihonshi*. Tokyo: San'ichi Shobo, 1994.

Shigematsu, Kazuyoshi. *Edo no Hanzai Hakusho*. Tokyo: PHP Kenkyujo, 1986.

———. *Nihon Keibatsu-shi Nenpyo*. Tokyo: PHP, 1986.

Shimizu, Shojiro. *Meiji-Taisho-Showa Norowareta Josei Hanzai*. Tokyo:

Yoshie Shobo, 1965.

Shimokawa, Koshi, ed. *Meiji-Taisho Katei-shi Nenpyo 1868–1925*. Tokyo: Kawade Shobo Shinsha, 2000.

——. ed. *Showa-Heisei Katei-shi Nenpyo 1926–1995*. Tokyo: Kawade Shobo Shinsha, 1997.

Shinji, Yoshimoto. *Kinsei Buke Shakai to Shohatto*. Tokyo: Gakuyo Shobo, 1989.

Shinoda, Kozo. *Meiji Kaika Kidan*. Tokyo: Sudo Shoten, 1947.

Shinomiya, Tsugio. *Hanzai no Keiko to Sosa no Kenkyu*. Tokyo: Nihon Keisatsu Shimbunsha, 1925.

Shiomi, Sen'ichiro et al. *Danzaemon Seido to Senmin Bunka*. Tokyo: Hihyosha, 1992.

——. et al. *Edo no Kasoshakai*. Tokyo: Akashi Shoten, 1993.

Soeda, Satsuki. *Satsujin to Ryukoka*. *Hanzai Koron*, November 1932.

Soeda, Tomomichi. *Tekiya no Seikatsu*. Tokyo: Yuzankaku Shuppan, 1970.

Suzuki, Koichi, ed. *Nyusu de ou Meiji Nihon Hakkutsu*. Vols. 2, 4, 8 & 9. Tokyo: Kawade Shobo Shinsha, 1995.

Taigyaku Jiken Arubamu: Kotoku Shusui to Sono Shuhen. Tokyo: Nihon Tosho Center, 1982.

Takada, Kyoko. *Osoroshiki Hanzai Kantei Yawa*. Tokyo: Ozorasha, 1999.

Takagaki, Shigezo. *Meiji Yonen Kishu Hanzai cho*. Tokyo: San'ichi Shobo, 1999.

Takagi, Tadashi. *Mikudarihan to Enkiridera*. Tokyo: Kodansha, 1992.

Takahashi, Bin. "Bakumatsu bunka no hiro to natta autoro tachi," pp. 112–117. *Bakumatsu no Mikata (Aera Mook)*. Tokyo: Asahi Shimbunsha, 1998.

Takayanagi, Kaneyoshi. *Edo Jidai Hinin no Seikatsu*. Tokyo: Yuzankaku Shuppan, 1981.

Takenaka, Tsutomu. *Kurohata Suikoden: Taisho Jigokuhen*. Vols. 1–2. Tokyo: Koseisha, 2000.

Takeyasu, Masamitsu. *Kotoku Shusui-ra no Taigyaku Jiken*. Tokyo: Keiso Shobo, 1993.

Taki, Shizuo. *Keisatsu Konjaku Monogatari*. Tokyo: Shinjinbutsu Oraisha, 1974.

Takigawa, Seijiro. *Nihon Gyokei-shi*. Tokyo: Seiabo, 1962.

Tamura, Eitaro. *Yakuza no Seikatsu*. Tokyo: Yuzankaku Shuppan, 1981.

Togawa, Masako. *Hieta Hono no Gotoku: Nippon Yofuden*. Tokyo: Peppu Shuppan, 1975.

Tokuoka, Takao. *Yokohama–Yamate no Dekigoto*. Tokyo: Bungei Shunju, 1990.

Toyoda, Joh. *Katsura Taro to Nichi-Ro Senso Shogun-tachi*. Tokyo: Kodansha, 1983.

———. *Saionji Kinmochi to Meiji Taitei Hogyo*. Tokyo: Kodansha, 1983.

Tsukuba, Akira. *Tsuyama Sanjunin-goroshi*. Tokyo: Soshisha, 1981.

———. *Showa 46 Nen, Gunma no Haru*. Tokyo: Soshisha, 1987.

Ueda, Tamotsu. *Hanzai Sosa kara Shikei made*. Tokyo: Kokumin Kyoikukai, 1937.

Uematsu, Tadashi. *Minzoku to Hanzai*. Tokyo: Yuhikaku, 1947.

Ujiie, Mikito. *Oedo Shitaiko*. Tokyo: Heibonsha, 1999.

Umayahara, Shigeo. *Gendai no Fuzoku Hankashi*. Tokyo: Tenbosha, 1982.

Wamaki, Kosuke. *Nippon Dorobo-den*. Tokyo: Mainichi Shimbunsha, 1993.

Yakuza to iu ikikata (Bessatsu Takarajima No. 56). Tokyo: Takarajimasha, 1986.

Yamamoto, Shigeru. *"Nihon Iminshi ni Miru Hanzaisha-sho"* in *Hanzai Geppo*, No. 2, 1993, Tokyo.

Yamamoto, Takeshi, ed. *Tosa no Jiyuminken-ka Retsuden*. Kochi: Tosa Shuppan-sha, 1987.

Yamanaka, Keiichi. *Ronko Otsu Jiken*. Tokyo: Seibundo, 1994.

Yamashita, Tsuneo. *Meiji Tokyo Hanzaireki*. Tokyo: Tokyo Hokeigakuin Shuppan, 1988.

Yamatani, Ichiro. *Datsugokuma Shiratori Yuei*. Abashiri, Hokkaido: Okhosk Shobo, 1979.

Yamazaki, Tetsu. *Monogatari: Nihon Kindai Satsujin-shi*. Tokyo: Shunju-sha, 2000.

Yanagida, Morihide, *Zatsugaku Oedo Omoshiro Jikenbo*. Tokyo: Nitto Shoin, 1992.

Yokokura, Tatsuji. *Yoriki, Doshin, Meakashi no Seikatsu*. Tokyo: Yuzankaku Shuppan, 1994.

Yoshihara, Ken'ichiro. *Edo no Johoya*. Tokyo: NHK Books, 1978.

Yoshimi, Toshiya, and Kinoshita, Naoyuki, eds. *Nyusu no Tanjo: Kawaraban to Shimbun nishiki-e no Joho Sekai*. Tokyo: University of Tokyo Press, 1999.

In English:

Apter, David E., and Sawa, Nagayo. *Against the State: Politics and Social Protest in Japan*. Cambridge: Harvard University Press, 1984.

Beckmann, George M. *The Modernization of China and Japan*. New York: Harper & Row, 1962.

Blakemore, Thomas L., trans. *The Criminal Code of Japan (1954)*. Tokyo: Charles E. Tuttle Co., 1954.

Edmonds, I.G. *Solomon in Kimono: Tales of Ooka, A Wise Judge of Old Yedo*. Tokyo: Pacific Stars & Stripes, 1956.

Enbutsu, Sumiko. *Chichibu Japan's Hidden Treasure*. Tokyo: Charles E. Tuttle Co., 1990.

Farrell, James Gordon. *The Siege of Krishnapur*. New York: Carroll & Graf, 1985.

Gaute, J.H.H. & Odell, Robin. *Murder 'What Dunit'*. London: Harrap Ltd., 1982.

Gulik, Robert Hans van. *T'ang Yin Pi Shi = Parallel Cases under the Pear-Tree: A 13th Century Manual of Jurisprudence and Detection*. Westport, Connecticut: Hyperion Press, 1979.

Gulik, Sidney L. *Evolution of the Japanese: Social and Psychic*. New York: Fleming H. Revell Company, 1903.

Hall, J. Carey. "Japanese Feudal Laws, Parts I~IV." *Transactions of the Asiatic Society of Japan*. Vols. 38 and 41. Tokyo, 1911, 1913.

———. "Japanese Feudal Laws, Part IV. The Edict in 100 Sections." *Transactions of the Asiatic Society of Japan*. Vol. 41, 5. Tokyo, 1913.

Hane, Mikiso. *Peasants, Rebels and Outcastes: The Underside of Modern Japan*. New York: Pantheon, 1982.

Ihara, Saikaku (Kondo, Thomas M., and Marks, Alfred H., trans.) *Tales of Japanese Justice*. Honolulu: University Press of Hawaii, 1980.

———. (Wm. Theodore de Bary, trans.). *Five Women Who Loved Love*. Tokyo: Charles E. Tuttle Co., 1956.

Jansen, Marius B., ed. *Changing Japanese Attitudes Toward Modernization*. Princeton: Princeton University Press, 1965.

La Motte, Ellen A. *The Opium Monopoly*. New York: The MacMillian Company, 1920.

Mertz, John. "Murder Makes the Nation: Novelizing Japanese Crime Trials in 1881." *Journal of Popular Culture*, Vol. 31.2, Fall 1997.

Martin, Peter. *The Chrysanthemum Throne: A History of the Emperors of Japan*. Phoenix Mill, Sutton Publishing Ltd., 1997.

Michaelis, G. *Beitrag zur Kenntniss der Geschichte des Japanischen Strafrechts* (Contribution to knowledge about the history of Japanese criminal law): *Bemerkungen ueber die rechespflege under den Tokugawa* (Remarks about administration of justice under the Tokugawa). Achtunddreissigstes Heft (leaflet No. 38). Tokyo, February 1888.

Najita, Tetsuo, and Koschmann, J. Victor. *Conflict in Japanese History: The Neglected Tradition*. Princeton: Princeton University Press, 1982.

Nakamura, Kichisaburo: *The Formation of Modern Japan as Viewed from Legal History*. Tokyo: The Centre for East Asian Cultural Studies, 1962.

Notehelfer, F.G. *Kotoku Shusui: Portrait of a Japanese Radical*. Cambridge: Cambridge University Press, 1971.

Nouet, Noel. *The Shogun's City: A History of Tokyo*. Kent, England: Paul Norbury Publications, 1990.

Perrin, Noel. *Giving up the Gun*. Boston: G.K. Hall, 1979.

Sato, Masayoshi. *The Shogun's Gold: A Novel of 19th Century Financial Intrigue*. Tokyo: Kodansha International, 1991.

Satow, Ernest. *A Diplomat in Japan*. Philadelphia: J.B. Lippincott Company, 1921.

Schreiber, Mark. *Shocking Crimes of Postwar Japan*. Tokyo: Yenbooks, 1996.

Seidensticker, Edward. *High City, Low City*. Cambridge: Harvard University Press, 1991.

———. *Tokyo Rising*. Tokyo: Charles E. Tuttle Co., 1991.

Shand, W.J.S. *The Case of Ten-Ichi-Bo, a cause celebre in Japan*. Tokyo: Tokyo Methodist Publishing House, 1908.

Shapiro, Sydney. *The Law and Lore of Chinese Criminal Justice*. Singapore: Times Academic Press, 1990.

Triplett, William. *The Flowering of the Bamboo: A Bizarre International Mystery*. Kensington, MD: Woodbine House, 1985.

Waley, Paul. *Tokyo Then and Now*. New York: Wetherhill Inc., 1991.

Ward, Robert E. *Political Development in Modern Japan*. Princeton: Princeton University Press, 1968.

Wigmore, John Henry, ed. *Law and Justice in Tokugawa Japan, Parts I-X*. Tokyo: The Japan Foundation, 1975.

Williams, Harold S. *Tales of the Foreign Settlements in Japan*. Tokyo: Charles E. Tuttle Co., 1958.

———. *Shades of the Past: Indiscreet Tales of Japan*. Tokyo: Charles E. Tuttle Co., 1958.

Yamamoto, Tsunetomo *Hagakure: The Book of the Samurai* (William Scott Wilson, trans.) Tokyo: Kodansha International, 1983.

日本犯罪史
THE DARK SIDE

2001 年 9 月 7 日　第 1 刷発行

著　者　マーク・シュライバー
発行者　野間佐和子
発行所　講談社インターナショナル株式会社
　　　　〒112-8652　東京都文京区音羽 1-17-14
　　　　電話：03-3944-6493（編集部）
　　　　電話：03-3944-6492（営業部・業務部）
　　　　ホームページ　http://www.kodansha-intl.co.jp
印刷所　共同印刷株式会社
製本所　黒柳製本株式会社

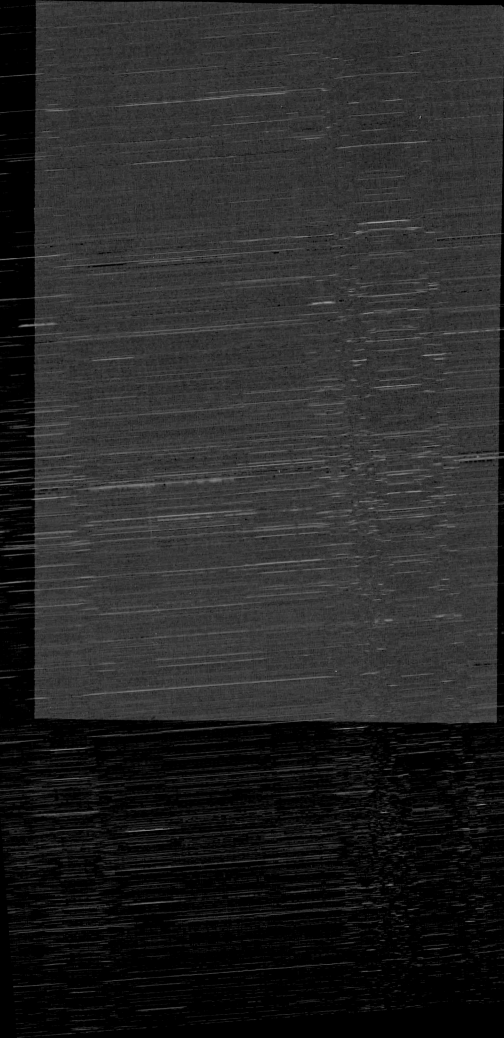